"As a seasoned and highly effective educator, Ms. Meyers has distilled both the science and art of teaching masterfully from A-Z! This book should be required reading for educators and included in teacher training programs everywhere!"
—**Eric Bethel**, *Instructional Superintendent, DC Public Schools*

"This book is a treasure chest of jewels teachers will rediscover again and again! It includes countless strategies that will empower educators everywhere on the path to unlocking the brilliance of their students!"
—**Dr. Jasmine Brann**, *Principal with DC Public Schools*

"Every educator, new and seasoned, needs to read this book! It provides real-world examples of peers using research-based strategies in classrooms like their own. While social media offers quick glimpses, this book explains the research behind effective strategies and how to implement them. It also gives parents the chance to collaborate with schools, fostering a stronger partnership for student success."
—**Grace Wilson**, *Assistant Principal with DC Public Schools*

"Having worked alongside Alicia Meyers for four years, I've seen firsthand her passion for education and her gift for making learning accessible and engaging. *The A-to-Z Teaching Toolkit* is a goldmine of practical strategies, creative insights, and ready-to-use resources that empower both educators and caregivers. This book is a true game-changer for anyone looking to inspire young minds, create meaningful learning experiences, and instill change!"
—**Brooklyn Beeler**, *Mental Health Advocate, School Counselor*

"Alicia Meyers is nothing short of inspiring. Her passion and energy make learning exciting and meaningful. Her students thrive academically, socially, and emotionally, and it's clear how much they adore her. I've learned so much from watching her in action! *The A-to-Z Teaching Toolkit* is a true reflection of her talent, dedication, and love for teaching."
—**Lindsey Daugherty**, *Kindergarten Teacher with DC Public Schools*

"As a picture book author and former homeschooling parent, I found *The A-to-Z Teaching Toolkit* to be a must-have addition to my home library. It provides insight, problem-solving steps, how-to guides, examples, and resources on everything from navigating big emotions, supporting neurodiverse learners, implementing classroom incentives, and basic building blocks that ensure any child is set up for success. Being able to reference this incredibly thorough resource has given me the confidence to tackle any educational issue I'm up against."

—**Brenna Jeanneret**, *Picture Book Author and Former Homeschool Parent*

The A-to-Z Teaching Toolkit for Early Childhood and Elementary Educators

The A-to-Z Teaching Toolkit for Early Childhood and Elementary Educators is your one-stop shop for the contemporary early childhood and early elementary classroom, offering an A-to-Z collection of invaluable resources, strategies, and systems to use in your teaching. If you're looking for . . .

   a) Research-backed ideas and strategies to recalibrate your classroom practices
   b) Creative anchor charts, sentence starters, and examples of classroom visuals
   c) Step-by-step, comprehensive action plans and lists
   d) Tried-and-true tools and materials to add to your classroom
   e) Niche picture book suggestions that support the A through Z concepts
   f) Approaches for consistency and open communication between home and school environments

. . . then you've found the right book! *The A-to-Z Teaching Toolkit for Early Childhood and Elementary Educators* is key reading for educators, caregivers, future teachers, and families. Join author Alicia Meyers as she opens the door to her classroom to journey through the ABCs of teaching.

Alicia Meyers is a first-grade teacher in Washington, DC, with more than 15 years of experience in Title I schools, teaching preschool to second grade.

Other Eye on Education Books Available from Routledge
(www.routledge.com/eyeoneducation)

The Co-Teaching Power Zone: A Framework for Effective Relationships and Instruction
Elizabeth Stein

Optimizing Early Auditory Development for Communication and Education: Strategies for Ages 0–8
Kimberly A. Boynton and Darah J. Regal

A New Vision for Early Childhood: Rethinking Our Relationships with Young Children
Noah Hichenberg

Unpacking Privilege in the Elementary Classroom: A Guide to Race and Inequity for White Teachers
Jacquelynne Boivin and Kevin McGowan

Reimagining the Role of Teachers in Nature-based Learning: Helping Children be Curious, Confident, and Caring
Rachel Larimore and Claire Warden

Teaching Higher-Order Thinking to Young Learners, K–3: How to Develop Sharp Minds for the Disinformation Age
Steffen Saifer

Promoting Language and Early Literacy Development: Practical Insights from a Parent Researcher
Pamela Beach

The A-to-Z Teaching Toolkit for Early Childhood and Elementary Educators

Best Practices for Classroom Management and Student Engagement

Alicia Meyers

Routledge
Taylor & Francis Group

NEW YORK AND LONDON

Designed cover image: Getty Images

First published 2026
by Routledge
605 Third Avenue, New York, NY 10158

and by Routledge
4 Park Square, Milton Park, Abingdon, Oxon, OX14 4RN

Routledge is an imprint of the Taylor & Francis Group, an informa business

© 2026 Taylor & Francis

The right of Alicia Meyers to be identified as author of this work has been asserted in accordance with sections 77 and 78 of the Copyright, Designs and Patents Act 1988.

All rights reserved. No part of this book may be reprinted or reproduced or utilised in any form or by any electronic, mechanical, or other means, now known or hereafter invented, including photocopying and recording, or in any information storage or retrieval system, without permission in writing from the publishers.

Trademark notice: Product or corporate names may be trademarks or registered trademarks, and are used only for identification and explanation without intent to infringe.

ISBN: 978-1-041-01979-4 (hbk)
ISBN: 978-1-041-01978-7 (pbk)
ISBN: 978-1-003-61720-4 (ebk)

DOI: 10.4324/9781003617204

Typeset in Palatino
by Apex CoVantage, LLC

To my past, present, and future students, families, and fellow educators—A through Z . . .

Contents

Meet the Author xi
Acknowledgments. xii
Where It Started: "Welcome to Camp!" xiv

Introduction: From My Desk to Yours 1

A is for Arts Integration. 6

B is for Books and Blankets 19

C is for Conflict Resolution. 31

D is for De-escalation. 40

E is for Engagement 51

F is for First Week Fundamentals. 62

G is for Goals and Growth 73

H is for Hobbies 84

I is for Incentives. 98

J is for Jobs 110

K is for Kid-tiques 120

L is for Learning Checks 130

M is for Menus 139

N is for Neurodiversity 151

O is for Organization 162

P is for Partnerships 173

Qu like in Conse/qu/ences 187

R is for Representation 196

S is for Self-Talk 206

T is for Teachable Moments 219

U is for Unfairness 227

V is for Virtual Learning 235

W is for Writing to. 248

X like in E/x/pectations. 263

Y is for You 274

Z is for Zen Den. 284

Conclusion 294

   A-to-Z Glossary 297
   Bibliography 301

Meet the Author

Alicia Meyers is a second-grade teacher in Washington, DC, with more than 15 years of experience in Title I schools, teaching preschool to second grade. As a neurodiverse author and teacher diagnosed with Tourette syndrome, Alicia is passionate about celebrating neurodiversity, social-emotional learning, building supportive communities for teachers and families, and the power of picture books. Her debut picture book, *TIC-ERRIFIC ME*, comes soon to a shelf  near you. When she's not teaching or writing, Alicia can be found in Arlington, Virginia, likely alphabetizing and color-coding everything in rainbow order. To learn more about Alicia, visit www.heyaliciamae.com or say *hey* on Instagram, X, or BlueSky @byaliciameyers

Acknowledgments

In the book *The Sociology of Art*, Arnold Hauser says:—

> "Every artist expresses himself in the language of his predecessors."

In this, I am no different. Like every artist, I've been shaped by those who came before—educators, authors, family, and friends—who've made me the teacher and writer I am today. Without them, this book would still be an idea.

Because we all know I love a good system, let's get to it: alphabetically, of course.

Beth Stillborn—Thank you for your keen eye on my first chapters and generosity toward the Kidlit community. Your detailed notes and quick tips sparked my excitement to keep writing!

Brenna Jeanneret—Thank you for 47 straight weeks of tedious, insightful critiques and letting me borrow that beautiful brain of yours.

Dr. Jasmine Brann—Thank you for your unwavering support throughout this journey. Your belief in what I do, not just in the classroom but in every creative endeavor, helps me honor my passions, inside and outside the classroom.

Grace Wilson—My affirmational angel. Thank you for being the genuine, encouraging leader that you are and constantly pointing out how much knowledge I have to share. You give me the confidence daily to turn my ideas into something bigger.

Jenny Cetlin—This book would not exist if it weren't for your encouragement to start writing it all down. Thank you for being my cheerleader!

Karen Keesling—Thank you for coming through at the final hour with your research-based insights and for your passion and partnership in our world of finding *Picture Books About . . .*

Mom and Dad—Thank you for supporting every talent, hobby, and passion in my life—and for restocking printer cartridges so I could print worksheets and play teacher in my makeshift classroom.

PBS, Totally Funny, and my Saturday Critique Crew—Thank you for your detailed critiques, powerful advice, and ever-present support.

Pyrrha Hallums—Thank you for taking me under your wing and teaching me everything I know, including how to dress appropriately in the winter.

Terri Clemmons—You were born to edit. Thank you for helping me organize my thoughts and for your patience with my lifelong struggles: the Oxford comma and when to hyphenate.

Valerie Bolling—Thank you for your heartfelt advice, check-ins, and constant championing of my work. I truly couldn't have done it without you!

> . . . And to every educator that I have crossed classrooms with, every family that has partnered with me on this journey, and every coworker that has become like family—

Thank you for inspiring me to continually learn, grow, and be the best teacher I can be, from A-to-Z.

Where It Started: "Welcome to Camp!"

My journey to becoming a teacher begins with a story of both *aspiration* and *desperation*.

Once upon a time, there was an embarrassingly uncoordinated fifth grader named Alicia, with braces that changed rubber band colors every two weeks like clockwork. Through her rose-colored glasses, teaching looked like the gig of a lifetime: summers off, full rein to boss others around, and complete control over snacks. Thanks to her fifth-grade teacher, Alicia's dream was about to come true. In a few days, she would join a club of other aspiring educators called "Teachers of Tomorrow," where once a week, select students would wear their honorary "ToT" t-shirt and bounce from classroom to classroom asking, "How can I help?"

Alicia, in her element, could barely sleep the night before—too excited to help students finish their work and help teachers create their bulletin boards. She was, after all, a career-driven, *basically* fully certified ten-year-old teacher.

Summer break in South Florida slowly approached, and the days would soon be spent outside with the neighborhood kids in unbearable heat. But Alicia just wanted to *teach*. So, she took matters into her own hands.

Showing off her stellar computer skills, she created a flyer and spread the news from mailbox to mailbox:

FREE SUMMER CAMP @ THE MEYERS' HOUSE
This Monday-Friday, 9am-12pm
Ages 4—8 are welcome
(Snacks Provided)

She cleaned the garage, set up foldable tables and chairs, dragged out her chalkboard, sharpened pencils, created worksheets, and (slowly) collected snacks from the pantry so her mom would not notice what was missing. She was ready. School was open!

On Monday morning, at 9:00 a.m. sharp, five kids arrived on her driveway ready for camp. Alicia's mom thought it was the *most adorable thing* to see neighborhood kids *playing school* with her. Around 11:00 a.m., the phone rang, and Mom answered with a "Hello?" When she came to relay the message that Anna was getting picked up early from camp, she muttered many words:

Unlicensed. Underage. Unsupervised. Uninsured.
Needless to say—there was no day two of camp.

I'm aware that this story is utterly ridiculous and leaves more questions than answers. But I must say, it was some of my finest work. My dream had come true, even if only for a few hours. Now, as a public school teacher of 15-plus years in Washington, DC, my personality and passion for teaching continues. Every day, I get to inspire my students to innovate, take chances, form friendships, and navigate this big, wide, complicated world. Plus . . .

. . . I get complete control over snacks.

Introduction: From My Desk to Yours

I have never had my own desk. Small group table, yes. Oversized carpet circle, of course. Desk designed for a six-year-old that I hunch over like a ninja turtle—absolutely. But not a desk I can call my own. So, where else as a teacher can I lay my hats?

Yes, my job is labeled as TEACHER, but in one day I am also part . . .

>Counselor,
>Therapist,
>Social Worker.

>>Security Guard,
>>Custodian,
>>Nurse.

>Office Manager,
>Accountant,
>Receptionist.

>>Computer Technician,
>>Librarian,
>>Art Teacher.

Public Speaker,
Presenter,
Mediator.

Friend,
Mentor,
. . . and often mistakenly called
Mommy.

It's the name of the game. Teaching is a job that requires you to be *on* in every capacity. It tests you every second, minute, and hour of the day. It has the highest highs and the lowest lows. It's a career that requires community, intentionality, and open-mindedness.

The book you have in your hands is an A-to-Z collection of strategies and systems that supplement the incredible work teachers are *already* doing. Little things that can make a big difference. But these ideas go far beyond the classroom.

This book shares systems, methods, and ideas that I've tweaked and tried over 15 years of teaching in inner-city charter and public schools. But every classroom I enter still teaches me something new. I am not the know-all, be-all teacher with the answers and solutions. I am the teacher that never feels fully seasoned but strives to grow each year in my craft. My hope for this book is to be a conversation starter for sharing our experiences and struggles. So, teachers, administrators, school support staff, counselors, coaches, parents, families, and picture book writers—let's band together as a community and inspire the next generation of learners . . . *together.*

This is only the beginning.

The Alphabetical Teaching Format

In 1584, the king of France received a compilation of alphabetically arranged names. This caused chaos, as many thought the list reflected a hierarchy of those more important, but the compiler had only intended to make the entries *easier to find* (Flanders, 2020). He used the alphabet as an organizational method to bring order and ease.

Like this list, our A-to-Z adventure is organized alphabetically to bring efficiency, consistency, ease, order, and structure to our everyday classroom—without hierarchy!

Imagine you are looking at an organized shelf with rows of alphabetized buckets. An abundance of options.

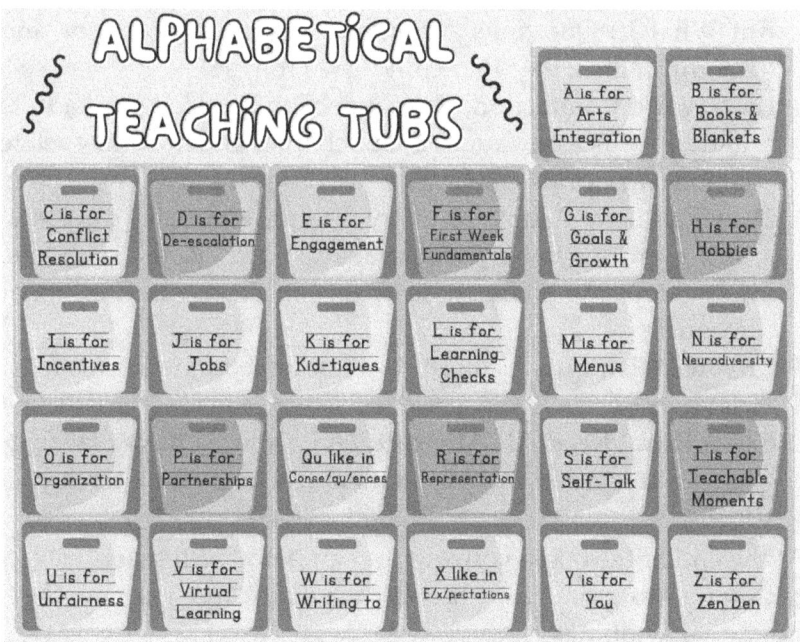

FIGURE INTRO.1 An alphabetical shelf of buckets representing each chapter

The chapters in this book, like buckets, hold ideas, systems, and strategies you can grab whenever you *want* or *need* them.

Within each bucket, alphabetically associated content is designed in a lesson plan format with the following categories:

I can _____ *so my students can* _____: The objective of the chapter. What we as adults will be able to *show* or *do* after reading, and how our students can benefit from the chapter

Definition and Similar Words: The meaning and context of our chapter, as well as synonyms

Our Alphabetic Association: The letter and practical skill/system/strategy we are zooming in on. Content that is chock-full of anecdotes, ideas, examples, and mnemonic devices

Where to Start: Three practical next steps that support and summarize our chapter

But What If: Questions and answers to misconceptions and modifications; the what-could-go-wrongs

Real-World Connection: The connection between us as adults and the principles taught in our chapter and how they relate to the real world

Dear Families: A note to every parent, guardian, caretaker, and family member with practical ideas to use at home. Educators can share these with families as an additional resource.

Chapter Wish List: A collection of aforementioned items from the chapter

Extra! Extra! Read All About It: Five picture books that reinforce our chapter and supplement teaching and learning

At the end of the book, you will find an **A-to-Z Glossary** packed with terms to guide you through your alphabet journey. Consider it your ultimate cheat sheet!

Whether you choose to read alphabetically from A to Z, backwards from Z to A, or close your eyes and point to a letter, each chapter will lead to an overflowing treasure chest of systems and strategies to use in the classroom.

Ready to dive in but not sure where to begin? Here's a guide to start your adventure. Pick a path that speaks to you!

First-Year Teachers	F is for First Week Fundamentals O is for Organization X like in E/x/pectations
Aspiring Teachers	O is for Organization P is for Partnerships Qu like in Conse/qu/ences
Parent/Caregivers	J is for Jobs N is for Neurodiversity S is for Self-Talk
Teachers of Five or More Years	B is for Books and Blankets L is for Learning Checks M is for Menus
A Teaching Refresh	R is for Representation V is for Virtual Learning Y is for You
Principals and Administration	A is for Arts Integration C is for Conflict Resolution P is for Partnerships
School Support Staff	C is for Conflict Resolution N is for Neurodiversity P is for Partnerships
Special Education Teachers	D is for De-escalation N is for Neurodiversity Z is for Zen Den
Coaches	I is for Incentives S is for Self-Talk U is for Unfairness
Early Childhood Teachers	A is for Arts Integration E is for Engagement T is for Teachable Moments
Kindergarten through Second Grade Teachers	B is for Books and Blankets J is for Jobs K is for Kid-tiques
Third through Fifth Grade Teachers	C is for Conflict Resolution G is for Goals and Growth W is for Writing To
Writers for Young Children	H is for Hobbies K is for Kid-tiques W is for Writing to

So, without further ado . . . in the words of A. A. Milne in *Winnie the Pooh*, "Perhaps the best thing to do is to stop writing introductions and get on with the book."

Are you ready to learn your ABCs?

A is for Arts Integration

> **[ARTS INTEGRATION]**: An approach to teaching and learning through which content standards are taught and assessed equitably in and through the arts (Riley, 2024)
> **Similar to** . . . the arts being incorporated, included, blended, or mixed (WordHippo, 2025)

I can <u>integrate the arts into classroom instruction</u> so my *students* can . . .

- Engage and stimulate their mind and body
- Enhance critical thinking and problem-solving through creative exploration
- Equitably access the arts
- Foster creativity, imagination, and innovation
- Practice personal self-expression

"Art is a place for children to trust their ideas, themselves, and to explore what is possible."
—Maryann F. Kohl (Kohl, 1998)

From an early age, my world revolved around the performing arts. From sixth grade through twelfth grade, I attended a magnet arts school where vocal music was not just a subject—but a way of life. In addition to my general education courses, my days were

DOI: 10.4324/9781003617204-2

filled with chorus, music theory, and vocal technique classes. This focus made me who I am as a creative—passionate about the arts. However, not every child is offered this same opportunity.

Now, as a public school teacher, I see firsthand how inequitable and inaccessible the arts have become to many. Every child might not have the opportunity to attend an arts school or program. Every family might not be able to afford additional programs, classes, and lessons. Every city might not offer the same opportunities in the arts. But, in the *school* environment, the arts *can* be equitable and accessible to all. Art can be for *every* child.

FIGURE A.1 Our Chapter A *why*

Let's kick off our ABC adventure by exploring the ABCs of arts integration.

Arts and Academics | Balance and blend | Content and creativity

When I think of arts integration opportunities in the elementary and early childhood classroom, the following general education blocks come to mind: reading, writing, speaking, listening, math, science, and social studies. However, any standard or subject taught in the classroom can be *balanced* and *blended* with the arts. This is where our fun begins!

Art comes in many forms and styles—circus arts, stand-up comedy, magic, or the spoken word—but for our A chapter, we will focus on the following **Five Artistic Avenues**: theatre, music, dance, visual arts, and communication arts (Tadesse, 2023).

> **Theatre:** Acting, costume design, improvisation, musical theatre, puppetry, scriptwriting, performing, set, sound, and light design, stage management, and storytelling
> **Music:** Instrumental and vocal music, choir, band, songwriting, composition, and music theory
> **Dance:** Ballet, jazz, hip-hop, tap, salsa, breakdancing, or any self-expression through choreography or physical movement
> **Communication Art:** The wide world of print, broadcast, and digital media including broadcast news, journalism, reporting, writing, screenwriting, commentating, and print media
> **Visual Art:** Drawing, painting, sculpting, pottery, photography, and graphic design

When integrating these five categories into the everyday classroom, we will keep four main goals in mind:

1. Keep it *meaningful*: Connect activities to learning standards
2. Keep it *authentic*: Connect to content in an authentic way, giving respect to various cultures, traditions, and history
3. Keep it *experimental*: Give students the room to make mistakes and space to try again
4. Keep it *experiential:* Incorporate reflection time and think of it as an experience

There is a myriad of ways to weave our five artistic avenues into the classroom.

Integrating Theatre

- Assign students a character, setting, problem, and solution to act out from a story. For a social-emotional focus, give a specific relationship to act out, such as a brother/sister, mother/daughter, or two friends.
- Build a set based on the current unit of study. For example: an ocean habitat or the National Mall for the March on Washington. Younger students can draw, build with blocks, make dioramas, or use molding clay.
- Have students write screenplays or commercials about a recent read-aloud or literacy unit
- Incorporate body movements and facial expressions to respond to read-alouds
- Re-enact historical events. Try playing "Who Am I?" and having students act like a historical figure by giving clues to their peers
- Re-imagine and act out alternate endings to stories
- Play charades with a theme. For example: During an animal unit, all answers are animals
- Practice reading with expression by doing imitations and a variety of character voices
- Provide brown paper bags to make puppet characters from books
- Use hand puppets and a puppet theater for students to re-enact read-alouds
- Use Reader's Theater scripts during needs-based small groups or guided reading time (See *K is for Kid-tiques* chapter for more ideas.)

Integrating Music

- Add a listening center device and headphones to your center/workstation block. Allow students to listen to instrumental music while working.

- Add sound effects to read-alouds. Many sounds can be found on YouTube or on white noise applications downloaded to your phone or device.
- Analyze and rewrite song lyrics
- Chant or rap expectations, transitions, or need-to-know phrases
- Compose music or songs based on a learning topic
- Find online playlists created to match picture books or ask students to pick a song that matches the emotion of a text
- Incentivize a karaoke party with a karaoke machine
- Incorporate instructional songs by artists such as Jack Hartmann or Harry Kindergarten
- Listen to different genres of music during work or reading time
- Make instruments out of recycled materials
- Research and write about the history of an instrument, genre of music, origin of music, famous musician, or musical practice
- Sing fingerplays like "Itsy Bitsy Spider," "Wheels on the Bus," or "Open, Shut Them"
- Study and listen to music written during different time periods

Integrating Dance and Movement

- Form letters and numbers with your body
- Incentivize a whole-class dance party
- Interpret the meaning of a new vocabulary word through movement
- Interpretively dance to a story
- Mimic peers through mirror movement
- Play freeze dance by starting and stopping music
- Provide brain breaks with stretching or yoga
- Study different forms of dance. Relate them to the cultures and parts of the world you are learning about in the

classroom. Try focusing on time periods and how dance has transformed through the ages
- Tell a story using body movement during read-alouds and poetry readings
- Use ribbons to interpret a song, story, or emotion

Integrating Communication Art

- Create a newspaper advertisement, article, or headline based on a topic studied

FIGURE A.2 Front page of a newspaper created by students about animal habitats

- Create a social media advertisement or post based on a topic
- Film a video responding to a question, debating, or sharing an opinion

- Interview an expert or peer: For example: After learning about perseverance, have students write three questions they would ask someone who has not given up on something difficult. Have them ask the questions and write down the responses.
- Practice storytelling: Start the first line of a story and have each child add one sentence. Watch the plot thicken! You can also use Story Cubes storytelling dice to think of a story.
- Prepare and give a speech as a character or historical figure
- Pretend to broadcast the news to discuss historical events or current events
- Use a voice-changing microphone for students to present to their peers
- Write a commercial based on the time period or unit being studied
- Write journal entries and sequels to stories read in the classroom

Integrating Visual Art

- Assemble a portrait using tangram shapes or construction paper shapes
- Build a diorama or three-dimensional project based on learning standards: For example: a solar system or animal habitat diorama
- Color, draw, paint, or sculpt while listening to a story
- Create a collage of a specific time period, event, or feeling/emotion
- Draw or paint in response to books or poems
- Fold origami paper to make an animal or symbol you are learning about
- Make character animal masks or crowns
- Paint to different rhythms and beats
- Sculpt a model of a character or their emotion shown in a book

FIGURE A.3 Sculpture and drawing response to *The Snurtch* by Sean Ferrell

- Study famous and historical artists who have a range of artistic styles
- Use a tablet, phone, digital camera, or instant camera to take photos documenting projects, school events, publishing parties, or celebrations. Allow students to incorporate photography into their projects.

By integrating theatre, music, dance, communication art, and visual art into the classroom, every child is able to participate, explore, learn, try, and access materials along with their peers. But the opportunities for arts integration don't stop there! Here are ways to broaden your school's commitment to integrating the arts into the classroom:

- Ask your local library if they have special passes or connections to museums, zoos, and other local learning experiences

- Collaborate with local organizations and community partnerships focused on arts enrichment and arts integration
- Connect families with local community centers, art museums, and community theaters
- Invite guest artists to speak at your school or resident artists to routinely work with students to plan a performance
- Pair with a buddy class (see *P is for Partnerships* chapter) to study one style of art. Join together to put on a culminating performance
- Put on an annual musical or talent show with a full audition process and backstage crew

FIGURE A.4 Elementary school talent show finale at a local theater

- Put on a seasonal show such as a winter concert, spring poetry slam, or fall art show. Celebrate important days or months such as Hispanic Heritage Month, Asian American and Pacific Islander Heritage Month, and Black History Month with performances from each class
- Research arts-based literacy programs/curriculums for the classroom
- Schedule in-school workshops for students in the arts
- Start extracurricular clubs for choir, dance team, publishing, film, art, fashion design, or podcasting
- Take advantage of professional development opportunities in the arts

- Take field trips to see shows, musical performances, dance performances, art exhibits, or tours with a behind-the-scenes look into the world of film, television, and broadcasting
- Watch filmed performances and musicals based on books read

When choosing what works for you, remember your arts integration ABCs! Together . . .

Arts and Academics | **B**alance and blend | **C**ontent and creativity

And when we keep learning *meaningful, authentic, experimental,* and *experiential* for our kids—that is when the magic happens.

Where to Start

1. Pick one of the five artistic avenues to integrate into your classroom
2. Look at your lesson plan/daily schedule. How can you blend art and academic content?
3. Connect with one to two community partnerships that can broaden learning

But What If . . .

. . . My School Does Not Have an Art, Drama, or Music Teacher?
Even more reason to integrate the arts the best you can into the classroom! Learn and explore the arts through professional development opportunities such as workshops and online courses. See if your school will fund art tools and materials. Email other schools in the district and ask to meet with their teachers in the arts to gather ideas and collect materials they are willing to give away.

. . . I Do Not Consider Myself Artistic or Feel I Have a Creative Skill Set?
Learn alongside your kids! Talk to them honestly about how even adults are not good at everything and have to try new things. Take an online class together or watch a YouTube video to learn something new.

. . . My Resources Are Limited?
Art is *everywhere*! You don't need the newest paint set or a grand piano in your classroom. Utilize art around you. Talk about graffiti, statues, and sculptures in your city or online graphics and media. Write songs and raps with paper and pencil or make shadow puppets on the wall with a flashlight. Art can be created with just your body and mind. Resources are a luxury!

Real-World Connection

Art is all around us—from street art to galleries, Broadway shows to concerts, or broadcast news to television favorites. Is there an artistic avenue you have always wanted to explore? Exploring, performing, and showcasing the arts can help our youngest learners grow up with artistic confidence. It can also open a world of career opportunities, like becoming a photographer, journalist, artist, graphic designer, interior designer, actor, choreographer, producer, stand-up comedian, author, poet, cinematographer, or museum curator.

Dear Families

Integrating the arts can also happen at home. During homework time, try incorporating ideas from our chapter to interpret, show, and respond to learning. Produce jingles, songs, chants, and rhymes to help your child learn.

Attend local educational shows at theaters and festivals. Utilize free opportunities at your local community center or with neighborhood non-profits.

Encourage your child's school to look into community partnerships and resident artist programs. Work with the PTA (Parent Teacher Association) or PTO (Parent Teacher Organization) to design a budget specifically for arts integration in classrooms. Help teachers create wish lists to get funding for arts-based materials they can use in the classroom.

A is for Arts Integration Wish List

- ★ Brown paper bags
- ★ Building blocks
- ★ Instant camera and film
- ★ Karaoke machine
- ★ Listening center device
- ★ Molding clay
- ★ Origami paper
- ★ Puppet theater
- ★ Puppets
- ★ Reader's Theater scripts
- ★ Ribbons
- ★ Student headphones
- ★ Story Cubes storytelling dice
- ★ Tangram shapes
- ★ Voice-changing microphone

Extra! Extra! Read All About It

Broadway Bird
Written by Alex Timbers; Illustrated by Alisa Coburn

Endlessly Ever After: Pick Your Path to Countless Fairy Tale Endings!
Written by Laurel Snyder; Illustrated by Dan Santat
    Great for Upper Elementary

Let's Dance!
Written by Valerie Bolling; Illustrated by Maine Diaz

My Brain Is Magic: A Sensory-Seeking Celebration
Written by Prasha Sooful; Illustrated by Geeta Ladi

Play This Book
Written by Jessica Young; Illustrated by Daniel Wiseman

A B C D E F G H I J K L M N O P Q R S T U V W X Y Z
is for **Arts Integration** because . . .
The way *we* and our *students* connect our creativity to learning matters

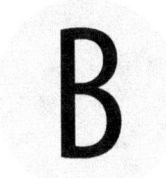

B is for Books and Blankets

> [BOOKS & BLANKETS]: A cozy, quiet reading time that encourages a love for reading (National Council of Teachers of English, 2021)
> **Similar to** . . . reflection, introspection, quiet time, or independent reading time (Thesaurus.com, 2023)

I can <u>**create a cozy, quiet reading space**</u> so my *students* can . . .

- Experience the joy of reading
- Look forward to a reading routine
- Relax in a safe space
- Re-read their favorite books
- Take time to decompress and lighten sensory overload

American author George R.R. Martin once said:—

> *"A reader lives a thousand lives . . . the man who never reads lives only one."*

Reading is an adventure—a first-class ticket to anywhere in the world and beyond. There are no limits to where we can go through a story. But to some, reading can feel like a chore.

DOI: 10.4324/9781003617204-3

A study from the National Literacy Trust showed that children who read for pleasure perform better academically, which leads to improved vocabulary, comprehension, and achievement in the general education classroom (Clark and Rumbold, 2006). Sometimes, as teachers, we focus so much on the standards that we forget to make time for the *pleasure* and *experience* of reading. Reading should be a celebration!

FIGURE B.1 Our Chapter B *why*

I *love* to read. To me, there is nothing better than grabbing my softest blanket, sitting by the fireplace, clicking on string lights, and curling up with my favorite book. So, during the daily classroom read-aloud, I hype up every book. Because when I get excited, so do my students. They match my energy, becoming increasingly intrigued and inquisitive about reading.

Books and Blankets, similar to independent reading time, is a routinely scheduled, protected period for cozy, quiet, reading (National Council of Teachers of English, 2021). It's a time of day when students can read *what*, *where*, and *how* they want—without feeling the pressures of performance or perfection. A time of day when they can just *be* with a book.

Similar to D.E.A.R. Time (Drop Everything and Read), when students silently read for long periods of time (Beverlycleary.com, 2024), Books and Blankets creates a safe space for quiet murmurs, as whispers of reading radiate throughout the room. For our B chapter, we will walk through the "Books and Blankets Basics"—your guide to setting a scheduled time for kids to read *what, where,* and *how* they want.

The Books and Blankets Basics:

1. B&B Environment
2. B&B Procedure
3. B&B Incentives
4. B&B Modifications
5. B&B Benefits
6. B&B and Beyond

B&B Environment

The Books and Blankets environment is a mellow, relaxing atmosphere where kids can decompress and focus on exploring books. Here are some ways to cultivate this environment:

FIGURE B.2 First-grade student sitting freely while reading during Books and Blankets

- Allow students to sit in spaces and in ways they typically aren't allowed to. For example: Students can safely sit on top of a desk if their two feet are sturdy on a chair, or they can use a cushion to lie under their desk.
- Display a timer on the board so students can gauge how much time is left
- Give students permission to take off their shoes when in their reading space
- Hang string lights around the room. When it is time for Books and Blankets to begin, turn off any overhead lights to transition to a calm atmosphere.
- Keep a collection of blankets in the classroom or allow students to bring a blanket from home
- Make a wide range of books available for students, as well as magazines, kid-friendly cookbooks, and devices to listen to audiobooks
- Play instrumental music such as piano, classical guitar, or light jazz
- Provide decorative pillows, stuffed animals, reading pointers, mini flashlights, and noise-cancelling headphones for students to borrow
- Turn on a virtual seasonal fireplace

B&B Procedure

The Books and Blankets procedure has four simple steps—the end goal being that students are practicing reading behaviors and perseverance. I like to write and anchor the procedure in student-friendly language, so they know exactly what to do:

1. We set the mood (For example: turning off overhead lights and playing soft music)
2. We pick our reading tools (For example: a blanket, stuffed animal, and bucket of books)
3. We find a special, cozy, solo spot
4. We *just keep reading!*

The process of book selection, or what many call "book shopping," can be done any way you like. Students can go "shopping" for their books in the classroom on Monday and return them on Friday using their book bin/book baggie, pick a bucket from the classroom library with the genre/topic they want to read that day, or grab the chapter book/graphic novel/middle grade novel they are working through from their desk.

At the beginning of the year, we talk about **reading behaviors**: how to hold a book, treat it with respect, sound out words, turn the pages one at a time, and read with a partner. We also talk about **reading stamina** and **reading perseverance**—the act of reading "longer and stronger" without giving up.

At first, Books and Blankets lasts only a few minutes, but as students practice the routine, the time increases. With inspiration from Dory in Disney's *Finding Nemo*, I like to tell them, "Just keep reading, just keep reading, just keep reading, reading, reading!"

While students are reading, the teacher can. . . .

- Give each child one *shine* (compliment) and one *grind* (skill to work on). For example: "Wow! You pointed to each word on the page! Next time, can you try to stop and stretch each sound in the word?"
- Read aloud to students
- Read their own book *next* to a student. My students love seeing me read in real time and tend to mirror my movements.
- Read with students one at a time around the room
- Take anecdotal notes on reading behaviors while a child reads to them

B&B Incentives

To make Books and Blankets extra fun and exciting, use incentives specific to *reading* that inspire students and encourage them to not give up. When you make this time of day a privilege and something to look forward to, you might hear kids asking, "Is it time yet?" "How long can we read today?" or "I can't wait!" You may even get some tears when there isn't time for reading on a particular day. Here are some ways to incentivize Books and Blankets time (see *I is for Incentives* chapter for more):

- Award reading badges or certificates of completion for milestones, such as reading for 15 minutes without stopping, reading every genre on the shelf, finishing a chapter book for the first time, or independently reading a picture book without teacher support
- Choose a leader to pick the music or virtual fireplace for the day. This is a great job for the DJ (see *J is for Jobs* chapter for more).
- Create cozy corners and crevices in the room that kids can read in. For example: The Seasonal Shelf, The Special Bookshelf, The Graphic Novel Zone, The Chapter Book Chairs, The Audiobook Area, or The Magazine Corner
- Display every classroom read-aloud book on a special shelf or location so students can freely access them
- Organize classroom library genres based on student interests
- Print out a variation of "Reading Genre BINGO," play a game of book trivia, or go on a scavenger hunt for specific words that practice phonics skills
- Schedule "Partner Reading Day" where students can pick a partner and read side-by-side or "Flashlight Friday" where each child can hold a mini flashlight under a blanket while reading their book
- Shout out a "Super Reader" who respected their books, tried their best, and stayed focused
- Use book-themed sticker reward charts to motivate readers and award incentives associated with books and reading. For example: After five stickers, a child can be the reading helper, sit with a special buddy, read in the teacher's chair, or pick a book from the teacher's bookshelf.

B&B Modifications

If a child is working on fluent reading or beginning reading behaviors, here are some ways to modify Books and Blankets time:

- Allow them to bring books from home that they know and love
- Download audiobooks for them to listen to through your local library
- Let students read leveled books or phonics passages previously practiced in needs-based small-group time
- Read digitally with a guided program such as RAZ-Kids, Vooks, Sora, or Epic
- Search for recently learned sight words using a mini magnifying glass
- Tell a story through illustrations and predict through pictures
- Use magazines with collections of visuals and crafts, such as *Highlights, High-Five, Cricket, Little Thoughts Press,* or *The Toy Press*

B&B Benefits

You might think that incorporating Books and Blankets into the day is a loss of instructional time or puts kids at risk of learning to read incorrectly, but research shows that the *volume* a child reads is incredibly important. The more one reads, the more knowledge is acquired about words, language, fluency, and the comprehension of complex texts (Allington, 2013). There are far more benefits to this time of day filled with student choice and student voice:

- Access to a wide range of themes, characters, settings, and experiences
- Agency over book choice and the position of reading
- Opportunities for encouragement through affirmation and motivation
- Practice of making choices for oneself
- Student excitement and engagement
- The development and growth of sustained reading stamina
- The experience of being part of a community based around books
- The opportunity to explore new topics

- Time to enjoy reading without being told or assigned what to read

B&B & Beyond

Books and Blankets has potential to go far beyond the classroom. Here are some ways to get your school and families involved:

- Add pictures to your classroom monthly newsletter to showcase star readers
- Host a "Birthday Books and Blankets" where the celebrant gets to pick when you do it, what music to play, and if kids can read with partners
- Invite students to a Books and Blankets Book Club during their lunch time
- Let students create and write their own books. Choose a day to read each other's work during Books and Blankets time
- Shout out one classroom a month on the announcements, detailing their hard work during Books and Blankets time
- Start a Books and Blankets club at your school or camp: Pair younger students with an older buddy to read together and work on reading-based homework. Let the students bring snacks and blankets with them.

Unlike other independent reading models, Books and Blankets is focused on the *act* and *practice* of the reading experience. The feeling of finding the perfect book for you can't be described in words. Every child deserves to have that moment! As teachers, let's provide the time and space for this magical experience to take over.

Where to Start

1. Set up your Books and Blankets environment
2. Make an anchor chart or visual of your Books and Blankets expectations

3. Model what this time looks like for the kids and slowly transition them to reading independently

But What If . . .

. . . Students Don't Know How to Read Yet?
Beginning readers can still experience the act of reading without knowing how to decode text. Use picture books or wordless picture books to show them how to tell a story through pictures, search for practiced sight words, or look for letters/sounds they know. Set up devices with audiobooks and digital websites with text-to-speech capabilities.

. . . A Child Is Faking Reading?
I say, *fake it till you make it!* Pretending and mimicking reading behaviors is natural for our beginners working toward becoming readers. At this stage, kids are still practicing how to hold a book the correct way, turn pages, move forward through a story, predict through pictures, and interact with text.

. . . My Schedule Does Not Allow Time for Books and Blankets?
Books and Blankets can happen *anytime*. For example: during breakfast, arrival, dismissal, transition times, after school as a club, incorporated into centers as a rotation, or for five to ten minutes after recess as a time for decompressing.

. . . A Child Is Making Noise or Distracting Others During This Time?
First, make sure you are praising the kids who *are* reading without distracting others. Then, ask the child if they need support from you or have any questions. Other solutions could be to . . .

- ♦ Invite them to visit the school library to explore new genres and books they might like to try (the *Dogman* series by Dav Pilkey has been a consistent obsession in my first-grade space over the years—so much that I now need multiple copies on hand. My students who once dodged reading *beg* to read or flip-o-rama these books!)

- Invite them to your teacher table when you see good choices in action
- Keep them in close proximity to you
- Personally incentivize their reading

. . . A Child Says They Are Done Early?
Remind them to, "Just keep reading!" Provide ideas for picture book re-reads such as reading in different voices, reading to stuffed animals, coming up with alternate endings, or reading with props such as oversized reading glasses, pointers, or finger puppets. Celebrate them when they re-read and try their best! If students are reading graphic novels, chapter books, or middle-grade novels, allow them to select their next book and start reading.

. . . My Collection of Physical Books Is Limited?
See if your local library provides educator accounts and check out a stack of books. Grab used books when you see them at Little Free Libraries or yard sales, download e-books or audiobooks, start a grant request through an organization like DonorsChoose to purchase new books, or ask parents to donate books they no longer need at home. Follow educator-friendly accounts on social media and keep an eye out for their giveaways and "Clear the List" calls, where people will purchase things off your teacher wish list and donate to your classroom.

Real-World Connection

Reading is at the root of everything we do. We read to follow directions, solve problems, communicate, text, email, and interact on social media. The opportunities for reading are *endless*.

Many adults I know dislike the act of reading because they have never experienced a book that was *fun* and *interesting* to them. In schools, if we only give standardized test passages or only have students read books on the summer reading list, then we are taking away from the fun and full *experience* of reading.

Not all of us had an adult model reading for pleasure or the resources for a fully stocked bookshelf. Books and Blankets provides this fun and free time to explore a range of books and be inspired by reading.

Dear Families

Good news! Books and Blankets can be done *anywhere*: at home, in the car, on the couch, or even on vacation. At home, designate a space with your child to keep books, a blanket, and stuffed animals. Hang string lights or use dimming lights/lamps. Play music from your phone, speaker, or a noise machine with a sound your child likes. Visit local libraries to replenish books and encourage reading through a variety of genres. Make Books and Blankets a once-a-week activity for the whole family!

Start by reading aloud to your child. Ask them to predict what might happen by looking at the pictures. Over time, slowly transition toward taking turns reading, ultimately having them fully read to you. Encourage the last few minutes to be time with just them and their book. Do a few minutes each day until their reading stamina grows. When they are finished, let them tell you about what they read and their favorite part!

You are incredibly influential in your child's reading journey. Show them how *you* would tell a story through pictures. Play audiobooks when driving in the car. Let them see *you* reading for fun and watch how their excitement grows for books!

B is for Books and Blankets Wish List

- Book boxes/book baggies for each student
- Book-themed sticker reward charts
- Child-sized superhero cape
- Cushions
- Decorative pillows
- Dimming lights or dimming lamps
- Finger puppets
- Fleece blankets
- Mini flashlights

- Mini magnifying glasses
- Noise-cancelling headphones
- Oversized costume reading glasses
- Reading badges or certificates
- Reading genre BINGO
- Reading pointers
- Small bookshelf
- String lights
- Stuffed animals

Extra! Extra! Read All About It

Are You Sitting Comfortably?
Written & Illustrated by Leigh Hodgkinson

Come, Read with Me
Written by Margriet Ruurs; Illustrated by Christine Wei

How Do Dinosaurs Learn to Read?
Written by Jane Yolen; Illustrated by Mark Teague

Shhh! I'm Reading!
Written by John Kelly; Illustrated by Elina Ellis

You Can Read
Written by Helaine Baker; Illustrated by Mark Hoffmann

A **B** C D E F G H I J K L M N O P Q R S T U V W X Y Z
is for **Books and Blankets** because . . .
The way *we* and our *students experience* reading m a t t e r s

C

C is for Conflict Resolution

[CONFLICT]: 1) A competitive or opposing action of incompatibles: an antagonistic state or action (as of divergent ideas, interests, or persons); 2) A mental struggle resulting from incompatible or opposing needs, drives, wishes, or external or internal demands (Merriam-webster.com, 2025)

Similar to . . . struggle, confrontation, discord, scuffle, tug-of-war, friction, disagreement, dispute, opposition, tension, tangle, clash, or contrast (WordHippo, 2025)

[RESOLUTION]: The act of answering, solving, determining, or analyzing a complex notion into simpler ones (Merriam-webster.com, 2025)

Similar to . . . resolve, perseverance, determination, verdict, decision, commitment, solving, ending, conclusion, answer, remedy, or fulfillment (WordHippo, 2025)

I can <u>teach and model healthy ways to resolve conflict</u> so my *students* can . . .

- ♦ Advocate for themselves
- ♦ Apologize without negating the apology
- ♦ Navigate conflict with their peers
- ♦ Take responsibility for their actions, big or small
- ♦ Voice their wants, needs, feelings, and boundaries

> *"The quality of our lives depends not on whether or not we have conflicts, but on how we respond to them."*
> —Thomas Crum (Crum, 1995)

Conflict is *everywhere*. It surrounds us. We experience conflict with family, friends, coworkers, neighbors, strangers, and within ourselves. We experience conflict when driving, at the store, and on social media. But most importantly, our classrooms are filled with young minds learning to navigate life and the conflicts it brings. Do any of the following sound familiar?

> "They pushed me!"
> "They said they weren't my friend anymore!"
> "I didn't do it!!"

Our kids work through conflict every day, but the resolution of conflict is something that is learned and practiced. Lucky us, we get to teach it!

FIGURE C.1 Our Chapter C *why*

Conflict is natural. Conflict is healthy. It helps us navigate our life and boundaries, stretching us as people. *The goal is not to delete or remove conflict, but to learn to handle it in a healthy, transformative way, bringing resolution, rather than escalation.*

Little minds and little eyes are watching our every move as trusted adults. They are watching how we respond to conflict and frustration, how we communicate effectively and ineffectively, and the language we use to solve problems.

One of my favorite ways to teach **Conflict Resolution** is through a four-step approach that I like to call: **The Recipe for Resolution**.

THE RECIPE FOR RESOLUTION

1 SAY IT
"I DON'T LIKE IT WHEN YOU _____."

2 OWN IT
"I APOLOGIZE FOR _____."

3 ACCEPT IT
"I ACCEPT YOUR APOLOGY."
"I DON'T ACCEPT YOUR APOLOGY YET. I NEED YOU TO _____."

4 RESOLVE IT
"WOULD YOU LIKE A..."

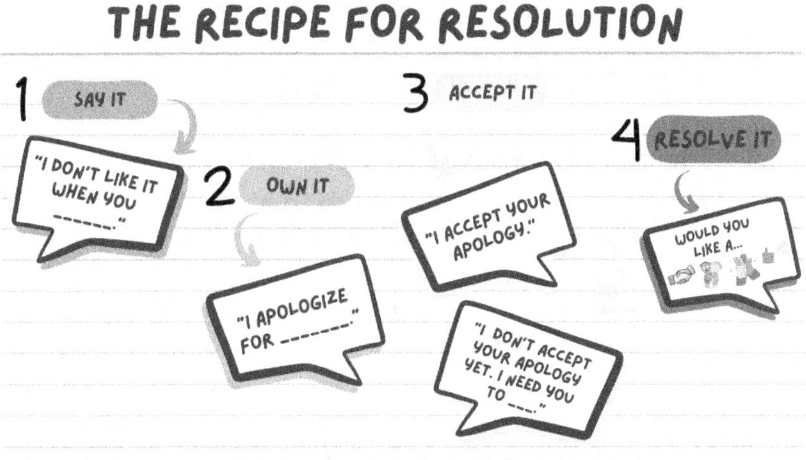

FIGURE C.2 The Recipe for Resolution steps

1) **SAY IT:** *"I don't like it when you _____."*
   Our first step focuses on finding your calm, taking a deep breath, and speaking up for yourself. Use a complete sentence to *state the behavior* you do not like using the words, "I don't like it when you _____." Upper elementary students can add details regarding how they feel. When teaching "Say It," discuss with students how important it is to speak up for themselves and identify their emotions before having their conversation.

2) **OWN IT:** *"I apologize for _____."*
   This step is about *owning your part by* taking responsibility, reflecting on the matter at hand, and apologizing. When ready to do so, sincerely use the words, *"I apologize for _____."* When teaching "Own It," lead a discussion about how to apologize sincerely with your tone, body language, and word choice. Talk about what happens when you are blamed for something you did not do, it was an accident, or you are not ready to apologize yet.

   Owning your part can also be done non-verbally by writing an apology on a sticky note. Leave a stack of sticky notes and a pencil near a designated conflict resolution area for students to use if needed.

3) **ACCEPT IT:** *"I accept your apology"* or *"I do not accept your apology yet"*
   This step ensures that both parties have listened, taken ownership, and are headed toward a resolution. The child who initiated the conversation decides whether they accept or do not accept the apology given. Teach two different sentences: *"I accept your apology"* and *"I do not accept your apology yet. I need you to _____"* (For example: I need you to say it again nicely or I need you to look me in my eyes.)

   If the apology feels insincere or is said in an unkind tone of voice, I tell students to state what they need, then give the friend some time to calm down and process if they are ready or not. It's important for our kids to be the gatekeepers of what they *will* and *will not* accept from others. When teaching "Accept It," talk about the meaning of *forgiveness* and the importance of feeling respected during conflict resolution.

4) **RESOLVE IT:** *"Would you like a _____ or a _____?"*
   This step concludes the conversation by showing that both parties have listened, agreed, and are willing to move forward. Give your students a list of options they can choose from to resolve their conflict and have them ask the other

child what they prefer. For example: "Would you like a handshake, high five, fist bump, or thumb kiss?"

In the past, I used the sentence, "It's okay, but don't do it again" to resolve conflict. But over the years, I realized that sometimes, it's *not* okay . . . and that's okay! Boundaries are crossed. People get hurt. When teaching "Resolve It," discuss how we can accept apologies and forgive, but we don't need to say the action is okay when it doesn't feel that way.

When teaching the **Recipe for Resolution**, make sure to state clear expectations, create a visual, model the behavior you want to see, and practice by role-playing.

To *teach expectations*, sit down with students to explain what conflict is, where they've experienced or seen it, and tell them what you expect in the classroom. For example, "If our feelings are hurt, we use our *words*, not our *hands*. Today, we are going to practice using our words to solve problems."

Next, *create a visual*—a colorful anchor chart to show the four steps. Add pictures of the children in action, let students help you write the words on the chart, and make it accessible to them at eye level so they can practice without you. You can even create a "Words Pledge" where the students can sign their name, stating that they will try their best to use their words from this point forward.

Last, *model and practice* the recipe routine with students. Act out each step and allow them to see firsthand what the expectation is from you. Make sure to discuss tone and volume of voice. Then, let them role-play with one another. This will take *a lot* of practice . . . Rome wasn't built in a day! Role-play various scenarios such as pushing, saying unkind words, breaking a class/school rule, and cutting in line.

Where to Start

1. Lead a family meeting to discuss each of the four steps to The Recipe for Resolution
2. Create a "Use My Words" anchor chart and post it in the classroom with pictures of the students practicing

3. Delegate a space to have conflict resolution conversations and praise when students resolve conflict independently

But What If...

...Students Are Talking Over One Another When Using The Recipe for Resolution?
Pass a stick, fake flower, ball, or stuffed animal back and forth to show whose turn it is to talk. The person holding the item holds the speaking power.

FIGURE C.3 Two students using a teddy bear stuffed animal to take turns talking

...A Child Is Refusing to Listen?
I tell students to "Try three before me," which means to attempt to use your words three times before inviting me in for support. Assist with advice such as, "Even when we don't agree, we still can hear and listen." If the child isn't ready to talk, I will have them ask, "Do you need a few minutes before talking?"

...A Child Didn't Do What They Are Being Accused of?
Sometimes, kids exaggerate or make up a story to get someone else in trouble. Sometimes a child flat out *didn't* do what they are being accused of. For me, it's very important to validate both stories while also asking questions. I want to know the who, what, when, where, and why, in order to have a full picture of

the conflict. Sometimes, this means talking to students one at a time, in a group, or asking the parties involved to sit together and come back when they have *one* story that they *both* agree on. I tell students to dig deep and think of one thing they can take ownership of or say, "I wasn't the one who did it, but I can help you figure out who did."

. . . A Child Is Playing Defense?
Sometimes, the listener reacts with tears, thinking they are in trouble or loudly declares, "BUT THEY DID IT FIRST!" or "I DID NOT!" I try to catch these moments as quickly as possible and dig into the who, what, when, where, why, and how. Then, we start from the beginning, making sure to *listen* to our friend.

. . . Their Conflict Resolution Is Disruptive?
Designate a corner/space in the room for students to use that is distanced from the whole-group carpet or main learning space. Give it a fun name like "The Words Window," the "Talk-it-out Territory," "The Resolution Rug," or the "Conflict Corner."

. . . The Problem Involves More Than Two Children?
If the problem involves two to four children, have them talk two-by-two and then swap. If the problem involves more than four children, stop what you are doing and hold a *family meeting* where all students are brought to the carpet and sit to discuss the conflict. Then, take time for the class to solve the problem *together* (see Qu like in Conse/qu/ences chapter for more).

. . . Their Apology Doesn't Sound Like an Apology?
Some words negate, invalidate, blame shift, or make an excuse for an apology. They cancel out the "I'm Sorry." I like to call this, *slicing out the sorries*. For example:

- "I'm sorry *you* . . ." places blame on the speaker.
- "I'm sorry, *but* . . ." negates the apology and gives an excuse.
- "I'm sorry *if* . . ." also places blame on the speaker.
- A sharp, "I'M SORRY!" checks the box, but dismisses the speaker.

Real-World Connection

How we communicate, listen, take accountability, and respond sincerely is all part of conflict resolution. Many adults have yet to master this skill—learning *how* to communicate can only *help* us. As adults, we forget that communication and solving problems can be *learned* through practice and experience.

Our kids are *sponges*. Their growing minds and little eyes are watching our every move. They look up to us. Copy us. Notice when we talk about our feelings—and when we don't. If we aim to react patiently, kindly, and with empathy during conflict, our students will follow suit.

When our kids see us apologize and put words to how we feel, it frees them to do the same. Our job as educators and parents is to help our kids resolve conflict in a healthy manner. Ask yourself how *you* respond to conflict: Do you run away? Avoid it because it makes you uncomfortable? Escalate out of frustration? Or apologize so it's over quickly?

Dear Families

Your kids are watching your every move. They pay attention to your daily interactions and empathize when you feel upset. Model what it looks like to take a deep breath, use your words, and resolve conflict.

If there is constant conflict between siblings, use the Recipe for Resolution at home. Teach your child the words to use to voice how they feel. Celebrate them when they independently resolve a conflict.

Connect with your child's teacher to see what words they use at school to resolve conflict. Try and repeat the same words at home so that your child is even more successful.

C is for Conflict Resolution Wish List

- Sticky notes and a pencil
- Talking tool: a stick, fake flower, or stuffed animal

Extra! Extra! Read All About It

How to Apologize
Written by David LaRochelle; Illustrated by Mike Wohnoutka

I'm Sorry *(The I'm Books)*
Written & illustrated by Michael Ian Black

One Little Word
Written by Joseph Coelho; Illustrated by Allison Colpoys

Ravi's Roar *(Big Bright Feelings)*
Written & illustrated by Tom Percival

The Rabbit Listened
Written & illustrated by Cori Doerrfeld

A B **C** D E F G H I J K L M N O P Q R S T U V W X Y Z
is for **Conflict Resolution** because . . .
The way *we* and our *students* handle conflict m a t t e r s

D

D is for De-escalation

> **[DE-ESCALATE]**: To decrease [specifically—behaviors] in extent, volume, or scope (Merriam-webster.com, 2025)
> **Similar to** . . . lower, ease, diminish, or reduce (WordHippo, 2025)

I can <u>provide a range of de-escalation techniques in the classroom</u> so my *students* can . . .

- Demonstrate strategies for self-soothing and self-regulating
- Feel supported in expressing their emotions
- Reflect on the impact of their personal behaviors
- Respond to others with love and empathy
- Understand how their behavior influences the surrounding environment

"It's not what happens to you, but how you react to it that matters."

—Epictetus

The behaviors we see at school can make or break our day, room, year, or job as a whole. But when we understand that kids are typically responding to their environment, we get a broader understanding of the root cause of their behavior.

In early childhood and elementary classrooms, children are not only learning to deal with their own emotions but are also picking up on behaviors from adults and the world around them, trying them on for size. They are figuring out who they are, what works for them, and what feels right, wrong, safe, or unsafe. A safe and loving adult is a crucial part of this process—to remind them they are loved no matter what and support them with processing situations.

In this chapter, we will dig into the importance of de-escalating behaviors and seeing the process through to the very end.

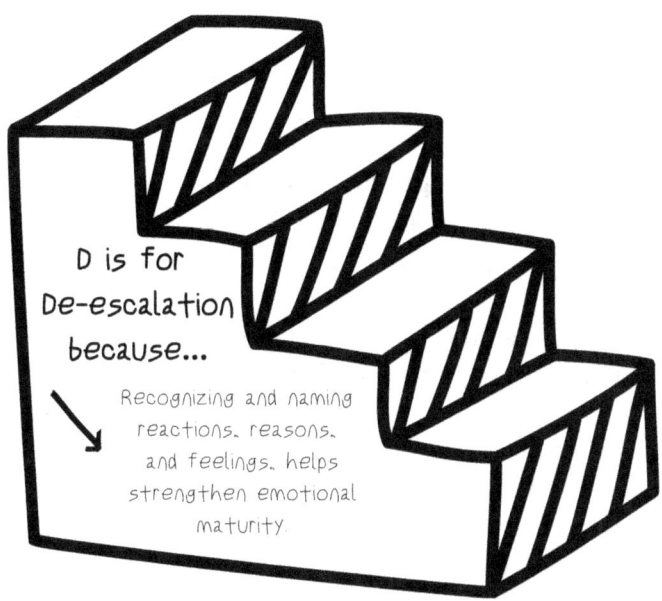

FIGURE D.1 Our chapter D *why*

The behaviors we focus on in this chapter are not the violent and unsafe behaviors that put you or other children in danger, but instead, the stomps and slams, hmpfs and humphs, *whys*, *NOs*, and *I don't want tos*. But to begin our conversation on healthy de-escalation, we must first journey through a sequence of steps called **The Flow of De-escalation**.

REACTION→ REASON → RESOLUTION → REFLECTION

The **REACTION** refers to the child's behavior; the response/action they took. The **REASON** is the *why* of the response and the emotion behind it. The **RESOLUTION** is the practice of using de-escalation strategies, and the **REFLECTION** concludes with a loving debrief, discussing how next time will be different, an affirmation, and a welcoming back into the environment. Let's dig a little deeper into this *flow*.

The Reaction

Think about a specific student and behavior you noticed recently that you would like to see change. If the child felt sad, frustrated, left out, or ignored by someone, how did they respond? What actions did they take? Did they cry, yell, whine, stomp, throw something on the ground, or run the other direction?

Take a moment to think about the environment around them. Is it possible they were feeling overwhelmed? Stressed? Confused? Tired? Was it too loud, hot, cold, or did music or noise distract them?

This is also the time for you to respond—cool, calm, and collected. Your response requires a soft, loving tone that gives firm and clear directions, without letting the behavior trigger you. Ask yourself, *How am I feeling? Am I ready to enter this conversation and space?*

Sometimes, this can feel impossible! If you need a breather before you begin, *take it!* It is important that we, as adults, de-escalate and enter conversations in a way that supports and leads. I admittedly must remind myself of this often.

Once you note the **reaction** of the child and feel ready to support them through this *flow*, it is time to move to the next stage.

The Reason

In the beginning, you will be doing heavy lifting as you walk the child through *The Flow of De-escalation*. The goal is for the child to get to the root of the inciting incident, identify their core emotion, and continue to the reflection stage.

Measure the mood. Then, ask yourself or the child a few questions, beginning with basic needs. Has the child slept, eaten, or drank enough water? Then, dig deeper. Does the child feel sick? Are they injured? Do they miss a family member? Have they lost someone or an animal recently and are grieving? Are they in the midst of a big move or change within their family dynamic? Did someone hurt their feelings? Remind the child that you are there to help.

Many of our students have experienced trauma at their young age, seeing and living through unfathomable things such as violent events, deaths, robberies, abuse, the death of a parent, or an incarcerated family member. With all of this on their shoulders, we still expect them to smile, raise their hand, stop their tears, and stay awake. I'll be honest . . . *I* personally would not be able to do that! Our kids are beyond resilient.

Once you have a good picture of the inciting incident, resonating trigger, and the reasoning behind it, see if the child can identify and name the emotion they are feeling. Feel free to use tools from your Zen Den to supplement this process (see *Z is for Zen Den* chapter). If the child cannot verbalize their emotion, state what you see. Then, ask them if that is a good way to describe how they feel. For example: "I see that you have tears in your eyes—that makes me think you feel sad. Is that how you are feeling, or is there a better word? Can you share it with me?"

Once you have a reason and an emotion, move to the resolution phase. If the child doesn't have a reason—that's okay. Help them identify their core emotion and begin to de-escalate.

The Resolution

Here is where de-escalation strategies come in hot. First, you'll want to teach and model your decided list of strategies, role-play different emotions and reactions, and keep a visual reminder anchored in the classroom. You can even put your de-escalation strategies on a key ring with visual cues, so students can flip through and choose what works for them in that moment. I know the weight of teaching the state-mandated curriculum is heavy and time to teach other material is hard to carve out, but teaching strategies for de-escalation will allow for more time the rest of the year as students learn to do it independently.

As students learn to move through *The Flow of De-escalation*, we can continue to empathize, support, provide strategies, and make new resources available to them. Try adding some of these de-escalation strategies to your collection (see *Z is for Zen Den* chapter for more):

- Ask for a hug from a teacher/friend
- Brush your arm or hand slowly with a sensory brush
- Color a picture
- Cover your legs with a weighted blanket
- Do a puzzle
- Go to a quiet space
- Grip the sides of a chair with your hands and pull upward
- Hug a stuffed animal
- Listen to soothing music or nature sounds
- Look at a picture of someone or something you love
- Read a book
- Rest your head and eyes
- Sit next to a friend or an adult
- Squeeze a stress ball or play with a fidget tool
- Take a short walk
- Take five deep breaths, bubble breathe, belly breathe, or use an expandable breathing ball to guide your inhales and exhales
- Taste something minty like a peppermint, sour like a lemon, or cold like an ice cube to connect with your body and senses
- Trace your hand with a finger. At the top of each finger, hold your breath for three seconds.
- Watch a sand timer or lava lamp move
- Wear noise-cancelling headphones
- Write or draw about how you feel in a journal

Encourage students to come up with their own ideas and add to the list throughout the year. If you have extra time, have each child make a personal key ring of their favorite strategies and allow them to use it when needed.

The Reflection

Now that the child has de-escalated, you can move to the final stage of reflection. This includes a loving debrief, discussion of what can be done differently next time, an affirmation, and a welcoming back into the environment.

Begin with a **loving debrief**, a one-to-one conversation with the teacher or adult. This conversation is best eye-to-eye, so try and get low to be on the child's level. Here, you can put together all the pieces: the reaction, reason, and emotion they are feeling. Narrate or ask the child to retell what happened and the choices that were made. Discuss how others might have felt on the outside and ask if there is anyone they would like to apologize to. To take it one step further—encourage students to ask their peers, "What can I do to help you feel better?"

Then, talk about what can be done differently next time and what was done well. Did they choose a strategy quickly and calm down independently? Did they use words to express how they felt? Did they name an emotion without support? What do they want to do differently next time?

Next, provide an affirmation, validation, or reminder of your unconditional love for them. For example, "I am here for you," "It's okay to feel this emotion," or "We all make mistakes—no mistake could ever change how much I love you." Who wouldn't want to know that after making a mistake, they are forgiven, loved, and accepted? This monumental moment models acceptance, forgiveness, love, and grace.

Last, welcome the child back into their environment. Ask if they would like a welcome that is *private* or *public*. If they choose private, whisper, "Welcome back," and offer a hug. If they choose public, have the class repeat, "Welcome back, (name)!"

This welcome reminds the child that you and their classmates love and support them. It brings resolution to their *flow* so they can comfortably transition back into what their peers are doing.

Where to Start

1. Choose five easy-to-implement de-escalation strategies to begin with and create a visual
2. Model how to use all five strategies with your students and show students where to go when they need time to de-escalate and work through their *flow*
3. Hang an accessible visual that identifies feeling and emotion words

But What If . . .

. . . A Child Shares Something That Sounds Like Abuse or Neglect?
As educators, we are mandated reporters. If a child shares something that leads you to believe they are in danger, report the situation immediately to the CFSA (Child and Family Services Agency) and then to your administration or school support team. Listen, empathize, and comfort the child, reminding them that your job is to keep them safe. Tell them, "I promise to only share this with people that can help keep you safe."

. . . The Child's Behavior Becomes Unsafe?
If a child is being unsafe to you, themselves, or other children, ask a teacher, behavior tech, or administrator for support. Move the other children away if necessary to ensure they are safe, reassure them that you will keep them safe, and ask another adult to be there as a witness.

. . . What Works for One Child Does Not Work for Another?
De-escalation is not one-size-fits-all like jeans were in the movie *The Sisterhood of the Traveling Pants*. The same thing won't work for every child. As teachers, we need an overflowing toolbox of de-escalation strategies and an understanding of what makes each child tick. If a child has an Individualized Education Plan (IEP) or 504 Plan, read the recommendations and

accommodations for additional ideas. Ask your school counselor, psychologist, or social worker for more resources or de-escalation strategies.

. . . A Child Is Unresponsive or Non-verbal?
Sometimes, asking questions can magnify the situation. Give the child time, space, and strategies to de-escalate *before* digging into the reaction and reason. Tell them you will move away so they can have space, but you will be close by when they are ready or need you. It's okay for the *flow* to be different for each child. What matters is looping back for the *reflection* piece. Maybe they would prefer to talk to another trusted adult at that moment or they would prefer to write it down instead of speaking. Maybe they would prefer to point to visual cues or written responses. Think of what the child needs to best *flow* through their process.

Real-World Connection

We have all had disagreements, arguments, disappointments, or traumas to work through in our lives. Whether at work, with our family or children, or driving on the highway, there are many opportunities to allow our emotions to take hold of us. But our reaction to these moments and our processing helps us grow.

The goal for our kiddos is to name their emotion and de-escalate before responding with a less-than-satisfactory choice. We want them to pause, process, replay, take ownership, apologize, and plan to do better next time. Our kids want to know they are forgiven, accepted, and loved even if they made a mistake. As adults, *we seek the same things*.

We have the unique opportunity to provide language and words as well as de-escalation strategies as our kids grow into healthy, communicative, and expressive adults that process their feelings head-on.

Dear Families

Your child is learning about the world by observing others. They are picking up and copying behaviors they see and responding to emotion the ways they know how. The good news is—responses can be taught.

When you are feeling a big emotion in front of your child, try narrating as you use de-escalation strategies to calm down. Label your emotion and explain why you chose a specific strategy at that moment in time to help you. Enter into the loving debrief with your child but allow them to ask *you* questions. Show them that de-escalation isn't just for kids; adults still must practice it too. If your child is going through a big change at home, or has recently experienced something traumatic, partner with their teacher, school counselor, or social worker for support both at home and at school.

Here are sentence starters to help guide the conversation through **The Flow of De-escalation**:

- **Reaction**: "I see you chose to (action)."
- **Reason**: When I see (action), it makes me think you are feeling (emotion). Does that word match how you are feeling? Can you tell me what is making you feel (emotion)?"
- **Resolution**: "When I feel (emotion), I like to (de-escalation strategy). What strategy would help *you* feel better?"
- **Reflection**:

    - *Loving debrief*: "Can you tell me what happened from the very beginning?" "How do you think that made (person) feel?" "When you (action), what could happen?"
    - *Next time*: "Next time when you feel sad, what could you do to help your heart feel better before (action)?"
    - *Affirmation*: "You are strong. You can do this." "I love you no matter what."
    - *Welcome back*: "Would you like to join us/me to finish (activity)?" "Welcome back!"

D is for De-Escalation Wish List

- Expandable breathing ball
- Feelings and emotions poster/chart
- Metal book rings and index cards to bind de-escalation strategies
- Noise-cancelling headphones
- Primary composition books to use as journals with space to draw and write
- Puzzles
- Sand timer or lava lamp
- Sensory brushes
- Stress ball or fidget toys
- Stuffed animals
- Weighted blanket

Extra! Extra! Read All About It

Allie All Along
Written & illustrated by Sarah Lynne Reul

How Do Dinosaurs Say I'M MAD?
Written by Jane Yolen; Illustrated by Mark Teague

Meltdown
Written by David Griswold; Illustrated by Merle Goll

The Color Monster: A Story About Emotions
Written & illustrated by Anna Llenas

The Snurtch
Written by Sean Ferrell; Illustrated by Charles Santoso

A B C **D** E F G H I J K L M N O P Q R S T U V W X Y Z

is for **De-escalation** because . . .

The way *we* and our *students* respond and resolve how we feel matters

E is for Engagement

> [ENGAGEMENT]: 1) The act of engaging emotional involvement or commitment (Merriam-webster.com, 2025)
> **Similar to** . . . participation, partaking, involvement, joining, collaboration, inclusion, contribution, or cooperation (WordHippo, 2025)

I can <u>use active engagement strategies in the classroom</u> so my *students* can . . .

- Feel motivated and excited to learn new things
- Follow tasks through to completion
- Have *fun* learning
- Show they are engaged through participation
- Stay focused during various activities

"In every job that must be done there is an element of fun . . . And every task you undertake becomes a piece of cake."
—Mary Poppins, in "A Spoonful of Sugar"

In the Disney movie, *Mary Poppins,* our beloved character carries a bag that holds anything and everything you could ever want or need. Her bag adds an element of *fun* to her story.

Imagine *you* have a bag of tricks, so to say. A collection of strategies that you can pull from at any time to engage your students and add an element of excitement to learning. *You* decide what to pull out of the bag depending on the needs of the child. Because, what works for one, might not work for another. What worked with last year's class might not cut it this year. Our **E is for Engagement** chapter is playful and practical, introducing engagement strategies that can be tossed into your bag of tricks and pulled out when needed.

FIGURE E.1 Our chapter E *why*

When I picture **engagement** in the classroom, I see students with their eyes on the speaker, hear sounds of excitement, and feel a sense of joy in the space. Students are focused, determined, paying attention, excited, and inspired to learn *more*. But how you get that engagement may change from day to day. Different strategies serve different purposes. So, zip open your bag as we gather four types of *tricks*: tricks that capture attention, inspire interaction, encourage learning, and those with tools that keep learning *fun*.

Tricks That Capture Attention

- Attention getters: Utilize call-and-response chants that can grab attention in a quick and easy way. For example: If the teacher says, "Class, class?" the students respond, "Yes, yes?" and stop what they are doing.
- Brain breaks: Incorporate breaks throughout the day to rest the brain—whether it be through song, dance, yoga, stretching, turn-and-talks, or other movements
- Chants and rhymes: To capture attention and quickly transition learners
- Hand clapping patterns: Clap a rhythm and have your students copy it
- Instruments or music: To signal transitions and gain attention—play a chime, ring a bell, bang a drum, or start a song
- Jokes and comedic hooks: Find ways to intrigue students and make them laugh. For example: When teaching numbers one through ten, start with, "Why is six afraid of seven?" "Because seven ate nine!"
- Make every minute count: Students should always have something to do that keeps them from being distracted. For example: If the slides on the board aren't loading and you need a moment to fix them, ask students to do a turn-and-talk with a partner to predict what they will learn about today.
- Match me: When students need to redirect their attention, say "Match me! "and have them copy your movement. For example: Putting your hands on your head or touching your shoulders. Continue changing the movement until you have gained the attention of the entire class.
- Physical responses: Have students share opinions through movement. For example: "Stand up if you think the answer is ten," "Raise two hands if you think the first letter is s," or "Snap if you think I need more details in my sentence."

- Real-world connection: Connect student learning to the real world. For example: When learning about airplanes, ask, "Tell me about a time *you* have seen or traveled on an airplane."

Tricks That Inspire Interaction

- Gamification: Use games like Kahoot, Jeopardy, Bingo, or "I Have, Who Has"
- Kagan Cooperative Learning Strategies: Use Kagan's many engagement strategies such as "Think-Pair-Share," "RoundTable," or "RoundRobin" so students can actively share their responses (Kagan, 2009).
- Minute to win it: Give kids one-minute challenges to solve with a partner or group. You can find hundreds of examples online, such as one minute to get a penny out of an ice cube when teaching perseverance or one minute to move as many goldfish as you can to a bowl using chopsticks while learning to count.
- Non-verbal signals: Use hand signals to share thoughts and explain thinking. For example: Shake a hand to show you disagree or put one fist on top of the other to show you want to add on and share.
- Partner work: Allow students to help and review each other's work.
- Partner combinations: Pair students for discussion times using creative combinations like peanut butter and jelly, ketchup and mustard, or macaroni and cheese. There are many ready-made resources for these pairings online!
- Peer-to-peer calling: Give students permission to call on the next friend to answer a question or share their opinion.
- Share the pen: Allow students to use the teacher marker on the board to participate during learning time.
- Share time: Carve out time for students to share their work with the class or talk about something special to them.

- Student self-surveys: Give kids a say and the opportunity to give feedback. Show them how feedback can create change. Use their ideas and opinions in the classroom.
- "Write the Room" or "Read the Room": Allow students to search for questions around the room and record their answers on paper. This brings a great mix of learning and movement!

Tricks That Encourage Learning

- Friendly competition: Allow students to challenge one another in a healthy way. Turn quizzes into competitive games, practice teamwork and sportsmanship, and encourage the celebration of others.
- Give choices by providing two options. For example: "Would you like to sit on your circle or in your chair?" This fosters autonomy and engagement in the learning process. Kids have a say and can make a decision that works for them.
- Junior teachers: Share the teaching experience with your students. Call on them to explain directions, re-state learning, or lead a routine. Let them hold the flashcards or oversee calling students one at a time to get started on work.
- Motivational cheers: Use cheers and chants to gain excitement. For example: The Fireworks cheer by Dr. Jean and Friends consists of clapping your hands together and shooting them up like fireworks while saying, "Pop, pop, pop, pop!" Dr. Jean has an amazing downloadable collection of cheers on her website. Print cheer cards, bind them, and continue to add new ones (Drjean.org, 2025).
- Point systems: Divide students into teams and give out points for above and beyond behaviors. For example: Teacher versus students, red team versus blue team, or left versus the right side of the room.
- Wait time: In Doug Lemov's *Teach Like a Champion*, he encourages leaving a few strategic seconds after you finish

asking a question and before taking responses. This gives processing time for your range of learners (Lemov, 2010).

Tricks With Tools That Keep Learning *Fun*

- Flexible seating arrangements: Provide a variety of seating choices such as stools, beanbags, cushions, or folding stadium seats in the classroom.
- Manipulatives: Many kids learn through touching and doing. Give tasks that require manipulatives and tools such as counting cubes, counting bears, number tracing cards, and magnet letters.
- Incorporate student interests: Do students like to build? Use blocks to teach addition and subtraction. Do they like superheroes? Write a math problem about their favorite hero. Do they like Minecraft? Add clipart of characters to your worksheets and anchor charts.
- Individual materials: Use manipulatives for whole-group and small-group lessons. For example: Counting cubes to teach counting or place value blocks to represent the hundreds, tens, and ones in a number.
- Messy materials: Pull out materials like paint or glitter. Listen, your girl loves a clean classroom. Honestly, when I pull out messy art supplies, a little part of my soul dies. However, we all know kids love a good mess! I've found that year after year, especially after the pandemic, kids need to touch, feel, play, and make a mess. If you have set clear expectations for where the materials go, how much is used, and how to clean it up, let them get messy! Paint that picture, glue that glitter, roll out that clay, and have *fun!*
- Real-life objects: Represent and model learning using real-life examples that students can explore with their five senses. For example: Adopt a pet turtle when learning about habitats or make a turkey sandwich step-by-step before teaching how-to writing.
- Special writing tools: Keep a stash of scented markers, sparkly pens, or fun-shaped erasers to use during special activities.

- Spin a wheel: Use a virtual spinner on the board and personalize the options. Allow students to spin the wheel and see what it lands on.
- Sticky notes: After asking a question, have students write their answer on a sticky note and add it to a poster or board.
- Teaching incentives: Keep a drawer with crowns, sunglasses, superhero capes, and inflatable microphones to sprinkle in a dash of *fun*.

FIGURE E.2 Child doing daily math work after earning the superhero cape for math time

- Technology: Search online for virtual flashcards, math manipulatives, e-books, games, or incentives to use on the classroom smartboard or screen.

Once you have filled your bag with tricks, be mindful of the amount you reveal at a time. We don't want to fill our bag, then proceed to dump it out all over the table. We want our kids to curiously ask "Ooh! Whatcha got in there?!" Start small, put strategies away before taking out another, and don't forget to have *fun*!

Where to Start

1. Make a list of the engagement strategies you would like to add to your bag of tricks

2. List the expectations that need to be taught before rolling out each strategy
3. Teach, model, and remember to *have fun!*

But What If . . .

. . . I Panic and Forget My Tricks?
Create a visual collection of your engagement tricks or write each one on a popsicle stick and choose from a jar at random. The more you use them, the more natural they will come.

. . . My Students Keep Talking and Working When I Use an Engagement Strategy?
Before using engagement strategies, teach your students how to listen for a bell that signals quiet, put their hands on their head when they hear your voice, or catch a bubble in their mouth when the lights turn off. If you have already taught the expectations and still have to give three or more reminders, stop the activity and re-teach the steps to ensure everyone understands. But keep in mind—there is such a thing as *healthy chatter* and *healthy laughter!*

. . . My Tricks Aren't Working?
Assess your delivery, personal excitement, and follow-through with your bag of tricks. When you share and teach about them, are you giving clarity? Are you excited about the trick when explaining or revealing it to students? When you say you will give them something, do you follow through? These are all important ways to build excitement, trust, and natural engagement before revealing your bag of tricks.

Real-World Connection

As adults, we aren't so different from our kids. When we aren't captivated, stimulated, or intrigued by the environment around us, we can lose focus. The same goes for our students! When we are disengaged, we might scroll on our phone, doodle, or start talking to others.

We need engagement, excitement, and motivation, whether extrinsically or intrinsically. Let's use our personal experience as a reminder to ensure our kids feel excited, encouraged, and inspired to learn more.

Dear Families

You can create your own *Bag of Engagement Tricks* at home! Try adding strategies to *your* bag that engage your child during homework time or in their day-to-day:

- Cook a meal or a snack together
- Create a homework corner/station with special materials like sparkly pencils, scented markers, or cushions on chairs
- Do science experiments and try new things together
- Encourage activities that incorporate play, creativity, and hands-on learning
- Explore the great outdoors to find inspiration for learning
- Go on treasure hunts or nature walks in search of something
- Learn to play a musical instrument together
- Motivate using incentives (see *I is for Incentives* chapter for more)
- Play games or sports together
- Read books together
- Re-arrange furniture or re-decorate a space
- Set goals with your child using colorful sticker charts
- Turn household tasks into games or timed challenges
- Use sidewalk chalk to solve math problems or hopscotch new words
- Use online videos with music, movement, and fun facts to reinforce learning, research information, or answer lingering questions

E is for Engagement Wish List

- Bell
- Chime
- Dr. Jean and Friends *Cheer Cards*
- Flexible seating options like stools, bean bag chairs, cushions, or folding stadium seats
- Inflatable microphones
- Kid-sized crowns
- Kid-sized sunglasses
- Manipulatives: counting cubes, counting bears, number tracing cards, or magnet letters
- "Messy materials" like paint or glitter
- Small drum
- Special writing tools like sparkly pens, scented markers, and fun-shaped erasers
- Superhero capes

Extra! Extra! Read All About It

Don't Push the Button! A Funny Interactive Book for Kids
Written & Illustrated by Bill Cotter

I Say Ooh You Say Ahh
Written & Illustrated by John Kane

Is Everyone Ready for Fun?
Written & illustrated by Jan Thomas

Shake My Sillies Out *(Raffi Songs to Read)*
Written by Raffi & Maple Lam; Illustrated by David Allender

Stomp, Clap, Wiggle, and Tap
Written & illustrated by Rachelle Burk

A B C D **E** F G H I J K L M N O P Q R S T U V W X Y Z

is for **Engagement** because . . .

The way *we* and our *students* engage in our own learning matters

F is for First Week Fundamentals

> **[FIRST WEEK OF SCHOOL]**: Five jam-packed days of introductions, routines, and setting expectations
> **Similar to** . . . introduction, opening, foundation, or beginning (WordHippo, 2025)
> **[FUNDAMENTALS]**: Serving as a basis supporting existence or determining essential structure or function (Merriam-webster.com, 2025)
> **Similar to** . . . essentials, principals, or basics (WordHippo, 2025)

I can **prepare to hit the ground running the first week of school** so my *students* can . . .

- Feel excited and comfortable in the classroom from day one
- Get to know their classmates and teacher
- Move through transitions with confidence
- Take ownership and responsibility for their space and materials
- Understand classroom routines and expectations

"The beginning is the most important part of the work."
—Plato (The Republic, 2000)

The first day of school for teachers is unlike any other job. On the first day of a typical nine to five, one might take a tour of the office, meet new coworkers, shadow mentors, learn how to use software, get assigned a desk—and personalize it. During the first week, one grows in experience, comfortability, and understanding as they adjust to new expectations.

This experience is similar for our students. When they arrive on their first day of school, they might take a tour of the building or their classroom, meet new classmates and teachers, learn how to use classroom resources, move through routines and transitions, get assigned a desk, and personalize it. During their first week of school, they grow in experience, comfortability, and understanding as they practice new expectations.

But for *teachers*, the first day is a whole different beast. On the first day of school, not only do we give a tour, provide opportunities for newfound friendships, teach and model expectations, and assign the desks, but we also plan the lessons, move the furniture, clean and organize materials, write the names, and create an environment that makes our kids feel welcomed. Our job is to hit the ground running and lay a strong foundation that supports the rest of the school year.

FIGURE F.1 Our chapter F *why*

When I think of the school year, I picture a roller coaster. A wild ride of ups and downs. We go *up, up, up,* building momentum during pre-service week, *down* the big drop the first week of school, *twist, turn,* and *loop* through the rest of the year, and push the brakes the last few weeks as we roll into summer.

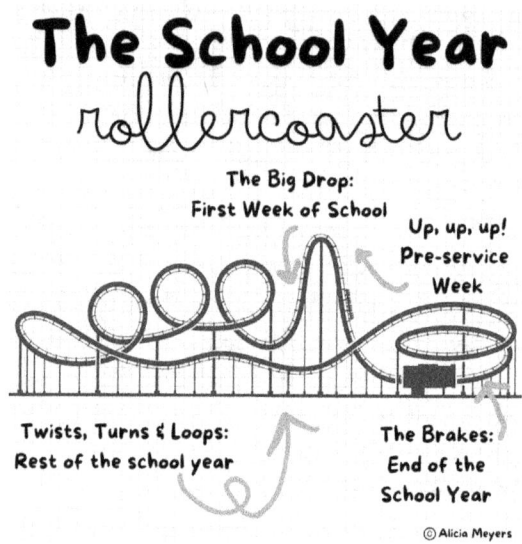

FIGURE F.2 The school year roller coaster

But what we do and teach the *first week* is fundamental. It sets the tone of our classroom—creates the culture, climate, and atmosphere. I remember the hours, days, and weeks I spent preparing over the summer before my first year of teaching. I wanted everything to be perfect. However, only 10% of my lesson plans were used as I realized management, expectations, routines, and transitions were far more important than jumping into content.

One of the goals of this A-to-Z journey is to work smarter, not harder, with a community of like-minded educators. Our chapter, **F is for First Week Fundamentals**, focuses on preparing a strong start to the first week of school. To me, a strong start means that students understand how the classroom operates, talk about how fun school was, and show excitement to return for week two. So, fasten your seatbelts, and let's zoom in on that big momentous drop—the first week of school.

The First Week of School Fundamentals

The WHO
The WHAT and the WHY
The WHEN
The HOW

The WHO

The WHO focuses on you and the students in your classroom through the incorporation of getting-to-know-you games and activities, so students can learn about each other, themselves, and their teachers. These can be done during morning meetings, carpet time, work time, recess, or even during transitions.

The WHO also focuses on representation and ownership in the classroom. This is when students decorate their desk, carpet, or cubby. Here are some ideas for ensuring that students feel welcomed and represented:

- Add getting-to-know-you tasks to center time. For example: Make vision boards, *Find Someone Who* boards, or *All About Me* flags that allow sharing about oneself.
- Allow students to choose their own desk, carpet, or line space. This shows them that from the beginning, you trust them and their choices
- Let students decorate name plates for their desk/table the first week of school
- Move books that represent students to the forefront of your library, so they feel represented, seen, and heard (see *R is for Representation* chapter for more)
- Take pictures of every child with a letter board and send it to families to celebrate their first day. You can also do this the last week of school and see how much they've grown!

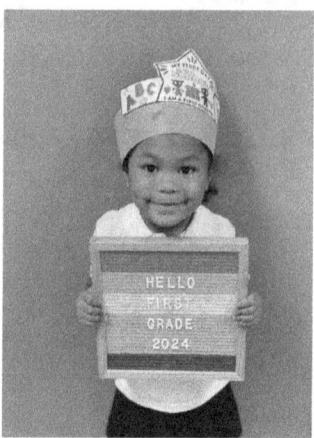

FIGURE F.3 First day of school letterboard

- Take portrait photos of all students and use them for desk plates, cubby tags, take-home folders, slideshows, center rotation cards, and anchor charts

The WHAT and the WHY

The WHAT and the WHY focus on what you will teach and why. The first week is prime time to prioritize your most important routines, transitions, and safety protocols.

Create a rough draft of a weekly lesson plan that lays out your priorities and helps you visualize your schedule. As the week goes on, circle any activities you didn't get to and move them to another day. Cross out items that are no longer necessary. There is no promise as to what the first week will bring, so it's important to stay flexible with your plans. Here are more ideas to help you prepare *what* to teach and *why*:

- Anchor your most important expectations or fundamental sayings of the classroom (see X *like in E/x/pectations* chapter for more)
- Ask students *why* they think the strategy or expectation you taught them is important and write down their answers

- Next to every expectation on your lesson plan, notate or think about *your why* behind it. It's important to have meaning behind the things we expect.
- Schedule time into your daily lesson plans to teach, model, and practice each important expectation, transition, and routine. Save time for reviewing as the week goes on!
- Share a list of all upcoming units and big learning standards with students. Make a checklist for what is coming up and check it off as you go.

The WHEN

The WHEN focuses on the schedule, routines, and transitions to introduce the first week of school that help you get from place to place or block to block:

- Add time-telling bulletin board pieces or labels around your analog clock so students can practice telling and keeping track of time
- Hang your classroom schedule with matching visuals so students can follow along throughout the day. Add a pointing-hand magnetic arrow that can be used to follow the schedule, so students know what happens next.
- Note all transitions in your lesson plan and add five extra minutes for them
- Post the times for bathroom breaks, snack times, lunch, and recess somewhere accessible in the classroom
- Use a small digital kitchen timer or digital clock to help students keep track of how much time is left in an activity or block

The HOW

Cue the song, "This Is How We Do It" by Montell Jordan. The HOW focuses on how we use materials and perform tasks in the classroom. Before students touch any material, it's important to explain *how* to use it. This helps prevent accidents, misconceptions, and misunderstandings.

If you are using pencils, there's a *how*. Say: "Pencils live in the pencil drawer. When they need to be sharpened, they go in the *To Be Sharpened* cup. The pencil sharpener's job is to sharpen them at the end of the day."

If you are walking to the cafeteria, there's a *how*. Say: "We stand in a straight line, directly behind our friend's head. We keep our hands to our side and keep a bubble in our mouth or stand in silent position. Our hands, feet, and objects like lunchboxes are kept to ourselves. If we are talking, we will have to go back and try it again quietly."

Before each block, center, or activity, notate the HOW. What do students need to know before I let them try independently? Try keeping a checklist for the first few weeks of all the *hows* and allowing students to check off the list as the week goes on.

FIGURE F.4 Example of a first week checklist of hows

Spend time on each transition until every child can follow your directions. It's okay to push the read-aloud to tomorrow so that you can ensure kids know how to clean up their workstations.

At the end of the day, we can plan for misconceptions and mistakes, but there is no way to know how the day will go with so many new, smiling (or crying) faces.

Our big, momentous roller coaster drop can look daunting the first week of school, but it doesn't have to be! The more you prepare, anticipate questions, and have strong expectations in place, the easier it will become year to year. The first week of school has grown to be my favorite week, and just like the night before my birthday . . . I can barely sleep out of excitement!

Where to Start

1. Make a list of your five most important WHATs with their WHYs. What five expectations/routines need to be taught for your first week to go smoothly? (see *X like in E/x/pectations* for more on creating your "Fundamental Five")
2. Anchor your schedule in the room with colorful visuals for students
3. Create your first week of school lesson plan and leave time for teaching and re-teaching routines, transitions, and practicing classroom expectations

But What If . . .

. . . A Child Says They Don't Want to Be There, or They Don't Fit in?
New things take time. Empathize with the child, get to know them, spend time with them, and begin to build a relationship. Ask their peer to volunteer as their buddy and partner with them through the first week of school.

. . . It's Mandated That I Teach Content the First Week of School?
The WHO, WHAT, WHY, WHEN, and HOW can be modified to content you are teaching. For example: If you have to do a daily read-aloud in week one, you can teach the expectation of carpet behaviors, how to do turn-and-talks/partner discussion, and

how to appropriately get the teacher's attention. You can stop throughout the story without losing the content piece.

. . . Parents Say Their Child Isn't Learning Anything Yet?
My motto is, "We walk the first week, so we can run the rest of the year." If a parent says their child isn't being challenged the first week, have a one-on-one conversation with them, explaining your values as a teacher. A positive classroom culture is important and built on the foundations of trust, safety, community, and comfortability. These are pillars to success, and as the classroom is a community, we need to create moments to make it feel like one.

Real-World Connection

We all know how important the first week is at any new job. It's prime time to establish ourselves, see the new layout of our days, and decide if it's somewhere we want to be long term. If we dislike our job, coworkers, or workspace, it can affect how we view the new commitment.

But think about how special it feels when entering a space and feeling welcomed, supported, safe, capable, and empowered from day one. It can transform the experience. During the first week of school, we have the capability to make this magic happen for our kiddos.

Dear Families

Momentum can also grow at home as the first week of school approaches. Here are some ways to build excitement at home:

- ♦ Do a daily countdown for the first day of school
- ♦ Learn about your child's teacher *with* your child by looking them up on the school website. Have your child write a letter for their teacher on the first day

- Pick out a special outfit or pair of sneakers for the first day
- Read picture books (see list below) at home focused on the first week of school and the feeling of being nervous/excited
- Talk with your child about how to introduce themselves, make new friends, and advocate for what they need. Help them build confidence about their new environment
- Wake up early and have a celebratory first-day breakfast or a special night-before dinner/dessert

F is for First Week Fundamentals Wish List

- Digital clock
- Pointing-hand magnetic arrow
- Small digital kitchen timers
- Time-telling bulletin board pieces/labels for an analog clock

Extra! Extra! Read All About It

Chu's First Day of School
Written by Neil Gaiman; Illustrated by Adam Rex

First Day Jitters *(The Jitter Series)*
Written by Julie Danneberg; Illustrated by Judy Love

Mr. S: A First Day of School Book
Written & illustrated by Monica Arnaldo

School's First Day of School
Written by Adam Rex; Illustrated by Christian Robinson

This Is a School
Written by John Schu; Illustrated by Veronica Miller-Jamison

A B C D E **F** G H I J K L M N O P Q R S T U V W X Y Z

is for **First Week Fundamentals** because . . .

The way *we* and our *students* start the year with momentum matters

G

G is for Goals and Growth

[GOALS]: 1) The end toward which effort is directed; 2) Aim (Merriam-webster.com, 2025)
   Similar to . . . goals, tasks, objectives, pursuits, undertakings, aspirations, or missions (WordHippo, 2025)
[GROWTH]: 1) Progressive development; 2) Evolution (Merriam-webster.com, 2025)
   Similar to . . . development, progress, advancement, improvement, or transformation (WordHippo, 2025)

I can <u>encourage setting goals and celebrating wins</u> so my students can . . .

- Build confidence and feel empowered in their learning
- Celebrate personal and peer growth
- Set and focus on specific tasks or goals
- Practice perseverance and develop a growth mindset
- Understand how small steps lead to big goals

"It does not matter how slowly you go as long as you do not stop."

—Confucius (n.d.)

Each of us is born with unique hopes and dreams. Some are easy to accomplish, while some feel near impossible. But to reach our goals in life, we have to learn how to *set a goal*, move *toward* it, persevere when it feels hard, appropriately handle rejection and disappointment, and celebrate our and others' wins.

FIGURE G.1 Our chapter G *why*

The topic of goal setting and school data can bring a load of concerns for both families and teachers. Families might feel out of the loop with what's being taught in the classroom, testing methods, standardized assessments, or their child's grades/scores. Teachers might feel overwhelmed and hopeless when looking at color-coded, gap-filled student data. They might feel the pressure trickling down from administration and become frustrated when day-to-day growth is not recognized. In my district, part of our pay for the following year is based on our student test scores and student surveys, so if the scores aren't up to par, panic can arise.

In the past, my administrator made a comment that stopped me in my tracks: "I'm not one of those Teachers Pay Teachers people with all the printouts. I care about the data."

Sir. *Sir*. We ALL care about the data. We bust our behinds for the data. We work daily for the data. We spend endless hours teaching toward and over-analyzing the data. This comment is where the divide lies for me between those who care about numbers more than the kids who provide those numbers. Getting the data and numbers we want goes far beyond teaching standards and required curriculums. There is an entire child to think about.

Our children aren't computers. We can't program them. What we *can* do is care about their data in a way that shows *why* and *where* students are struggling so we can start at the root and teach from there.

In my opinion, the school/district/state-mandated testing requirements tend to ruin the fun of goal setting and goal tracking. I see each learning standard as an umbrella goal. The process of mastering these standards can be *different* for each child. When I think of goals and growth, I think of celebrating *progress* toward a result, while thinking about the *whole child*.

This chapter is not about how to teach to the test. We aren't going to deep dive into numbers—but instead focus on the fun, encouraging, organized way of tracking data with data folders and spreadsheets, creating goals, using student goal trackers, celebrating wins, and analyzing data.

Tracking Data With Data Folders and Spreadsheets

To begin thinking through and keeping track of both goals and growth, it's important to have an organized, accessible system for two types of data: grades and evidence. I like to keep track of my student' grades and goals using two different systems: *data folders* and a *data spreadsheet*.

1. *Data Folders:* Using a three-pronged pocket folder for each child, create an easy grab-and-go location for all evidence

of student work and important documents. You can keep a range of items in these folders such as . . .

- Copies of progress reports and report cards
- Extra copies of login cards and passwords for student devices
- Family information sheets with all important contact information
- IEPs (Individualized Education Programs) or 504 plans
- Important work samples or portfolio pieces
- Incident reports
- Records of anecdotal notes
- Student goal-setting charts and trackers

The first week of school, let students decorate their data folder so they feel ownership in the data collection process. As a class, talk about the meaning of the word *data*, why it is important, the purpose of data folders, the location of said folders, and what is kept inside of them. At the end of the year, students can take them home, or the folders can be passed to their teacher for the following year.

2. *Data Spreadsheet:* Create a color-coded master spreadsheet in either hard or soft copy to keep all information in one location—easy to find and easy to track. Create a tab or section for each of the following:

- Assessment data scores: Create a column for beginning-of-year (BOY), middle-of-year (MOY), and end-of-year (EOY) assessments to track scores and growth
- Overall student grades: Keep track of students' grades for all tests, quizzes, projects, and big assignments, unless you have a separate gradebook (I personally like to keep a hard copy)
- Parent contact information: Parent names, phone numbers, email addresses, and emergency contact information for extended family
- Progress monitoring data: If progress monitoring throughout the year, keep track of student growth or concerns

- Progress report and report card scores: Keep track of all scores given out on report cards to double and triple-check your grade insertion
- Student information: Birthdays, student numbers, health notes, love languages, what students are motivated by, and usernames/passwords for online portals

Creating Goals

The creation of goals should be a filtration process that begins with the teacher. Start with the big picture and break down each goal. Ask yourself the following questions as you think through your goals for students:

1) Where does the *state/district* want them to be?
2) Where does my *school* want them to be?
3) Where do *I* want them to be by the end of the year?
4) How can this goal be broken down into smaller increments?

For example: In my district, the goal is to have 92% of students increase at least one benchmark level or leave at or above benchmark in the DIBELS assessment (Dynamic Indicators of Basic Early Literacy Skills). My school also uses this goal. When

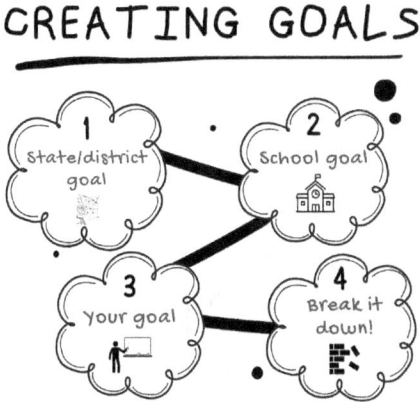

FIGURE G.2 Steps to creating student goals

looking at each section of the test, first-grade data typically shows me that word reading fluency and nonsense word fluency are the lowest-scoring sections. So *those* would become my biggest growth goals. Within that specific category, I then look at the *numbers*—where students need to be during BOY, MOY, and EOY to reach that goal—and break down where I want them to be throughout each month of the school year.

After setting classroom goals, think about the *whole child*:

- Accommodations: What accommodations are needed? Does the student have an IEP or 504 plan?
- Motivation: What excites and incentivizes them to work hard?
- Re-teaching: What can be re-taught for them to master this goal?
- Root concerns: What important skill do they still need to master? For example: To master decoding nonsense words, students must know their letters and letter sounds.
- Self-confidence: Are they confident about their abilities? Do they believe they can do it, or do they melt down when they have to try?
- Support: Who can help them meet their goals? Do they have support hours listed on their IEP? Are they in an intervention group? Do they have a parent/guardian/family member that can support them at home?

Using Student Goal Trackers

When setting goals with your students, it's essential to *let them be a part of the process*. Once you have picked your top two to three student-specific goals, use a visual tracker to help kids visualize their growth over time. Explain the goal, how to read the tracker, put a gold star sticker on the goal, and ask them "Where do *you* want to be by (specific time/date)?" Color in their beginning of the year data, have them write *when* they want to achieve this goal on their tracker, and talk about how exciting it will be to "beat the score" next time.

FIGURE G.3 Student goal chart for Nonsense Word Fluency in the DIBELS assessment

Each time you progress monitor a student, pull their chart from their data folder and let them color their updated score. Throughout the year, routinely send home copies of the updated student tracker.

Use stickers, highlighters, or colorful markers to bring attention to each step of their goal so students can understand where they are, follow along, and most importantly—see where they can get to.

Celebrating Wins

Every time the chart/tracker is updated, *celebrate*! Celebrate progress, perseverance, growth, and hard-working attempts every step of the way. Here are some ways to celebrate wins:

- Allow them to show their hard work to a teacher next door or an administrator
- Call or FaceTime a parent or family member
- Give a sticker or other incentive (see *I is for Incentives* chapter for more)
- Let the student color in their progress with a special pen or scented marker
- Make an announcement to the whole class so they can cheer for them

♦ Send home a copy of the student goal sheet with a sticker and handwritten note

Analyzing Data

Data is completely useless without *analyzing* it. As teachers, we must go deeper than the numbers. After setting and collecting data, take some time to reflect on a few questions:

♦ *Do any students need accommodations?*
♦ *How can I tag in a child's learning team?* (intervention teachers, after-school tutors, parents, guardians, or camp counselors)
♦ *What are they doing well?*
♦ *What are they still missing? Why are they still missing it?*
♦ *What social-emotional strategies would help them?*
♦ *What strategies did I see them use? How can a different strategy be helpful?*
♦ *When/how can I re-teach this concept?*

Where to Start

1. Use the creating goals chart from Figure G.2 to decide on your students' goals. How will you break them down into measurable pieces?
2. Create a manageable, student-friendly tracker or sticker chart to visualize said goals for each child
3. Schedule a time each week or month to check in with students on their goals and update their charts

But What If . . .

. . . There Isn't Enough Time to Do Goal-Setting Check-Ins?
Flexibility is key. Sometimes, things need to be rescheduled or cut for this to happen. But when you make one-on-one time to check

in with students, you'll start to see growth happen in front of your eyes and feel excitement buzzing. Is there a day of the week that is more flexible than others? I like to use Fridays for goal check-ins, progress monitoring, and bonus intervention groups.

. . . Students Aren't Showing Growth?
Find something positive to praise. Did you see a difference in their speed or fluency? How about their confidence? Did you see them refuse to give up? This is also a good time to pause and ask yourself if this is the best goal for this child. Goals can be adjusted. Break down their goal into smaller pieces and find a way to empower them so that they can see their success.

Real-World Connection

As adults, many of us set goals using vision boards, pictures, charts, accountability systems, calendars, and social media. Our self-talk affects the way we work toward our goals (see *S is for Self-Talk* chapter for more).

It's important that we teach our youngest learners how to empower themselves, work towards something without giving up, and celebrate one another along the way, just as we would as adults. Think about how motivation *toward* a goal can influence our kiddos as they grow up.

Dear Families

Good news! Goal setting and tracking can be done at home as well. Try to . . .

- ♦ Celebrate growth during homework time or when your child brings home finished work from school. Display their work and tell them how proud you are, specifying *why*.
- ♦ Track the number of books read, minutes read, or genres of books checked out at the library in a bar graph or thermometer outline with an incentive at the top

- Try to focus on the small wins instead of a specific grade or perfect score. Celebrate when they made a mistake, but it taught them something. Learning happens in the mistakes, too!
- Use colorful chore charts with incentives to track daily tasks

G is for Goals and Growth Wish List

- Gold star stickers
- Growth mindset affirmational stickers
- Motivational teacher stamps
- Three-pronged pocket folders (one for each child)

Extra! Extra! Read All About It

A Bad Case of the Almosts
Written by Janet Sumner Johnson; Illustrated by Alexandra Colombo

Flight School
Written and illustrated by Lita Judge

Mabel and the Mountain: A Story About Believing in Yourself
Written and illustrated by Kim Hillyard

Squirrel's New Year's Resolution
Written by Pat Miller; Illustrated by Kathi Ember

The Magical Yet
Written by Angela DiTerlizzi; Illustrated by Lorena Alvarez Gómez

A B C D E F **G** H I J K L M N O P Q R S T U V W X Y Z

is for **Goals and Growth** because . . .

The way *we* and our *students* set, work toward, and celebrate goals m a t t e r s

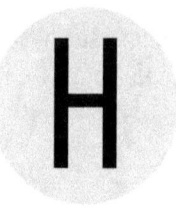

H is for Hobbies

[HOBBY]: A pursuit outside one's regular occupation engaged in especially for relaxation (Merriam-webster.com, 2025)

Similar to . . . recreation, entertainment, amusement, interest, pursuit, or specialty (WordHippo, 2025)

I can <u>encourage the exploration of hobbies in my classroom</u> so my *students* can . . .

- ♦ Correlate learning with fun
- ♦ Explore new interests, skills, and abilities
- ♦ Find commonalities and shared interests with others
- ♦ Practice self-expression
- ♦ Stay engaged through hands-on experiences

"Do what you love and love what you do."
—Ray Bradbury, author of Fahrenheit 451 (Bradbury, 2008)

Think about the kids in your classroom who thrive through creativity and exploration. What makes them tick? What makes them come alive? The first thing that comes to mind for me is a first-grade student I taught who had a passion for *art*. During phonics, he would doodle at the bottom of his dry erase board; during spelling tests, he would turn his letters into cute little monsters;

and during carpet time, he would gather tiny scraps of paper to create something with later. Not only did he love making art, but he was *great* at it. His creativity left me awe-struck.

I love to hear what careers, hobbies, and creative outlets intrigue my students, but I also love to witness the moment they feel inspired in the classroom by a new creative interest. I picture it like a seed being planted—the start of something beautiful.

In our **H is for Hobbies** chapter, we will water the seed of inspiration and watch it grow by compiling materials that foster the exploration, practice, and refining of hobbies and interests.

FIGURE H.1 Our chapter H *why*

From an early age, I loved to write and sing. In my free time, I wrote stories, made up songs, and performed in every school production. My music teachers helped me sharpen my craft through choir and one-on-one lessons, and my classroom teachers gave me the time and tools to build books. They encouraged me to enter writing contests, motivated me to follow my passions outside of school, and a few came to support my shows and performances on the weekends. I was extremely lucky to have resources and support surrounding me.

But while some families are able to purchase materials/equipment to explore a hobby, take a group class, or sign up for one-on-one lessons, others might not have access to the same resources and opportunities. Fortunately, the classroom is a place where we can make experiences, interests, and exploration *equitable* and *accessible* to all through the exploration of hobbies.

Begin by creating an area for all hobby materials to live. For example: The Hobby Corner, Hobby Drawers, or Hobby Baggies. My favorite storage technique is using drawers that can be removed and put back when students are finished.

Discuss the meaning of the word *hobby* with your students—something that interests you or that you enjoy doing and learning more about. Ask them what hobbies come to mind and make a list of their personal interests by writing their names next to each response. For each hobby, gather, sort, and organize materials by hobby name. When I began the process of "**Hobby Drawers**" in the classroom, I used what I had, then created a wish list asking for donations of gently used or new items. Then, during Fun Friday, free time, or morning work time, for 20–30 minutes, my students could freely grab a drawer and explore! *If students are interested in . . .*

- **Acting:** Allow them to role-play, improvise, write scripts, produce a show, or practice facial expressions. Fill your bucket with items such as puppets, masks, crowns, script templates, Reader's Theater scripts, costume pieces such as hats, gloves, a cape, a towel, or wigs, pretend microphones, playbills from real shows, a mirror to practice facial expressions, sound effect tools such as a small drum, bell, whistle, rain stick, or xylophone, and props like a baby doll, spoon, bowl, or cane.
- **Arts and Crafts:** Have a shelf or area for art supplies that students can access. Include items such as yarn, popsicle sticks, cotton balls, pipe cleaners, beads, sequins, buttons, felt, washable paint, watercolor paints, glue, markers, and a bound sketchbook with special drawing materials. Keep copies of *High Five* Magazine by Highlights for ideas

from their featured crafts section. Find kid-friendly YouTube videos that provide art tutorials or how-to books focused on the artistic process for kids.
- **Building:** Designate an area for building tools such as blocks, Lincoln Logs, or Legos. Provide materials to create with, such as blueprint paper, graph paper, protractors, and pencils. Make sure there is a flat surface for students to build on and an area to keep their project safe. Tearing down a building can be quite emotional after such hard work! Take a photograph or allow the child to draw their final structure and add it to a "building book" that holds their projects.
- **Cheerleading:** Keep a bucket of pom-poms for students with a notebook and pencil to write their own cheers. Print out popular cheers to read, choreograph, and perform. Add a badge on a lanyard for a "Cheer Coach" that one student can wear to teach cheers to a "squad."
- **Coding:** Give time and assistance for students to practice basic computer skills. Download applications/programs to student devices such as Minecraft, Scratch, Blackbird, Elementari, Vidcode, or EarSketch. Add in picture books such as *How To Code a Sandcastle* by Josh Funk; Illustrated by Sara Palacios, and other printed activities. Ask for donations of robot devices like Robot Mouse. Allow students to take the Elementary School course on https://code.org/ (Misstechqueen, 2023).
- **Cooking:** Provide recipe cards/templates for students to write their own recipes and collect kid-friendly cookbooks that students can read and explore. Add in dramatic play cooking materials and plastic dramatic play food. Create a playlist on YouTube of videos that teach kids how to cook or learn tips and tricks in the kitchen. As a bonus, cook in the classroom with the kids! Ask for donations for kid-friendly knives, bowls, and cutting boards. Invite a guest chef to visit the classroom and speak about cooking organically or fresh farm-to-table cooking. You can also request school funding to outsource companies such as FoodPrints, where students get to cook in the classroom.

- **Creative Writing:** Designate a writing space with various kinds of paper and writing tools such as glitter pens, scented markers, spiral-bound notebooks, and book-binding materials. Hang brainstorming ideas and pictures for inspiration. Add in a student dictionary and thesaurus with pictures. Keep a collection of poetry books nearby and allow students to write poems.
- **Dancing:** Create a YouTube playlist of technique videos for kids and various styles of dance. Add a standing mirror to the classroom so students can create routines while seeing their reflection. Ask parents to donate any gently used dance shoes like ballet slippers or tap shoes. Add a tutu, silk ribbons, top hat, folding fan, or dancing cane. Collect picture books that focus on styles of dance and movement—like *Let's Dance!* by Valerie Bolling; Illustrated by Maine Diaz.
- **Drawing:** Play step-by-step drawing videos from *Art for Kids Hub*. Get a special kit of supplies students can use during free time or when working on projects. Get a sketchbook they can call their own and keep it in the classroom. Download digital art platforms or applications they can use with technology. Outside of hobby drawer time, let one student be the 'art lead' and teach art lessons to students on Fun Friday. Ask them to help draw the pictures on classroom anchor charts. Have them assist with creating school banners, signs, murals, and decorations for events. Connect them with the art teacher for more opportunities.
- **Fashion Design:** Let students use a sketchbook to design outfits. Order a fashion design craft kit or design book that allows students to dress models and characters. Keep old fabric and clothing items and let them cut and design new creations for a mini mannequin. Ask for their advice to plan outfits for school performances or other events. If the school is designing new t-shirts, recommend that this child is part of the planning process.
- **Gardening:** Add small seeds, soil packets and pots, fruit and vegetable seeds, and a mini watering pot to this drawer. Allow the child to plant seeds in the classroom or outside

if there is a designated space, and track plant growth over time. Add picture books about plants and the gardening process. For extra activities, let a leader take the class on a nature walk, give students the responsibility of watering and taking care of a plant, or do an outdoor project where students see the fruit of their work in a real garden.

- **Jewelry Design:** Keep a collection of various beads, charms, and string in the classroom to create necklaces, bracelets, and rings. Allow students to make jewelry for dolls and stuffed animals.
- **Knitting:** Have child-friendly knitting needles and yarn available. Add a how-to book with step-by-step directions on how to begin knitting. Let students work on their project a little bit each day. Let them create a knitting circle during hobby time. Ask them to knit something for the classroom, like a coaster for a cup or a shirt for a baby doll.
- **Learning Languages:** Download Duolingo for the classroom or other online programs. Keep books in the classroom that serve as resources for learning new languages. If possible, connect the child with teachers or students who are fluent in the language. Use online literacy resources such as RAZ Kids https://www.raz-kids.com/ to read books in languages such as Spanish. Encourage students to write bilingual books by translating a sentence per page into the language or by finding cognates (words in different languages that are spelled similarly). To learn American Sign Language, bookmark https://www.handspeak.com on student devices or read *Mara Hears in Style* by Terri Clemmons; Illustrated by Lucy Rogers.
- **Magic:** Collect items that kids can use to perform and learn magic tricks such as a deck of cards or coins. Get a magician's cloak, hat, and wand, as well as a kid's magic kit or trick book. Find picture books and websites where students can watch tutorials and learn new tricks. Let them write a script to a magic show and perform for their classmates—costume and all!
- **Musical Instruments:** Collect donations for new or gently used musical instruments and allow students to use them

during fun/free time. Bookmark kid-friendly YouTube videos that give free lessons on the basics to playing a new instrument. Let them put on a special pair of headphones and take their online lesson with an instrument that you have access to such as a guitar, keyboard, or flute. Give students a notebook to write songs and lyrics in and let them perform for their friends. Students can also create their own instruments out of recycled materials, such as a tissue box guitar or a rainstick made with rice.
- **Painting:** Have a tabletop easel and special paint smock that the child can use. Ask them to paint something based on the lesson/content—like a character's feeling in a book or an alternate ending. Hang butcher paper and let them paint murals for each new unit of study (For example: Space or animal habitats) or a painting for the bulletin board.
- **Photography:** Ask for donations of disposable cameras, old digital cameras, or polaroid cameras that students can use to document certain parts of the day. Choose a student to take pictures during class events or field trips. Create a job as the resident photographer (see *J is for Jobs* chapter for more). Let students use free photo editing programs and watch kid-appropriate videos about photography and editing techniques.

FIGURE H.2 Student practicing photography skills at a hobby drawer

- **Sculpting:** Gather a bucket with materials such as molding clay, cookie cutters, and molds. Allow students to create sculptures in response to content. For example: Students can sculpt the character's facial expression to show how they felt at the end of a book.
- **Singing:** Have students write songs to transition or retell a story. Let them perform during share time or sing karaoke during brain breaks. Collect old microphones to play with during free time. Use a bedazzled microphone that they can use throughout the day when presenting or performing. Connect them with the music teacher for extra resources/opportunities.

FIGURE H.3 Two students practicing singing skills using microphones from a hobby drawer

- **Sports:** Add a microphone and thrifted suit jacket to let students act as the commentator to a sports game. Keep a dry erase coach's clipboard for students to draw out plays with small magnets to act as the players. Add in materials to write sports-based stories. For extra ideas: create/read stories based on sports to engage students, write math word problems based on the sports they are interested in, connect with the physical education teacher for additional ideas, and encourage them to try out for school teams to learn more.

- **Yoga:** Ask for donations of yoga mats and blocks. Add yoga time into movement breaks through online videos like Cosmic Kids Yoga on YouTube or FLOW on GoNoodle.

Hobby time also creates an opportunity for **Loose Parts Play**, where students can play with objects, materials, or items that can be manipulated, moved, touched, or explored for playtime. This concept, theorized by Simon Nicholson, typically done at the preschool level, highlights that kids should have the opportunity to openly and naturally toy with materials or "loose parts" to build on investigative critical thinking skills (Brightwheel, 2023; Nicholson, 1971).

If you would like to go *beyond* the classroom, there are a variety of ways to include creative hobbies and interests in your school:

- Get books from the library based on student interests and hobbies
- Host a "Hobby Day" or "Hobby Fair" where students can showcase their skills
- Organize a theme-based or interest-based classroom library
- Plan a field trip based on student interests
- Plan projects based on learning to align with student interests
- Start a school club based on a specific hobby (for example: knitting club)

Where to Start

1. Create a wish list or donation request with the items you want
2. Collect books for children focused on hobbies and *how-to* do them step-by-step

3. Create a list of local organizations for parents that encourage the exploration of hobbies. For example: classes at a community center, after school programs, vocal or music lessons, Saturday open gyms, dance studios, or children's museums that host events

But What If . . .

. . . My Schedule Doesn't Allow Time?
Incorporate creative time into academic blocks. Use project-based learning to allow creativity to flow or assign at-home projects to culminate learning. When planning, ensure there is a balance between hobbies that stretch curiosity, imagination, physicality, and creation. Start a club before school, after school, or a lunch bunch with a small group. Connect with specialty teachers such as the drama, art, or music teacher and ask them for tips, tricks, or curriculum support.

. . . A Parent Doesn't Want Their Child to Do a Specific Hobby?
If a family chooses not to participate in an activity, that's okay! Talk to the family about the positive aspects of hobbies and the benefits they can bring to their child as a young learner who is exploring and trying new things. Highlight people and characters who participate in activities that challenge the norm. A great picture book to share is *Except When They Don't* by Laura Gehl; Illustrated by Joshua Heinsz.

. . . I Don't Have the Resources to Provide Said Materials?
Create a DonorsChoose grant request or Amazon Wish List. Research accounts on social media that have "Clear the List" opportunities—where online viewers will purchase items on your wish list to give back. Ask churches, temples, or local organizations to support. For example: Ask a local yoga studio to donate yoga mats, a plant store for gardening materials/seeds, or a music store to donate unsellable items or to repair a donated item. You never know who is willing to help!

Real-World Connection

As adults, we have hobbies and interests just like our students. Following our dreams in adulthood means adjusting our work schedule, priorities, and budgets. We have to do our own research, spend money, buy materials, and attend classes or webinars. However, our kids could find their passions at an early age if we create the time and make materials accessible. We have connections, networks, and partnerships that can help.

Take the time to explore your own interests and hobbies. Find things that you enjoy! Do you want to be an artist, singer, or writer? Once you start exploring and pursuing your dreams, *share your experiences* with the kids! Sing, draw pictures, and write stories with them. Play sports, do yoga, or learn to knit a scarf with them. Model what it looks like to grow as a learner who has passion and perseverance.

Dear Families

Keep an open mind as your child explores their creative side. Use the ideas and resources above to encourage creative time for hands-on exploration. Inquire about after-school programs at your child's school with a creative focus.

If your child has a business venture they want to pursue, encourage them to try! Help them make a simple business plan, create a company name, gain a sponsor, and support them in reaching their goal. For example: selling homemade bracelets or paintings.

If your child tries something and doesn't like it, that's okay! Encourage trying new things, persevering through things when they feel hard, and deciding when something is not the right fit for you. Most importantly, support your child, answer their questions, and be a *partner* to them.

H is for Hobbies Wish List

- Art supplies such as yarn, popsicle sticks, cotton balls, pipe cleaners, beads, sequins, buttons, felt, washable paint, watercolor paint, glue, or markers
- Beads, charms, and string to make jewelry
- Blank recipe cards or index cards
- Bound sketchbooks with special drawing materials
- Building blocks like Magna-Tiles, Lincoln Logs, or Lego bricks
- Building materials such as blueprint paper, graph paper, protractors, and pencils
- Child-friendly cookbooks
- Child-friendly knitting needles and yarn
- Copies of *High Five Magazine* by Highlights
- Costume masks, hats, gloves, a cape, towel, or wigs
- Crowns
- Dance materials such as a tutu, silk ribbons, top hat, folding fan, or dancing cane
- Disposable camera, digital camera, or polaroid camera
- Dramatic play food/kitchen tools
- Drawers, buckets, or tubs to store materials divided by hobby
- Dry erase coach's clipboard with small magnets to function as players
- *Except When They Don't* by Laura Gehl; Illustrated by Joshua Heinsz
- Fashion design craft kits
- Gently used or new dance shoes such as ballet slippers or tap shoes
- *How To Code a Sandcastle* by Josh Funk; Illustrated by Sara Palacios
- iPad or tablet to practice coding
- Kid-friendly knives, bowls, and cutting boards
- Kids magic kit, trick book, and a deck of cards

- *Let's Dance!* by Valerie Bolling; Illustrated by Maine Diaz
- Magician's cloak, hat, and wand
- *Mara Hears in Style* by Terri Clemmons; Illustrated by Lucy Rogers
- Mini mannequin and various fabrics
- Molding clay, cookie cutters, and molds for sculpting
- New or used musical instruments
- Playbills from shows
- Poetry books for children
- Pom-poms for cheerleading
- Popular cheers, a notebook, and a pencil
- Pretend microphones/bedazzled microphones
- Props such as a baby doll, spoon, bowl, or cane
- Puppets
- Reader's Theater scripts
- Robot devices like Robot Mouse
- Script templates for screenwriting/film writing
- Small seeds, pots, soil packets, and a mini watering pot
- Sound effect tools such as a small drum, bell, whistle, rain stick, or xylophone
- Special writing tools such as glitter pens, scented markers, spiral-bound notebooks, and book-binding materials
- Standing mirror and handheld mirror
- Student dictionary and thesaurus with illustrations
- Suit jacket
- Tabletop easel and paint smock
- Yoga mats and yoga blocks

Extra! Extra! Read All About It

Be a Maker
Written by Katey Howes; Illustrated by Elizabet Vuković

Bloom: A Story of Fashion Designer Elsa Schiaparelli
Written by Kyo Maclear; Illustrated by Julie Morstad

Extra Yarn
Written by Mac Barnett; Illustrated by Jon Klassen

Louise Loves Art
Written & illustrated by Kelly Light

Who Do You Want to Be When You Grow Up?
Written by Paula Faris; Illustrated by Bhagya Madanasinghe

A B C D E F G **H** I J K L M N O P Q R S T U V W X Y Z
is for **Hobbies** because . . .

The way *we* and our *students* creatively express ourselves m a t t e r s

ns about

I

I is for Incentives

> **[INCENTIVE]**: Something that incites or has a tendency to incite determination or action (Merriam-webster.com, 2025)
> **Similar to** . . . motivation, encouragement, boost, drive, influence, or commitment (WordHippo, 2025)

I can <u>inspire in the classroom using incentives</u> so my *students* can . . .

- Build momentum for learning
- Have *fun* at school
- Practice goal setting and growth mindset initiatives
- Stay motivated and focused on tasks
- Work toward something meaningful

"The more difficult the journey, the sweeter the reward."
(Erin Andrews, n.d.)

Incentives in the classroom are like the gas we put in our cars. They get us moving, give us a destination, and push us to have a mindset of *doing*. What inspires *you* to work toward a goal? What motivates *you* to take action?

Every kid, class, and school year are different. The incentives that worked with one group may not work with another, but

DOI: 10.4324/9781003617204-10

having a readily available collection of ideas will bring variety and excitement to each child's learning journey.

In our **I is for Incentives** chapter, we will walk through a collection of tried-and-true, kid-friendly incentives that encourage the behavior you want to see and create an atmosphere of positivity and productivity.

FIGURE I.1 Our chapter I *why*

I grew up hearing the word *reward*, which holds a different meaning than **incentive**. While a *reward* is a prize given after performing a behavior, an **incentive** is a tool for motivation—used to encourage a behavior and presented *before* the behavior is performed.

Rewards recognize—
Incentives influence.

Rewards are given after—
Incentives are introduced before.

Rewards acknowledge—
Incentives motivate.

Incentives tie to targets. Merge with milestones. Go with goals. They direct our kids toward a positive learning experience and give them a destination. But let's be real: If we want to keep our classroom buzzing, we need a flood of ideas that can cater to every student. Sticking to the same old routine gets *boring*!

To mix it up and keep things fresh, we are going to build an **Inventory of Incentives**—a plethora of incentives that keep the energy high and the excitement alive.

When creating an Inventory of Incentives, add ideas that are unique to you, your kids, and your classroom. Show your students that you listen to them when they talk about their interests. Keep your incentives current, fresh, and exciting for your students. Boredom becomes lackadaisical learning. If your students are into Spiderman, add pencils and stickers that have Spiderman on them. If they enjoy science, get a slime kit. If they like trucks, get a tablecloth decorated in trucks and let them use it as a special spot to work. I once had a student who would do anything to zoom in on Google Maps and see the world. We made "Google Maps time" an incentive for getting his daily work completed.

Ensure your incentives go beyond snacks and candy. Snacks could motivate me all day, every day, but incentivizing them can be controversial. Kids can be motivated in ways that don't include sugar or food! Also, make sure to get parent/guardian approval before putting anything on a child's body, such as temporary tattoos, stickers, ChapStick swipes, and stamps, due to allergies/personal preference. I like to get this approval in writing at the beginning of the year.

You don't necessarily have to spend money to incentivize. If a student likes Bluey, laminate a picture and put it on a stick. Have Bluey give them kisses when they are working hard. If a student likes reading chapter books, let them earn time to put on noise-cancelling headphones and curl up with a book from the school or classroom library.

Over years of teaching, I've accumulated a hodgepodge of ideas from students, trainings, social media, and other classroom teachers that I threw into my bag and made work for me and my students. Here is a glimpse into my collection of incentives—my inventory. What would *you* add to *yours*?

FIGURE I.2 Inventory of Incentives Chart Part 1

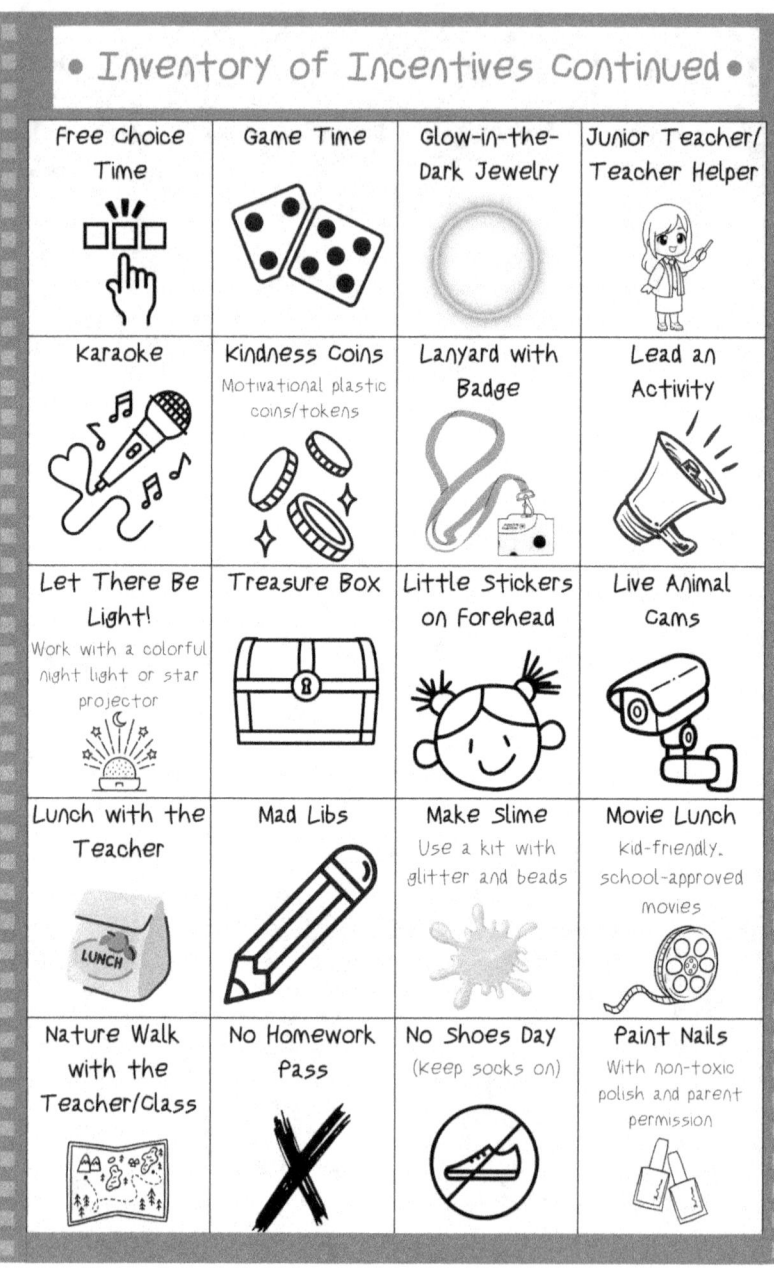

FIGURE I.2 (Continued)

FIGURE I.3 Inventory of Incentives Chart Part 2

Inventory of Incentives Continued

Smelly Swipes Swipe the top of the hand with a sweet smelling lip balm	**Special Chair** The teacher's chair, a cushion, or a decorated stool	**Special Writing Materials** Use a special gel pen, marker, or highlighter	**Stamps** Earn a stamp on your hand
Sticker Charts Add a sticker as you work toward a bigger incentive	**Stuffed Animal Day** Hug or hold a stuffed animal while working	**Teacher Play Time at Recess** Ten minutes to play with your teacher one-on-one! (PBIS)	**Trophy** Give out miniature trophies for above and beyond behavior/work
Under the Desk Work Work under the desk with a cushion	**Virtual Field Trip** Take a 360-degree tour of the White House, museums, or aquariums	**Virtual Roller Coaster Ride** Fasten your seatbelts and take a virtual roller coaster ride on YouTube!	**Visit Another Classroom/Techer** Be a helper, work with other students, or join in for some fun!
Watercolor Magic Draw on white paper with a white crayon and paint over with watercolors	**Wave a Wand** Use a magic wand throughout the day to shout out leaders	**Wear a Crown**	**Wear a Special Sash**
Window Markers Draw a picture on the classroom window	**Work in the Tent**	**Wrapping Paper** Wrap student desk with wrapping paper for the day	**Write with Paint Pens** Use paint pens to decorate the desk area (Tip Comes off with hand sanitizer!)

FIGURE I.3 (Continued)

Using *Class Dojo* (Classdojo.com) is one of my favorite virtual methods for tracking student behavior. On this website, students can earn points for a variety of categories such as working hard or teamwork. To encourage earning points, students get an incentive for every ten points earned. In the beginning of the year, we decide as a class what our incentives will be. We write down a bank of ideas, vote with stickers, and put them in order from smallest to biggest. For example: When students make it to 10 points, they get to go to the treasure box, but when they make it to 50 points, they get to change their name for the day. When students reach their goal, they write their name on the chart and patiently wait to earn their incentive until I am able to give it to them.

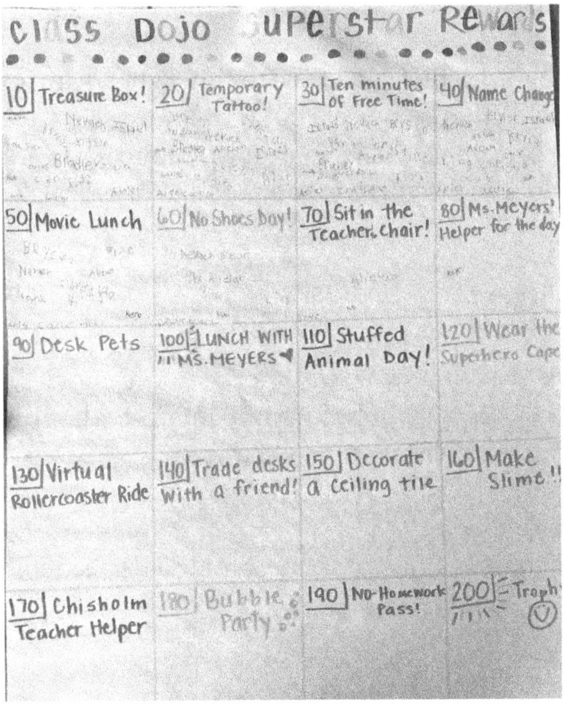

FIGURE I.4 Example of Class Dojo incentive chart—mid school year

Once you have created your Inventory of Incentives, divide said incentives into three categories to guarantee a healthy balance of whole group, small group, and individual incentives. For example: In my class, a virtual field trip is for the whole group, lunch with the teacher is for a small group, and the superhero cape is for individual students. Once you pick your incentives and create your inventory, make an anchor chart that reminds and encourages students of what they are working toward. For more incentive ideas, check out PBIS Rewards' *Ultimate List of PBIS Incentives*. PBIS Rewards (Positive Behavioral Interventions and Supports) is a framework used by schools to improve school culture and student behavior (PBIS Rewards, 2023).

I'm a firm believer that if a child earned an incentive, they should get to keep it. For example: If a child earned *lunch with the teacher* but threw an eraser across the classroom during work time, then the child would get a logical consequence regarding the eraser (see *Qu like in Conse/qu/ences* chapter for more) but would still have lunch with me.

I struggle with this from time to time when I am at peak frustration with a child's choices, but remind myself, "They already earned it. I can create a new, logical consequence to address their behavior, but the incentive is still theirs to have."

Where to Start

1. Ask students to share their favorite movies, television shows, sports, hobbies, and interests. Use this data to drive your selection of incentives.
2. Create your own Inventory of Incentives—an ever-evolving list
3. Purchase, gather, or request materials needed

But What If . . .

. . . My Students Get Upset When Others Earn an Incentive Before Them? Have a whole-group meeting to discuss the feelings and emotions that come when we feel disappointed, sad, frustrated, or not good enough. Talk about how it's okay to feel these emotions, but it's what we do *next* that matters. I tell my students

to breathe deep, tap their brain, and say "I'll get it next time!" I tell them these words work like *magic*! When people see you accepting disappointment, they are far more likely to think of you next time.

. . . My School Budget Doesn't Allow for Money to Put Toward This Initiative?
See if your Parent Teacher Association (PTA) can fund any purchases, create an Amazon wish list, GoFundMe, DonorsChoose, or ask parents/school partners to donate. Incentives can also be created with items you already *have* or require no materials at all. For example: a dance party, free time, picnic lunch, or nature walk.

Real-World Connection

As adults, we've experienced incentives in our careers and hobbies, and some of us use them to motivate ourselves. For example: When an office incentivizes a high number of sales to earn a paid vacation. Incentives can be used in our daily lives to encourage ourselves to do a specific action or behavior—the same way incentives can be used to encourage our kiddos as they cross the finish line and practice perseverance. What would your Inventory of Incentives look like if made to motivate *you*?

Dear Families

What inspires you? What helps you work toward and look forward? When thinking about the difference between rewards (given after performing) and incentives (presented before the behavior to encourage), what rewards do you use at home that can be transformed into incentives?

What is one goal that your child can work toward? What are specific routines and skills you want them to practice? For example: Working hard at homework time or picking up toys after playing. Think about how you can motivate your child *toward* these behaviors and start adding to *your* Inventory of Incentives.

Try adding a family movie night, game night, museum trip, bookstore or library visit, day without chores, drawing contest, or video game time.

Last, if you are cleaning out toys or books, ask your child's teacher or school if they would like any items donated. Teachers famously spend their own money to stock supplies and will be very appreciative if it checks something off their list!

I is for Incentives Wish List

- Animal erasers and clear plastic mini cupcake containers for desk pets
- Blank student certificates
- Board games (educational and/or fun)
- Bubbles/bubble machine
- Butcher paper
- Claw machine for kids with prizes inside such as mini stuffed animals or rubber ducks
- Color-changing night-light
- Fidget toys
- Flashlights (handheld or headlights)
- Gel pens
- Glow-in-the-dark necklaces or bracelets
- Hello name tags
- Karaoke machine or microphones (can also use YouTube)
- Kids' jewelry-making kit with charms
- Kindness coins (motivational plastic coins/tokens)
- Lanyards with plastic ID badge holder
- Mini stickers
- Miniature trophies
- Motivational button pins
- Multicolor pom-poms for arts and crafts and a jar
- Non-toxic nail polish for kids
- Scented ChapSticks
- Scented markers (non-toxic and washable)
- Scratch-and-sniff stickers
- Sidewalk chalk

- Slime kit
- Smiley face, heart, or star stamps
- Star projector
- Stuffed animals
- Tiny trinket prizes for treasure box such as pencils, stickers, and erasers
- Twenty-four-piece puzzles
- Unifix cubes (colors of the rainbow)

Extra! Extra! Read All About It

Earn It! *(A Moneybunny Book)*
Written & illustrated by Cinders McLeod

Jabari Tries
Written & illustrated by Gaia Cornwall

My Favorite Book in the Whole Wide World
Written by Malcolm Mitchell; Illustrated by Michael Robertson

When Grandma Gives You a Lemon Tree
Written by Jamie L. B. Deenihan; Illustrated by Lorraine Rocha

Y is for Yet: A Growth Mindset Alphabet
Written by Shannon Anderson; Illustrated by Jake Souva

A B C D E F G H **I** J K L M N O P Q R S T U V W X Y Z

is for **Incentives** because . . .

The way *we* and our *students* work and are motivated toward a goal m a t t e r s

J is for Jobs

> **[JOB]**: 1) A specific duty, role, or function; 2) Something that has to be done (Merriam-webster.com, 2025)
> **Similar to** . . . position, task, duty, mission, effort, role, contribution, or responsibility (WordHippo, 2025)

I can <u>provide a classroom job for every child</u> so my *students* can . . .

- Be accountable for a shared space
- Learn about responsibility
- Practice independence
- Take ownership of their environment
- Work as part of a team

"No one can whistle a symphony. It takes an orchestra to play it."
—H.E. Luccock (Luccock, n.d.)

Think about your first job. What did it feel like to be responsible for something? Were there high expectations or low expectations? How did you perform based on those expectations? How did it feel to get hired or fired?

For my first job, I answered phones, took orders, brushed garlic on fresh knots, and scooped blazing hot soup into cups at an Italian restaurant. I experienced the real world—*real* fast. I learned about efficiency, task responsibility, making and owning mistakes, doing things independently, and the hiring and firing process.

Our kids should be kids, yes. But they are ready for an introduction to the skills we hold in a job, such as accountability, ownership, responsibility, and independence. Classroom jobs are a way to teach that magic while taking the heavy load off your back. Using jobs, we can create an environment that is seen as a *shared* space—where everyone is encouraged to contribute.

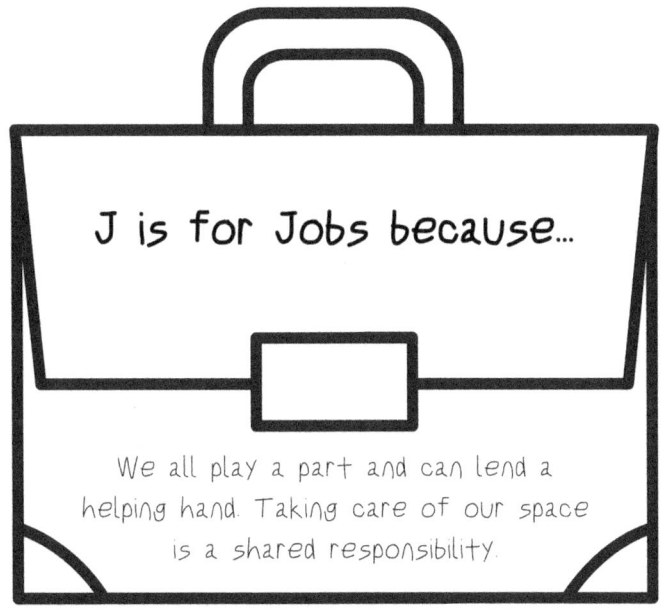

FIGURE J.1 Our chapter J *why*

Think about your classroom. Who is doing the heavy lifting to keep it functioning like a well-oiled machine—you or the students? What percentage of that responsibility lies with you and what percentage lies with students? The teacher sets the tone, but the teacher doesn't have to do *all* of the work. Tasks can be delegated to kids—it's *their space too*, after all!

Classroom jobs can teach students about responsibility, independence, accountability, and ownership. *Responsibility*, meaning students are trusted with performing their job according to your expectations. *Independence*, meaning students can perform their job on their own or with the support of a friend. *Accountability*, meaning students remember and do their job daily/as needed, and *ownership*, meaning students are chosen to own or perform a job during a designated time frame.

Let's break the rollout of classroom jobs into four parts: job titles and availability, choosing and hiring, modeling expectations, and firing and rehiring.

1. **Job Titles and Availability:**
   There are varying philosophies about jobs in the classroom. Some believe all should help with classroom responsibilities, some think kids should come up with jobs as they see a need, and some create five jobs at a time and rotate student names. What works for *me* is to provide enough jobs for *every* child. This creates a culture that says, "Everyone here is needed, everyone plays a part, and everyone is important to us."

   Think about each area of your classroom and the materials that live in it. What jobs can be delegated to the kids? For example: Watering a class plant or feeding a class pet. Write down the amount of jobs possible in your classroom and create catchy titles that the kids would enjoy. Here are a few of my favorite job titles and responsibilities to use in the early childhood and elementary classroom:

   - **Attendance Taker:** Takes daily attendance (I have the child do this on the website *Class Dojo* while I simultaneously submit in our school system. This provides a back-up attendance record when there is a substitute or attendance isn't submitted.)
   - **Calendar Captain:** Leads the daily calendar time at the board
   - **Counselor:** Consoles friends who are feeling big emotions. Takes them to the Zen Den (see *Z is for Zen Den* chapter for more), rubs their back, or walks with them to the water fountain

J is for Jobs ◆ 113

FIGURE J.2 The calendar captain leads the class at morning meeting time

- **Cubby Patrol:** Checks cubbies throughout the day to make sure nothing has fallen on the floor and returns items left behind to students
- **Disinfector/Sanitation Station/Health Department:** Gives the class one pump of hand sanitizer before lunch and after recess
- **DJ:** Chooses the songs for brain breaks and movement breaks
- **Door Holder/Door Manager:** Holds the door when the class transitions
- **Electrician:** Turns the lights on and off when asked
- **Errand Runner:** Runs errands if the office or another teacher needs something
- **Gardener:** Waters class plants and monitors science projects
- **Handy Helper:** Helps the teacher
- **I.T. Computer Helper/Computer Technician:** Helps students log in to websites and makes sure devices are charging when the class leaves for the day
- **Janitor/Custodian:** Sweeps or vacuums the room
- **Librarian:** Keeps the classroom library clean and organized
- **Line Leader:** Leads the line when walking with the class in the hallway

- **Paper Collector:** Collects papers, work, and homework for the teacher
- **Resident Photographer:** Documents important events with the classroom device
- **Shoe Manager:** Ties students' shoes when asked
- **Table Cleaner:** Wipes and cleans the tables
- **The Substitute:** Performs jobs when students are absent
- **Toy Manager:** Organizes the toy shelf
- **Weather Reporter:** Helps lead the weather report for the day
- **Veterinarian:** Feeds, gives water, and takes care of any class pets

Student jobs can be posted in a variety of ways, both physically and digitally. I personally prefer to use magnets with each child's name written and hang them under the board, front and center of the classroom. You can also have students design the job board.

2. **Choosing and Hiring:**
Once you have your list of jobs and students' names written, kids can begin to *choose* their job for the week. Choosing jobs should be exciting and something students look forward to. There is something for everyone! Rather than rotating names, let the students choose their jobs one at a time every Monday morning. The moment they see you on a Monday, you'll likely hear, "Don't forget new jobs!" or "We have to choose new jobs!"

Giving choices rather than a fixed rotation schedule provides additional teachable moments for social-emotional learning (see *T is for Teachable Moments* chapter for more). Every week, at least one student is disappointed that the job they want has been taken. We talk about what to do when we feel disappointed. If we don't get the job we want, we point to our brain and whisper, "I'll get it next time."

Some students like to repeat jobs, so the expectation is to pick a different job than the week before. Then, other students have the opportunity to choose something new. As weeks go on, you'll notice trends of those who like to organize, clean, support, or take the lead.

3. **Modeling Expectations:**
   Every classroom job needs to be *taught*. The first week of school, I like to go over a few jobs at a time and make my expectations clear. Expectations must be set from the day they are introduced and reviewed often. If a child makes a mistake, remind them of the expectations and show them again or have a friend show them how to do it. Give another chance if they forget the expectations—there are a lot of jobs to learn! Strong expectations are especially helpful when there is a substitute because your students already know what they are expected to do. The classroom should be able to operate with or without you.

   Here are a few examples of how I expect jobs to be done: The *Line Leader* stands in the first spot, waits for the teacher's direction, stops when told, and sets the example with a quiet line body. The *Shoe Manager* asks permission before tying shoes, moves with the friend off the carpet or to the wall in the hallway to stay safe, and asks the teacher for help if they are still learning how to tie laces. The *Calendar Captain* comes up to the board immediately after attendance is taken, uses the pointer to ask the class for the month, year, date, and day of the week. Then, changes the date written and calls the weather reporter up to continue the morning routine.

4. **Firing and Rehiring:**
   Classroom jobs are a privilege. In the classroom, we talk about how when we are adults, we get hired for jobs we are good at or want to try and we can get fired for jobs if we do not perform well or make our best choices. If we get fired, then someone else can quickly be hired because

the job must get done! Sometimes, after being fired, you can get rehired if you make better choices and prove you are responsible enough to do the job well.

Firing is a **logical consequence**. This means students are only fired if the problem concerns their job performance. They are not fired for what happened at recess or for talking too much during math, because it had nothing to do with their job (see *Qu like in Conse/qu/ences* chapter for more). Most times, if a child gets *fired* from their job, it's just for the day. Then, we discuss what actions they need to take and what they need to do differently to be rehired the next day.

Where to Start

1. Make a list of your preferred classroom jobs, ensuring there is one for *every* child
2. Create a visual that lists all available jobs and simple expectations
3. Put each child's name on a magnet so they can select their preferred job on hiring day

But What If . . .

. . . My Students Forget the Expectations?
Anchor the expectations on a hanging chart, create a flipbook with all jobs and expectations, meet with students one-on-one to model, explain, and practice, or write a class book during shared writing about classroom jobs and add it to your classroom library.

. . . A Child Refuses to Choose a Job on Hiring Day?
Choosing jobs is not a way to force students into cleaning. If a child does not want to choose a job, put their name away or let them hold it until they are ready. Then, continue hyping up the

selection process with the rest of the class. Let the child know when you will allow them to try again if they change their mind and want to join the team.

... A Child Is Absent or Tardy on Hiring Day?
Put their name somewhere easily accessible. My routine is to hang names on the board next to the calendar so students can grab and choose their job without me having to remind them. Majority of the time, they are the ones who ask and remember!

... A Child Has a Tantrum Over Not Getting the Job They Wanted?
I have a firm logical consequence that if you throw a tantrum over a specific job, you aren't ready to be hired for it yet. I have a one-on-one discussion with the child to help them de-escalate and remind them that there is an abundance of jobs. We get a new chance every week (see *D is for De-escalation* chapter for more).

Real-World Connection

As adults, jobs are how we make a living in this world. Applying, hiring, firing, meeting expectations, and doing a job well are important skills and processes we learn through *experience*. Although classroom jobs are unpaid and volunteer-based, the act of keeping a job builds confidence, community, respect, and *purpose*, which helps us grow as human beings.

The more practice our kids get with being responsible for something, owning tasks, lending a hand, and being accountable, the greater their gain will be in the real world.

Dear Families

Good news! Jobs can also happen at home. Similar to chores and routines, jobs can be used to encourage and incentivize. Think about your child's interests and jobs that would align. For example: If your child loves art, they can oversee the organizing and tidying of art materials. If they love reading, they can oversee organizing the reading shelf. The idea is to foster independence, ownership, and accountability at home *and* at school. Teach *how* you want a job done step-by-step and praise your child when they have completed it—meeting all expectations.

You can modify any of the jobs from above for the home environment and give them a catchy title. Feel free to also use some of these bonus jobs:

- **Mail Deliverer/Postal Worker:** Gets and opens the mail with an adult
- **Mayor:** Makes important decisions when two choices are given by an adult
- **Pet Patrol:** Helps take care of pets
- **Receptionist:** Politely answers the phone and writes down messages
- **Sous Chef:** Supports an adult in the kitchen when cooking

J is for Jobs Wish List

- Badge or necklace for the errand runner to wear when they need to run an errand
- Bottle of hand sanitizer
- Handheld vacuum, broom, and dustpan for the janitor
- iPad/digital camera delegated for the photographer
- Non-toxic wipes for the table cleaner
- Pointer for the calendar captain and weather reporter
- Watering pot for the gardener

Extra! Extra! Read All About It

A Job for Kingsley
Written & illustrated by Gabriel Evans

Career Day
Written by Anne Rockwell; Illustrated by Lizzy Rockwell

Here Come the Helpers
Written by Leslie Kimmelman; Illustrated by Barbara Bakos

Mi Comunidad! My Community!
Written by 123 Andrés; Illustrated by Mónica Paola Rodriguez

Tinyville Town Gets to Work!
Written & illustrated by Brian Biggs

A B C D E F G H I **J** K L M N O P Q R S T U V W X Y Z
is for **Jobs** because . . .

The way *we* and our *students* practice responsibility and accountability m a t t e r s

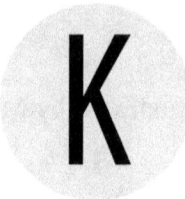

K is for Kid-tiques

> **[KID-TIQUES]**: A tried-and-true term I've coined to describe the child-centered, creative, artistic process of critiquing, internalizing, and comprehending stories
> **Similar to** . . . personifying, representing, expressing, illustrating, mirroring, appraising, discussing, interpreting, internalizing, summarizing, rephrasing, or re-telling

I can <u>use the literary, creative process of Kid-tiques</u> so my *students* can . . .

- Develop a passion for storytelling and world-building
- Experience the process of revision in writing
- Have the space to be artistic, creative thinkers
- Strengthen comprehension skills and attention to detail
- Use drama and art to enhance understanding

"Those who do not think outside the box are easily contained."
—Nicolas Manetta (Manetta, n.d.)

Learning to read and write is only the *beginning*. Comprehending a story's plot structure is only the *start*. There is a whole world of creativity and dreaming waiting for us beyond a book.

In this chapter, we will discuss a creative process I like to call **Kid-tiques**—six artistic literary techniques that can be done in the classroom or at home to enter *into* stories. Kid-tiques are an imaginative, artistic process to support visualizing, internalizing, and comprehending stories—a literary practice in which every child's opinion and idea is valued, represented, and heard.

FIGURE K.1 Our chapter K *why*

Kid-tiques create opportunities during the literacy learning block for problem-solving, creative thinking, arts integration, and dreaming as storytellers. Ideally, they are used for published picture books, stories written by students, polished manuscripts without illustrations, or shared writing pieces where kids can explore the world of acting, drawing, editing, reading, writing, publishing, and marketing. This method consists of six Kid-tique techniques.

The Six Kid-tique Techniques

1. Hidden Storytime
2. All Hands on Deck
3. Advisory Board
4. Draw It!
5. Broadway Stars
6. Play Publishing

1. **Hidden Storytime:**
   For this first technique, students *visualize what they hear*. Begin by reading a story out loud to students while *hiding* or *covering* the words and illustrations, allowing them to fully immerse in what they hear. During the story, observe the following:
   - Do the scenes or lines you expect a reaction from attain said reaction?
   - Does the way you read affect the way students respond? When you expressively read bold words, italics, words written in all capital letters, or large/small print distinguishing voice levels, does it translate?
   - What facial expressions are the kids making while listening? Do they look excited? Confused? Bored? Enticed?
   - What words/phrases elicit verbal responses versus non-verbal responses from students?
   - When only hearing the words, can students comprehend what is happening without seeing pictures? When only showing illustrations, can students comprehend what is happening without hearing words?

   Hidden Storytime gives students the opportunity to visualize when listening to specific words, details, or context clues. While reading, don't forget to be extra expressive like you are putting on a show!

2. **All Hands on Deck:**
   For this technique, students use simple sounds and non-verbal reactions to share how they feel *during* the

read-aloud. Teach and model a selection of non-verbal cues that can be used to share thoughts, opinions, and immediate reactions about the story. For example:

- "Laugh if something is *funny* to you" (You'd be surprised how many kids feel too nervous to laugh out loud during a story.)
- "Make a WOW face if something is *interesting* to you"
- "Point to your heart if you *connect* with a part of the story"
- "Point to your smile if you are *enjoying* a part or feel *happy* about something"
- "Put your hands over your eyes if a part is too *sad* or *scary*"
- "Shrug your shoulders and put your palms out if a word *doesn't make sense*"
- "Tap your brain if you are *confused* by something in the story"

Throughout the read-aloud, ask students to share their specific reactions using details and examples from the text. Have students discuss with a partner or in small groups to continue the creative process.

3. **Advisory Board:**
Picture books are written *for* kids and *about* kids—their opinion matters! For this technique, students *share their opinions* about the story. If you allow them the space to freely express themselves, their observant minds will tell it to you straight—with the purest intentions! I can't tell you how many times I've laughed out loud at a manuscript or read a published book and thought, "My class is going to LOVE this!" But lo and behold, there was not one giggle in the room and a sea of hands with questions of confusion.

After reading the story out loud, set up a "meeting space" for students to discuss their opinions by putting tables together or having them sit in a circle. Display a collection of sentence stems that can be used when expressing their opinion and sharing their perspective. For example:

"I'm not sure what they meant by _____,"
"I think it would be (funny/cool/better) if _____,"
or "I liked it when _____, but what if _____ happened instead?"

Show students how to kindly agree, disagree, add thoughts, ask questions, and challenge responses in a respectful way. At the end of the meeting, see if the group can come to a consensus about the story.

4. **Draw It!**

   For this technique, *hide* or *cover* the illustrations. After reading the story to students, ask them to draw a character, scene, or moment the way they imagined it. You can choose this moment or leave it up to them.

   Highlight or re-read lines that describe the character, setting, or scene, and ask students if what they drew matches. Then, reveal the illustrations and analyze the similarities and differences between details they heard and their picture. Ask students:
   - "Did your picture match what we read?"
   - "If you were an illustrator, what would you *add* to the picture?"
   - "What did you imagine the character would look like and why?"
   - "What specific words helped you draw your picture?"
   - "Why did you pick *this* moment to draw? What helped you picture it clearly?

5. **Broadway Stars:**

   For this technique, students will become Broadway stars by listing all materials needed to make a story come alive. Then, they will perform it!

   Print out copies of the text for each child. *After* reading, make a list with students on chart paper of props, costumes, and music needed for the story to come alive on stage. Then, split students into teams and let them discuss their plan (Can be in small groups, individually, or two-by-two—the world is your oyster!).

Give students ample time to internalize, choose their part to play, and rehearse. Then, open the "stage" to act out a specific scene or retell the full story and watch it come to life! Choose a child to hold a Hollywood movie scene clapper as the whole class says, "ACTION!" With permission, record the performance and allow students to watch it back like a movie. This technique can also be done with purchased or downloaded Reader's Theater cards: scripts that list parts for students to read aloud while pretending they are characters in a play.

6. **Play Publishing:**
    For this last technique, students explore the world of publishing, editing, and marketing. *After* reading, go beyond what an author or illustrator does and discuss what publishers, editors, and marketing teams do in the industry to make stories come to life. For example: If we were *publishers*, *editors*, or worked in *marketing*, we might . . .
    - Brainstorm the plot for a sequel
    - Create a book jacket
    - Create an advertisement for a magazine or website
    - Create back matter for the story by researching the topic
    - Create press releases and list ideas on how to publicize an upcoming book
    - Design a front and back cover
    - Edit a book by deleting unnecessary words and fixing punctuation, grammar, and spelling errors
    - Prepare for media interviews by writing questions and answers
    - Write a blog post, film a video, or record a podcast reviewing the book
    - Write and film a commercial for the story
    - Write an alternate ending or an alternate beginning

Where to Start

1. Think about where a Kid-tique could fit into your schedule. I typically attach them to my read-aloud or writers' workshop block.
2. Choose one book, story, or text to focus on, and one or two Kid-tique techniques
3. Collect any props, pointers, paper, and other materials needed for the process

But What If . . .

. . . A Child Does Not Want to Participate?
Every child is different—some like to be front and center, while some like to be backstage. But during Kid-tiques, everyone has a place in the creative process. If a child does not want to perform, speak publicly, or display their work for everyone to see, give them another way to express themselves. Can they be the director, cameraperson, or videographer? Can they help you select the stories and hide the pictures?

. . . A Child Does Not Think Their Idea Is Valuable?
Art begins with an idea. Every idea is valuable. Talk to students about how ideas are the start of something bigger. Read picture books about creating, dreaming, innovating, problem-solving, and making mistakes. When the child has an idea, make sure they know how invaluable it is that they shared it with you and others.

Real-World Connection

We all have different skills, talents, hobbies and interests. The Kid-tique process can inspire and aspire kids to follow passions they have never considered before. Think about all the careers available to our kids as they grow as creatives . . .

- Actor
- Advertising Analyst
- Art Director
- Author
- Backstage Crew
- Book Buyer
- Brand Strategist
- Camera Operator
- Casting Director
- Communications Manager
- Composer
- Content Coordinator
- Copywriter
- Costume Designer
- Digital Marketing Manager
- Director
- Editor
- Graphic Designer
- Illustrator
- Lighting Designer
- Literary Agent
- Marketing Director/Marketing Assistant
- Producer/Executive Producer/Associate Producer
- Production Coordinator/Production Assistant
- Prop Designer
- Publicist
- Publisher
- Run Crew
- Scenographer
- Screenwriter
- Social Media Manager
- Sound Designer/Sound Operator
- Stagehand
- Stage Manager
- Video Editor

Dear Families

You don't need a classroom to do a Kid-tique! When reading your favorite picture books with your child, explore the six techniques the same way they would in the classroom! Provide opportunities for them to visualize, use non-verbal reactions while you read out loud, draw, debate their opinion, perform, edit, add on, and learn to market! Enter this creative process *with* them or allow siblings to participate.

If you homeschool your child and they do not have a peer to interact with, *Hidden Storytime, All Hands on Deck, Draw It,* and *Play Publishing* can still be done. During discussion times, partner with your child and be a safe place to express their opinion. For *Advisory Board*, try letting your child record their opinion and play it back for you. Then, record your response and let them listen to it. This allows for each opinion to be heard in full. Last, for *Broadway Stars*, talk about the definition of a "one-person show" or let them cast you for a part in their production!

K is for Kid-tiques Wish List

- Chart paper for *Broadway Stars* to make a list of costumes, props, and materials
- Hollywood movie scene clapper to begin a scene during *Broadway Stars*
- Reader's Theater cards
- Your favorite picture books!

Extra! Extra! Read All About It

Aaron Slater, Illustrator
Written by Andrea Beaty; Illustrated by David Roberts

How This Book Was Made
Written by Mac Barnett; Illustrated by Adam Rex

Night Play
Written & Illustrated by Lizi Boyd

The Fantastic Bureau of Imagination
Written by Brad Montague; Illustrated by Kristi Montague

The Wrong Book
Written by Drew Daywalt; Illustrated by Alex Willmore

A B C D E F G H I J **K** L M N O P Q R S T U V W X Y Z
is for **Kid-tiques** because . . .
The way *we* and our *students* interpret, and reflect upon writing matters

L

L is for Learning Checks

> **[LEARNING CHECKS]**: A quick check for understanding and progress toward mastery
> **Similar to** . . . knowledge checks, progress checks, quizzes, or measurable data (WordHippo, 2025)

I can <u>use learning checks to break down standards and data</u> so my *students* can . . .

- Build confidence in a positive testing environment
- Feel empowered by seeing proof of their progress
- Master key learning standards
- Practice skills in a quick and easy way
- Set and work toward achievable and measurable goals

"Believe you can and you're halfway there."
—Theodore Roosevelt (n.d.)

Testing can be a daunting word. For some, the process comes easy. But for many of us, including me, testing triggers anxiety, negative self-talk, and foggy thinking. Living with Tourette syndrome, taking tests caused my motor and vocal tics to get significantly worse. My vocal tics would distract and frustrate others in the room, as well as distract and frustrate *me*.

Every child tests differently. With our youngest learners, my hope is that we can create testing environments that tame emotions rather than trigger them. But to do this, our kids have to work out their testing muscles like you would in the gym. They need exposure, affirmation, celebration, support, and preparation in a *positive environment*.

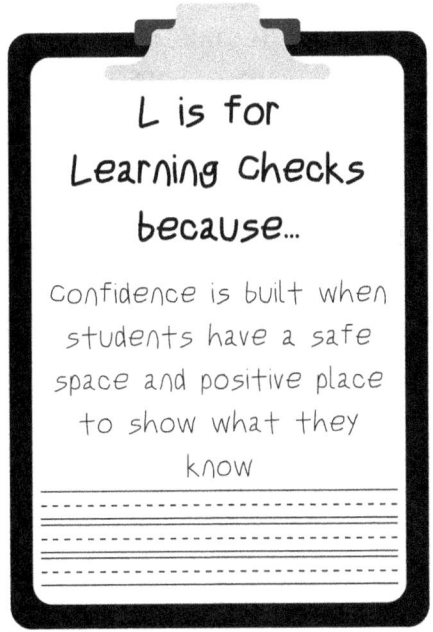

FIGURE L.1 Our chapter L *why*

Building muscle takes time, repetition, and perseverance. Confidence in testing isn't much different. There is way too much pressure on teachers to make sure students ace their standardized tests. We need a system that builds up to the big event and takes off the stress.

My favorite method of working toward mastery with our youngest learners is through **Learning Checks**—monthly one-on-one check-ins that gather data for the mastery of building block skills. Through learning checks, we focus on mastery goals rather than performance goals: the achievement of *learning* versus the achievement of *performing* (Svinicki, 2010). Mastery goals encourage our kiddos to grow intellectually within *themselves*, without the competition of others and the stress of performance (Rapposelli, 2021).

Learning checks are not just about tracking and crushing goals—they are about boosting a growth mindset. To begin planning for learning checks, start with a month-by-month grid of the semester, with a box for each subject for which you want to collect data. For example: phonics, reading, math, or writing. Then, add your assessment periods, units, or big standards for each month.

Monthly Learning Checks

	Example: January	Month:	Month:	Month:	Month:
Phonics	Glued Sounds				
Reading	Sliding finger				
Math	2D/3D Shapes				
Writing	Capital letters				
Other	MOY Testing				

FIGURE L.2 Example of a monthly planning template

Next, ask yourself: "What do students need to know this month in order to grow toward the mastery of their goals?" For example: In early first grade, students are expected to sound out CVC words (words with a consonant-vowel-consonant pattern). But before they can master that, they must identify letters and sounds one at a time and blend the sounds together to make a word. When thinking of questions for your learning checks, try filling in this sentence: "In order for my students to _____, they first need to fluently _____."

Learning checks can come in any format, but I prefer to create a slideshow that can be flipped through on a tablet, computer, or phone. When creating each month's learning check, be as creative as you like! Try adding pops of color to your slides and monthly seasonal themes. Create a cover slide, followed by a slide with directions, one slide for each question, and a final slide at the end with a scoring sheet. I like to attach the scoring sheet so that parents know exactly how their child will be graded. Print out one copy of the grading sheet for each child. Then, once the check is complete, make a copy to send home to families and put the original in the child's data folder.

FIGURE L.3 Example of a mastery question slide

NAME: _____				DATE: _____			
you	for	your	or	four	all	#4	
Write		Write		Write			
Write		Write		bl	br	gr	
gl	sk	scr	pr	1+1	2+2	3+3	
4+4	5+5	Score: ___/24				___%	

FIGURE L.4 Example of a grading slide

If you have access to a color printer, print a colored copy of the learning check for students to practice with in the classroom. Laminate the slides and connect them with a binder ring so students can flip through them at their leisure and encourage parents to print the slides out as flashcards and practice throughout the week. If possible, pair students with a partner to quiz each other. You can also practice the slides daily in the classroom during morning meeting or other whole-group times.

Talk about test-taking strategies in the classroom and what it means to *try your best*. Learning checks are like the pit stop at a NASCAR race—a quick check to make sure the race car is prepared and ready to zoom ahead!

Tell students they might see questions that are too easy, too hard, or just right—like in *Goldilocks and the Three Bears*—but the goal is to *show what you know*. Chant together, "Show me what you know, show me what you know, show me, show me, show me what you know!"

For learning check, standardized test, or other assessment days, give kids extra affirmation and love, and turn on your excitement switch. Build confidence by reminding your students how much you believe in their capabilities, how big their brain is, and how much they have learned this year. This check has nothing on them!

You can use learning checks to check in on report card standards or for an extra layer of data. But remember, the purpose is to build confidence in the testing arena, not add stress!

Where to Start

1. Map all important dates, units, and big standards on your monthly grid
2. Create your first monthly learning check slideshow and send to families
3. Build excitement around learning checks to both students and families

But What If . . .

. . . A Student Needs Accommodations?
First, look for recommended accommodations on their IEP or 504 plan. If they do not have a plan, think of accommodations that will boost their self-confidence. Provide a silent space to take their learning check without students in the room, let them wear noise-cancelling headphones, stand up to take the check, or give them a comfortable cushion to sit on. Let them close their eyes and take the test without a time limit.

. . . Students Continue to Be Anxious About Their Learning Check?
Standardized tests can bring forth heavy test anxiety. When students feel anxious, their cognition levels lower, which impacts their success on a test (Rapposelli, 2021). Talk to students about *stress-release strategies* they can try in those moments:

- Ask a friend for a pep talk
- Close their eyes and count to ten
- Declare an *I Am statement* in the mirror (see *S is for Self-Talk* chapter for more)
- Do deep-breathing exercises
- Drink cold water

- Hold a stuffed animal or stress ball
- Meditate
- Release the wiggles: dance, move, or stretch the body
- Sit in a comfortable chair or on a cozy cushion
- Smell or taste cinnamon or peppermint: A study by the University of Cincinnati found that taking a whiff of peppermint helps people concentrate when taking tests that require focus (Brand, 2007).
- Take a quick walk
- Tell a joke
- Think about something silly/funny
- Wear a superhero cape to remember how powerful they are

Real-World Connection

Testing isn't just for kids; we do it too as adults! Certifications, clearances, finals, driver's license exams, and extended learning are all part of the adult testing world. As we grow up and experience taking tests, we can't let it decide *who we are* and *what we are capable of*. I grew up telling myself *I am bad at tests, tests make me seem dumb,* and *my tics always get in the way*. It has taken me years to flip the negative self-talk and work on a healthy way to deal with testing, especially as a teacher. If our kids see tests as a chance to flex their thinking muscles, it could open doors for the next generation and the way they respond to testing in the real world.

Dear Families

There is *always* more to learn. When *you* realize that you don't have the answer to something, instead of feeling down or frustrated, model the excitement of an opportunity to learn something new. Show your child how to find information—whether that be through books, videos, online research, or asking someone.

Make a note of all your child's testing dates and add them to your calendar. The week of every test, make it an exciting and fun countdown. Celebrate the upcoming day rather than push learning or force last-minute studying. If your child's teacher uses the method of learning checks, practice the slides daily with your child. Make it into a game like Go Fish, hopscotch, or a scavenger hunt.

The night before their learning check (or any assessments), be mindful of screen/technology time, make sure your child gets plenty of sleep, and ensure they have taken any necessary medications, including allergy medicine. On the day of the learning check, ask them how it went. Did they feel ready? What do they still want to practice? What could they do differently next time as they continue to grow?

L is for Learning Checks Wish List

- Binder rings
- Chair pad/chair cushion
- Costume superhero cape
- Noise-cancelling headphones
- Stress ball
- Stuffed animal
- Sugar-free peppermint or cinnamon candies

Extra! Extra! Read All About It

A Little Spot of Anxiety: A Story About Calming Your Worries
Written & illustrated by Diane Alber

Big Test Jitters
Written by Julie Danneberg; Illustrated by Judy Love

I'm Trying to Love Math
Written & illustrated by Bethany Barton

The Little Engine That Could: *90th Anniversary Edition*
Written by Watty Piper; Illustrated by Dan Santat

The Pout-Pout Fish and the Worry-Worry Whale
Written by Deborah Diesen; Illustrated by Dan Hanna

A B C D E F G H I J K **L** M N O P Q R S T U V W X Y Z

is for **Learning Checks** because . . .

The way *we* and our *students* feel confident in showing what we know m a t t e r s

M

M is for Menus

> **[MENU]**: A comparable list or assortment of offerings (Merriam-webster.com, 2025)
> **Similar to** . . . *a la* carte, spread, list, checklist, record, inventory, agenda, or lineup (WordHippo, 2025)

I can <u>use menus to track work, progress, and data</u> so my students can . . .

- ♦ Finish work to completion
- ♦ Keep their family up to date on what they are learning
- ♦ Practice independence, ownership, and agency
- ♦ Prioritize tasks by making choices
- ♦ Visualize weekly expectations

"The child's inner need: help me to do it by myself."
—Maria Montessori (Montessori, 1949)

Can I tell you a secret? Center time, also known as the workstation block in many early childhood and elementary classrooms, has historically held first place for the most chaotic part of my day. In a 45-minute timeframe, I am expected to lead multiple small-group lessons, manage student behavior, control the volume, answer questions, monitor who is in and out of the classroom for bathroom, water, and nurse visits, and ensure students are effectively working on their tasks at hand—while still being challenged. Now, add on the extra time it takes to prepare centers, make copies, and grade student work—there is never enough time in the day.

The center/workstation block is a *small* time that holds *big* value. I desperately needed a *system* that could help me plan, teach, track, collect data, and consistently communicate with families. Inspired by **choice boards**, student **menus** were born.

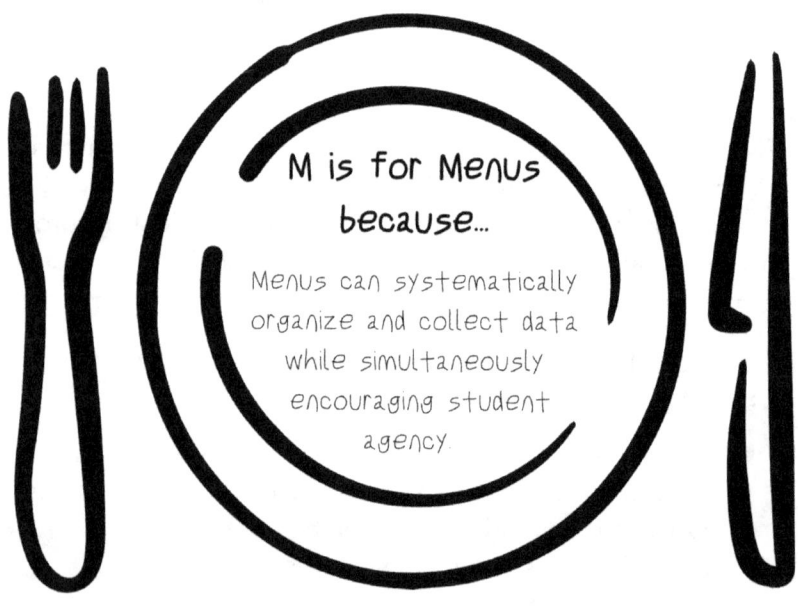

FIGURE M.1 Our chapter M *why*

When I took a moment to zoom out and reflect on my center block, I realized I needed *ten* specific systems to make it run like a well-oiled machine. I needed a way to . . .

1. Balance paper activities with hands-on activities
2. Consistently update parents on what we were learning

3. Easily collect work samples for data meetings, progress reports, parent-teacher conferences, and the monthly bulletin board display
4. Have students work independently so I could lead non-interrupted small groups
5. Incentivize the completion of weekly tasks
6. Observe and collect evidence on student work ethic
7. Provide choice and differentiate work for students
8. Tie social-emotional learning into work time
9. Track finished and unfinished work
10. Visualize scheduling conflicts (for example: holidays, field trips, and celebrations)

After much trial and error, I created **menus**: a visual board of tasks presenting all student work/expectations for the week. Through one template, my ten needs were met! Students could work together, help one another, ask for support, track work in progress, make choices, prioritize to complete tasks, visualize upcoming projects, field trips, or assessments, work toward manageable goals, and show their family how hard they worked each week. Families were able to see firsthand what we learned, how hard their child worked, and could support me with finishing any necessary tasks.

Preparing a Menu

To create your own menu board, begin by creating your menu template. My typical template leaves space for students to write their name and date, includes 12 boxes for the title and picture clue of the assignment, and distinguishes between literacy and math tasks. When creating your own menu template, think about the length of your academic block, how often you want students to switch activities, and what would be feasible for them to complete by the end of the week. Then, choose the amount of boxes that work for you.

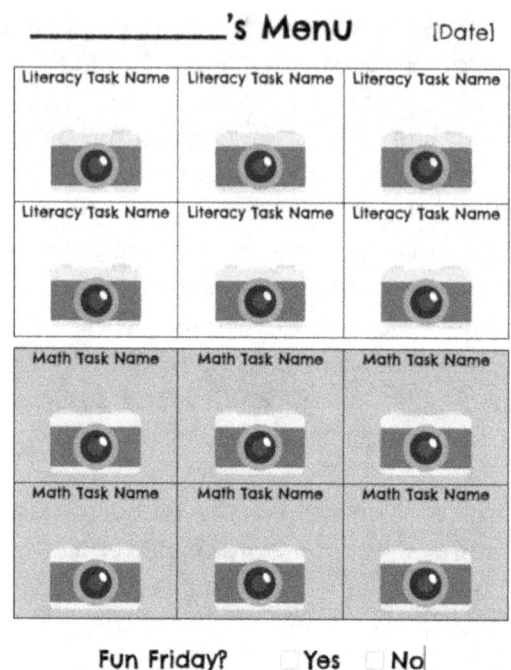

FIGURE M.2 Sample of a bare menu template

Once you have created your template, it's time to add in your activities. I balance activities by adding a center each week for technology, library, writing, sight words, word work, and something creative for hands-on fun. From week-to-week, centers can roll over, switch, or be modified by switching a few materials. When planning, you can insert activities for important tasks like finishing a mandatory assessment or completing a project for the bulletin board. Then, by the end of the week, you can see clearly which students need to complete work.

Once you've created your template, print a menu for each student and attach all work that needs to be finished by the end of the week. You can also give each child a pocket folder to keep all papers organized and collect the empty folders on Friday. This will help decrease the amount of lost papers, while keeping finished work in one location.

FIGURE M.3 Sample of a menu organized by activity with 16 boxes

Teaching Menu Expectations

Before rolling out this new system, reflect on the following questions:

- *How many students can be at a center at once?* For example: three at a time
- *How will students mark work as completed?* For example: By drawing an X through the box with a designated "menu marker" near the teacher's desk. If the assignment is incomplete, students can draw a slash (I like to say "Half an X").
- *What should students do if they finish their menu before Friday?* For example: Students can redo their centers, help a friend, or do extra lessons on district-mandated computer programs.

- *What should students do if they need help while the teacher is leading a small group?* For example: I tell students to *ask three before me*. After asking three friends for help or clarification, they can switch to a different activity until I am available. I like to use an LED night-light touch lamp that lights up *red* when I am closed for questions and *green* when I am open. For students who are visually impaired or experience color blindness, use a sign that reads open/closed.
- *What will clean-up time look like?* Will there be music, a timer, or student jobs to help? For example: When it is time to clean up, set a timer for one minute. When the timer goes off, students must freeze *straight like a pencil* with their hands by their sides.
- *Where will the materials/bins live?* For example: All materials belong on the designated center shelf, in their coordinating bins.

On the first day of each week, give students their new menu packet. Walk through the materials, steps, and expectations for each center. Model the activity with students and then show them how to clean and put it away when finished. At the end of the week, check each menu, the work attached, and sit with students to fix errors or re-do activities to ensure mastery and growth. On Friday, if the menu is complete, draw a large smiley face and give students free time to explore the hobby drawers or other creative activities (see *H is for Hobbies* chapter for more).

Collecting Data With Menus

Menus give us daily data. Pay close attention to your students during centers and observe/take **anecdotal notes** on the following:

- Which students ask for help when they need it?
- Which students attempt to copy others?
- Which students check off their work as finished when it is in fact—not finished?

- Which students need more support?
- Which students rush to be the first one done?
- Which students spend their time on one activity and are not finishing their work?
- Which students turn work time into play time?

Incentivizing Menus

Hype up menus by incentivizing above and beyond work. Use stickers, stamps, or scented markers to draw stars or smiley faces. Send pictures to parents or make announcements to the class to show when students prioritize important work first. Incentivize completion of work by including **Fun Friday** time—a chance for free-choice activities. Over the years, Fun Friday has brought me new songwriters, musicians, cheer captains, architects, illustrators, and authors!

Over the years, menus have become a staple in my classroom, grade level, and school. Teachers from pre-kindergarten through fifth grade have adapted the template and made it their own! Some teachers have added spaces for their signature to show work has been completed, checkmark boxes for completed small-group time, smiley faces to color and track behavior, and classroom expectations to remind students of what they are looking for. As teachers, we want our kiddos to practice independence, perseverance, decision-making, prioritizing, and goal setting. Menus are just *one* way you can foster these practices in your early childhood or elementary classroom.

Where to Start

1. Make a list of your weekly **centers**. Add each name and picture into your menu template
2. Create a bucket that matches each station. For example: sight words, fluency, writing, or number recognition
3. Designate a space where students can wait for support and mark off their completed work without interrupting

your small group. For me, this space is near my desk with a scented marker velcroed to the table. Paper clips and binder clips are nearby for menus that come apart, and tape is available for papers that have ripped. One line of painter's tape on the floor clearly marks where students can stand if they need support from me.

But What If...

...A Student Finishes Their Menu Before the End of the Week?
If a student finishes early, they can repeat centers on their menu, help a friend, or go on district-mandated computer programs. You can also create a *bonus menu* with additional options.

FIGURE M.4 Example of a *Bonus Menu*

M is for Menus ♦ 147

... I Have a Substitute Teacher for the Day or Week?
The classroom should be able to operate with or without you in it. When there is a substitute, prepare a special substitute menu and leave directions within your sub plans. This eliminates leaving busy work and having to interrupt the classroom routine when you are not there.

FIGURE M.5 Example of a *Substitute Menu* for a full week

... I Want to Differentiate Work for All Learners?
Within each bucket, **differentiate** the *activity* inside. Use folders to divide the activities.

... Packets Come Unstapled or Extra Papers Need to Be Added?
Provide paperclips or binder clips for students to keep papers together or have students put their menu inside a basket labeled "staple requests" when they need the *teacher* to staple them. If

a significant amount of school is missed, send a menu home of work to complete.

. . . The Menu Is Too Difficult for a Student?
Differentiate the activity within the center or prepare a unique menu for their specific needs.

. . . I Want to Show Parents and Families How Menus Work in the Classroom?
Use a parent-specific menu for Back-to-School Night or Meet the Teacher Day. Add the tasks you want *parents* to complete or the areas of the classroom you want them to see. Model how students X each task and earn Fun Friday when work is complete.

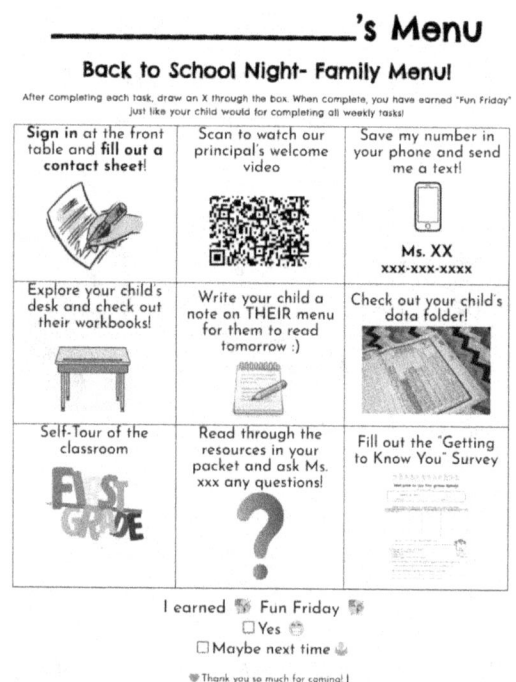

FIGURE M.6 Example of a *Back-to-School Night Menu* for families to use.

Real-World Connection

Some adults prefer to complete a task in one sitting, whereas others need to take breaks. Some complete tasks one at a time, whereas others prefer to juggle multiple projects. Some do the bare minimum to finish, whereas others are perfectionists and spend time trying to get it flawless.

Our kids are going to enter the real world and decide which way they will lean. We have the chance to teach them how to self-regulate, prioritize tasks, finish tasks to completion, and follow expectations. Menus are one way to introduce those skills!

Dear Families

If your child's teacher uses menus, there are many ways to support this system at home. Every Friday when your child brings home their menu, sit with them and go through their work. Ask them what they learned and practiced, what was easy or challenging for them, and which tasks were incomplete and why. You can learn a lot about your child's week by looking at one piece of paper! Partner with your child's teacher when work needs to be completed due to behavior, leaving school early, or absences.

Menus can also be used at home to keep track of weekly chores, summertime learning, or for children who are being homeschooled. Create a menu of work you need completed for the week and an incentive for finishing work early. Use your creativity and make menus your own!

M is for Menus Wish List

- LED night-light touch lamp
- Mr. Sketch scented markers
- Multi-purpose storage baskets

- Painter's tape to create a line for menus to be checked
- Paperclips or binder clips
- Velcro to attach the menu marker to its designated spot

Extra! Extra! Read All About It

Charlie Chooses
Written by Lou Peacock; Illustrated by Nicola Slater

My Magical Choices
Written by Becky Cummings; Illustrated by Zuzana Svobodová

Not Perfect
Written by Maya Myers; Illustrated by Hyewon Yum

The Perfect Percival Priggs
Written & illustrated by Julie-Anne Graham

You Can Do It, Bert!
Written & illustrated by Ole Könnecke

A B C D E F G H I J K L **M** N O P Q R S T U V W X Y Z

is for **Menus** because . . .

The way *we* and our *students* prioritize and complete tasks matters

N

N is for Neurodiversity

[NEURODIVERSITY is the umbrella term, followed by sub-definitions]

[NEURODIVERSITY]: *(Noun)* The diversity or variation of cognitive functioning in people. Everyone's brain is unique, and each person has different skills and abilities (Exceptional Individuals, 2023)

[NEURODIVERSE]: *(Adjective)* Term that describes those that identify as neurodivergent

[NEURODIVERGENT]: *(Adjective)* Term that describes those with a neurodivergence

[NEURODIVERGENCE]: *(Noun)* Atypical cognitive functioning

[NEUROTYPICAL]: *(Adjective)* Those whose cognitive functioning falls within "the norm"

Similar to . . . Neurodiversity to me is synonym-free. It's as unique as the term itself!

I can <u>**celebrate and embrace neurodiverse learners in my classroom**</u> so my *students* can . . .

- Accept and appreciate differences
- Build self-esteem and confidence
- Cultivate compassion and empathy
- Discover and celebrate individual strengths
- Feel empowered, loved, and accepted

In the 2009 animated film, Fantastic Mr. Fox says:

> *"We are all different, but there's something kind of fantastic about that, isn't there?"*

No two brains are exactly alike. When I was a child, this used to be labeled as having a *disability*, which for many carried a negative connotation. The word left a resonating feeling that being different meant *less than, inconvenient,* or *incapable*.

As someone who has personally struggled with Tourette syndrome since childhood, the disability label haunted me. *What if the label made my peers and teachers view me differently?* I already felt far from "normal" and didn't need outside opinions.

But the neurodiversity movement has re-invented the way we look at each other. The way *I* look at myself. It is a movement of celebration and inclusion that, instead, appreciates differences. To me, it says, "I am me because my brain works uniquely."

The term **neurodiversity** was introduced by sociologist Judy Singer (Corker and French, 1999) and later explored through her book, *Neurodiversity: The Birth of an Idea*. She writes that the term *neurodiversity* was the culmination of research and personal experiences, as her family was affected by a disability that society did not see as acceptable (Singer, 2016).

I believe Judy helped shift our stance to focus on the *strengths* and *abilities* brought through our unique cognitive functioning. Specifically, helping me see that my difference isn't a deficit, but a part of who I am.

It is estimated that 15–20% of our population presents a form of neurodivergence (Cancer.gov, 2022). That means with a class

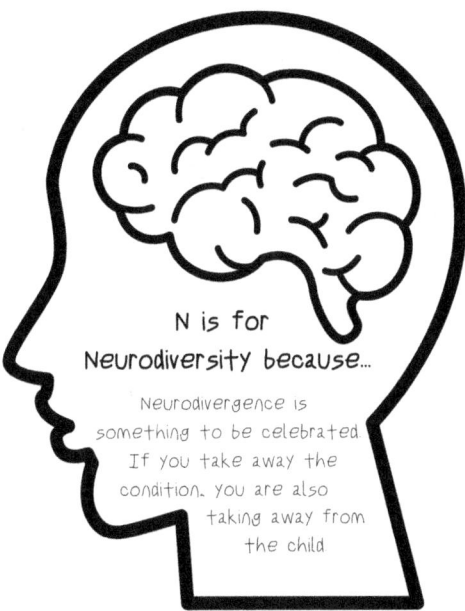

FIGURE N.1 Our chapter N *why*

size of 20 children, at least three or four students may identify as neurodivergent. The term *neurodiversity* can include:

- Acquired Neurodiversity or ABI: Brain injuries after birth such as traumatic brain injury (TBI), encephalitis, stroke, and mental health illnesses such as obsessive-compulsive disorder (OCD), schizophrenia, and bipolar disorder
- Attention Deficit Hyperactivity Disorder or ADHD: Challenges with attention and impulse control
- Auditory Processing Disorder: Challenges with processing sound, following spoken directions, and remembering things heard
- Autism Spectrum Disorder or ASD: Challenges with communication, social skills, and repetitive behaviors
- Developmental Language Disorder: Challenges with understanding, learning, and speaking a language
- Down Syndrome: Developmental, physical, and mental challenges due to an extra Chromosome 21

- Dyscalculia: Challenges with math and numbers
- Dysgraphia: Challenges with writing and spelling
- Dyslexia: Difficulty reading, writing, and spelling
- Dyspraxia: Challenges with movement and coordination
- Hyperlexia: A strong interest for letters, numbers, logos, maps, and other visuals
- Intellectual Disability: Challenges with life skills, self-care, and cognitive abilities
- Irlen Syndrome or Meares-Irlen Syndrome: Challenges with processing visual information
- Sensory Processing Disorder: Difficulty processing one or many of the five senses
- Synesthesia: When one sense is felt as another. For example: Seeing music as colors
- Tourette Syndrome: Causes involuntary tics, movements, and sounds
- Visual Processing Disorder: Challenges with interpreting information seen
- Williams Beuren Syndrome: Challenges with cognitive development, the endocrine system, and physical features of the body (Khaliq, 2023; Byrd, 2010; NIDCD, 2023; CDC, 2024; Exceptional Individuals, 2024; familydoctor.org editorial staff and Cook, 2024; Cleveland Clinic, 2017)

In the classroom, I've noticed a range of social, emotional, and behavioral hurdles with my neurodivergent learners. For example:

- Being around large groups
- Breaking routines
- De-escalating
- Identifying emotions
- Fitting in/navigating social behaviors
- Following along/following directions
- Making eye contact
- Reading body language
- Self-regulation
- Sensitivity to light, sound, temperature, or touch
- Sensory overstimulation

- Speech and language challenges
- Tics (motor and/or vocal)
- Transitioning between activities or locations in the building

But as teachers, we hold the light to shine upon *positive* traits and characteristics. We can shift our energy to find the special skills and attributes of our students, rather than focusing on their deficits (Armstrong, 2012). Our neurodivergent kiddos *also* have . . .

- Artistic abilities
- Attention to detail
- Creativity
- Empathy
- Enhanced language skills
- Enhanced learning abilities
- Exceptional memory
- Extreme focus
- Heightened interests
- Innovation
- Musical talents
- Pattern recognition
- Special interests

As teachers, we decide how to set the tone in our classroom. We show our students how unique the brain is and empower them so that they in turn can empower others. It begins with us.

It is important for us as educators to provide **supports** and **modifications** for each learner in our classroom, neurodiverse or not. Supports are *strategies* and *resources* that benefit the child and create an equal opportunity in their environment (*What Are Learning Supports?* n.d.), while modifications are changes made to the work, expectation, or teaching of a child. Here are ways to get started in the classroom:

- Administer tests in a quiet environment and use privacy boards/desk dividers
- Allow movement and brain breaks. Use a mini trampoline for when students need to get their energy out

- Assign classroom jobs that showcase strengths and interests (see *J is for Jobs* chapter for more)
- Be aware of environmental sensory overload, including the level of noise, light, colors, heat, and temperature of the air
  - For light: Reduce the amount of fluorescent lights/bright-wattage bulbs. Use dimming lights. Allow the child to choose a desk next to a window with natural light. Allow usage of sunglasses if lights are too bright.
  - For noise: Use noise-cancelling headphones and create quiet working spots. Headphones are especially helpful when there are loud noises like a fire drill or construction nearby.
  - For smells: Stay away from the use of air fresheners, aerosol sprays, and scented perfumes/lotions
- Be flexible: What works for one child may not work for another. What works on Monday, might not work on Tuesday.
- Build a strong relationship with children and their family/caregivers. Continually connect with them to share strategies.
- Change the environment: This can include asking a student to run an errand within the school building, put something away, help pass out materials, or take a routine walk with another staff member.
- Encourage those with tics to let them out. Give them a safe space to do it.
- Focus social-emotional lessons on sensitivity, empathy, and celebrating neurodiversity
- Give the option to work alone during group/partner work time
- Give verbal directions one step at a time. Repeat directions one-on-one if needed, using visuals to show each step.
- Have students create "offices" the first week of school by creating a barrier with a standing file folder. Allow them to grab their "office" anytime they want privacy at their desk.
- Post pictures of classroom routines, transitions, and schedules

- Post visuals of students throughout the classroom. For example: pictures of students doing desired tasks, pictures of students on anchor charts, and social stories about their day
- Provide **flexible seating** such as wiggle cushions, carpet squares, stools, bean bag chairs, or yoga balls
- Purchase books with large print or dyslexia-friendly fonts
- Repeat directions one-on-one if needed, using visuals to show each step
- Provide voice recording buttons that can repeat directions
- Speak with students before a big change. For example: rearranging the room, having a substitute, or attending a meeting
- Stick a Velcro strip on desks or chairs for students to touch for texture-based self-stimulation
- Supplement learning with picture books
- Use chair bands on chair or desk legs for self-stimulation
- Use **non-verbal signals** throughout the day. Print out pictures of each signal and hang them up for children to reference.
- Use **sensory stim toys**—tools that help children calm their body, such as stress balls, pop-its, fidget spinners, or smooth rocks found in nature
- Use tools to assist with time management, such as online timers, sand timers, egg timers, or countdown clocks
- Utilize an expert: Gather new ideas from teachers and support staff within your school's special education program, or from teachers themselves who identify as neurodivergent
- Write and display sentence stems for social situations such as asking to play, making new friends, or setting a boundary

I would not be the person I am today had I not grown up with Tourette syndrome. It is a part of who I am. It taught me patience, self-regulation, calming techniques, boundaries, and how to advocate for myself. I am unique and there is *no one* like me. The same goes for each of our kids. No two brains work the same.

But most importantly, their differences are not a disability. Their differences are a strength.

Where to Start

1. Pick three supports from this chapter to add to your classroom setup
2. Adjust your classroom schedule to ensure there is time for brain breaks and transitions
3. Meet with families to build a strong partnership and put together a plan for success

But What If . . .

. . . None of My Students Identify as Neurodiverse?
The world extends beyond our classroom. Students may have family or friends that identify as neurodiverse. It is just as important for us to build awareness as it is to provide accommodations and encouragement in the classroom.

. . . A Child's Condition Is Too Severe for the General Classroom Environment?
Refer to your district/school's special education process and begin advocating for the child. Start the IEP (Individual Education Program) or 504 plan (provides supports within the classroom) process. Take detailed anecdotal notes. Bring together a team of teachers that have a relationship with the child and can support them and you throughout the day.

. . . One of My Students Has Multiple Conditions That Fall Under the Neurodiverse Umbrella
Find the commonalities and overlaps in their symptoms and needs. Set them up for success from day one by making modifications and preparing a comfortable environment. Do your research, talk with their family, meet with their previous teacher, reference their IEP or 504 plan if they've qualified, and gather as many ideas as possible.

... Students in the Classroom Are Unkind to Neurodiverse Learners? Find the root of the unkindness. Are they jealous of the modifications/tools their peer has? Are they seeking similar attention? Do they not fully understand what their classmate is experiencing? Create a community from day one that highlights how each of us is unique, including positive character traits that we can see in one another. Host a lunch bunch with students to talk about how they can reframe their thinking.

... My Students Do Not Understand Their Neurodiverse Classmates? Use picture books and videos to showcase a variety of neurodivergent conditions. Bring in neurodiverse adults or parents to share their story. Learn about celebrities who also identify as neurodivergent. Allow students to ask you questions and learn more.

Real-World Connection

There are many ways we can partner with the neurodiversity movement, celebrate our kids, and continue learning:

- Celebrate Neurodiversity Awareness Month, Neurodiverse Celebration Week, National Autism Awareness Month, National ADHD Awareness Month, and National Down Syndrome Awareness Month
- Continue to learn through books, documentaries, podcasts, and asking questions
- Donate to organizations that focus on neurodiversity awareness
- Introduce children to careers that align with their strengths (Armstrong, 2012)
- Partner with local organizations

Dear Families

You are the expert regarding your child. However, your child's teacher can be a partner and resource to bounce ideas off. Don't be afraid to ask them for support. Ask the teacher what tools are working for your child at school and share what works at home. Use the wish list at the end of this chapter to try new tools. If you have social, emotional, or behavioral concerns, consult your child's doctor or arrange a meeting with the special education team at your child's school.

Create visual schedules, chore charts, and social stories using your child's photograph. Keep a collection of sensory stim toys and noise-cancelling headphones in both the house and car. Break directions into small steps when doing homework or household tasks. Allow brain breaks and flexible seating when reading, writing, or doing homework. And most importantly, continue to shine light on the strengths and positive traits of your child, speaking into and celebrating their uniqueness.

Before the first day of school, write a letter to your child's teacher about your child's strengths, areas of growth, triggers, how to approach them if they are upset, special interests, routines that work at home, and any other pertinent information. This sets up your child for success from day one.

N is for Neurodiversity Wish List

- Bean bag chairs
- Books with large print or dyslexia-friendly fonts
- Chair bands
- Dimming light bulbs
- File folders to create "offices": homemade privacy boards
- Individual carpet squares
- Koosh balls (spaghetti string balls)
- Mini trampoline
- Noise-cancelling headphones
- Privacy boards/desk dividers for students
- Sensory stim toys: stress balls, Pop Its, fidget cubes, or fidget spinners
- Sentence strips
- Student stools
- Student sunglasses

- Time management tools: sand timers, egg timers, or countdown clocks
- Velcro strips
- Voice recording buttons
- Wiggle cushions
- Yoga ball

Extra! Extra! Read All About It

Brilliant Bea: A Story for Kids with Dyslexia and Learning Differences
Written by Shaina Rudolph & Mary Vukadinovich; Illustrated by Fiona Lee

I Am Me: A Book of Authenticity
Written by Susan Verde; Illustrated by Peter H. Reynolds

The Boy with Big, Big Feelings
Written by Britney Winn Lee; Illustrated by Jacob Souva

Too Much: An Overwhelming Day
Written by Jolene Gutiérrez; Illustrated by Angel Chang

Wiggles, Stomps and Squeezes Calm My Jitters Down
Written by Lindsey Rowe Parker; Illustrated by Rebecca Burgess

A B C D E F G H I J K L M **N** O P Q R S T U V W X Y Z

is for **Neurodiversity** because . . .

The way *we* and our *students* celebrate our uniqueness matters

O

O is for Organization

[ORGANIZATION]: The way in which something is done or arranged (Cambridge Dictionary, 2025)
Similar to . . . structure, arrangement, system, method, order, neatness, or efficiency (WordHippo, 2025)

I can <u>keep a clean, clear, and organized space</u> so my *students* can . . .

- Develop healthy habits
- Feel safe and secure in an orderly environment
- Minimize distractions around them
- Productively and efficiently focus on learning
- Understand the parameters of their space

"For every minute spent in organizing, an hour is earned."
—Benjamin Franklin (n.d.)

Organization is at the heart of our A-to-Z adventure. The alphabet alone, in all its forms and languages, is an organizational system that provides structure and order to the chaos of everyday life. As educators, we hold the power to create and design our own organizational systems that can work just as seamlessly, making everything from lesson planning to classroom management easier. Whether you choose to organize materials, re-arrange furniture, or structure routines, thoughtful and intentional organization can transform the classroom environment.

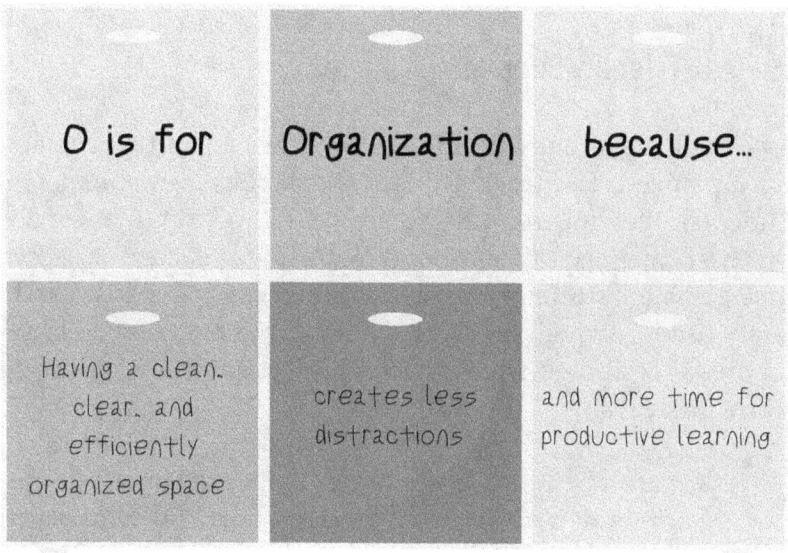

FIGURE O.1 Our chapter O *why*

When I think of an organized classroom, I imagine a *clean, clear,* and *efficiently organized* space where everything has its place. A room where efficiency, creativity, and productivity collide in the best way possible and confidently say, "I've got this!"

When a classroom is *clean,* it becomes a healthy environment free of germs and dirt. When it's *clear* of clutter, it allows for distraction-free, productive learning. And when a classroom is *efficiently organized*, systems are in place that minimize wasted time and make life easier. In this chapter, we will focus on **The Categories of Classroom Organization**: simple ways to create a clean, clear, and efficiently organized environment for both you and your students.

The Categories of Classroom Organization

1. Student-Friendly Supplies
2. Teacher Tidiness
3. Established Routines
4. Pre-modeled Expectations

Student-Friendly Supplies

As adults, we initially decide where things go and how spaces are organized. Eventually, this responsibility can shift to the students, allowing *them* to take ownership over their space. Our first category of classroom organization is creating accessible areas for **student-friendly supplies**: supplies that can be safely used, reached, taken care of, and put away by children. Try making student-friendly supplies easily accessible in the following ways:

- Create an area for student-friendly cleaning supplies such as non-toxic table wipes, brooms and dustpans, a handheld vacuum, disposable gloves, hand sanitizer, a duster, and small plastic shopping bags to collect trash
- Hang data trackers and anchor charts low enough or at student eye level so that each child can clearly see them
- Label buckets and drawers with both text and a picture. Labels written in student handwriting are always a bonus to add ownership and agency.
- Organize construction paper, markers, crayons, and colored pencils in rainbow order. For example: *All red coloring utensils go in the red drawer.* Organizing by color makes it quick and easy to find what you need without missing work time.
- Sort books by genre, topic, or learning objective. Put a sticker or graphic icon on the book so that students can match it to the correct bucket when cleaning up.
- Use clear, stackable storage bins with lids for student shelves so that they can see what is inside. Tape a

matching label onto the physical shelf so that students can put the container back in the correct spot.
♦ Sort materials according to teacher versus student zones. Keep your personal supplies behind your desk, small-group table, or near your easel. Give a tour of the classroom to ensure students know what areas are off limits, what zones are only for teachers, and what areas are safe versus unsafe.

Teacher Tidiness

How we organize our personal space, data, lesson plans, and teaching materials directly affects how we show up each day. In a cluttered classroom, every minute spent searching for items, shoving things away in places they do not fit, and re-inventing the wheel to create new materials is time that could have been time spent on other things. Before digging into the reorganization of your space, do a *Decluttering State of the Union*. Throw away trash or out-of-date papers, refurbish or donate furniture that can be easily fixed, and give items that are no longer needed to families or other teachers who are low on supplies. Decide what fits in your post-pandemic world of teaching and keep only what you deem necessary. Then, begin tidying up what is left:

♦ Create a substitute binder that has your classroom roster, schedule, list of emergency contact information, allergies, dismissal routines, computer login codes, extra work, and seasonal activities that can be used throughout the year. This makes it easy for the substitute to locate all essential information. Update this information regularly when new students enter/exit your classroom.
♦ Create a system to track everything ingoing and outgoing. For example: student home-school folders, newsletters, student work, notes to parents, behavior trackers, and homework. Designate a space for these items to live,

such as a large basket. Anytime you have something to send home to families, put it in that basket.
- Keep as many teacher materials near your desk space, table, or teaching area as possible, to allow for more student-accessible areas. If you have a shelf of materials purely for planning purposes, cover the shelf with a piece of plain color fabric that can roll down like a curtain and keep visual stimuli low.
- Organize all hard-copy materials into binders labeled with the learning topic. Create digital folders that match the binders and store the soft copy of the same items. This creates a simple grab-and-go method for when you need to make a copy, a co-worker or parent needs a resource, or you are in a pinch.

FIGURE O.2 Example of color-coded binders with soft copy resources

- Store all data, goal trackers, exit tickets, and anecdotal notes inside individual student data folders (see *G is for Goals and Growth* chapter for more). Designate a data basket or binder to keep all folders/documents in one place, as well as a master data folder/binder to keep all templates you use throughout the year.

Established Routines

If we want to keep our organizational systems functional and have our kids follow suit, we need to establish daily routines. Set aside time throughout the day when cleaning and organizing happens so that students can independently complete tasks. For example: When entering or exiting the classroom, transitioning from centers, or packing up for dismissal.

During arrival each morning in my classroom, we take down chairs and make sure everything is in its place. (This is especially important if after-school care or before-school care uses your space.) After workstation rotations/center time, we put away everything we have taken out, tidy up work bins, and push in all chairs. At dismissal time, four students volunteer to wipe the tables with non-toxic wipes and stack the chairs, three students volunteer to sweep, and the rest of the students are on *clean and clear* duty—putting things back in their place. The goal is that our classroom looks *better* than we found it that morning.

Pre-modeled Expectations

Every expectation must be modeled, every organizational system explained, and every reason understood. Front-loading the *why* ensures students attach meaning to everything they do.

Having clear expectations is especially helpful when a substitute or other adult is using your space. When I come back from days off, I know my classroom space will look how I left it because my students know exactly *what to do* and *how to do it*, with or without me. Try rolling out your expectations using the following ideas:

- Explain and show where each item lives and *why*. For example: "All crayons, markers, and colored pencils go in their matching color drawer so that the color we need is easy to find."

- Model how you want a space to look. For example: When teaching students to organize their desks, create an anchor chart that shows where each item belongs. I tell my students that books are stacked on the left, papers go on top, and our pencil pack goes on the right so that everything fits and does not fall onto the floor. This can also be done with areas such as cubby spaces, the classroom library, and center areas.
- Model your expectations for *how* things are cleaned and *why*. For example: "If you are chosen to wipe and stack, you take one wipe, close the lid of the wipes, clean the top and sides of the desk, and stack the chair like this so that the custodian can come and vacuum under the tables when we go home."
- Use classroom furniture such as shelves, tables, carpets, rolling dividers, or curtains so that separation and privacy is given. Create "coves" in the classroom by turning shelves sideways and set boundaries by using colored painter's tape on the floor.
- When it is time to transition, do a final check as a class to ensure the room is ready. Talk about how it makes us feel when we leave/enter a clean space versus a messy space. This takes *time*—make sure to leave lots of it!

Where to Start

1. Reflect on your space and designate a place for every item to live. If an item does not have a home or practical use, donate it.
2. Pick three routines that are most important to you or need the most practice. Create an anchor chart to teach and practice said expectations. For example: If my students need to practice putting books back in their matching library bucket, I can create an anchor chart that shows how to sort the books by picture icons.
3. Create a bucket of student-friendly, non-toxic cleaning materials for your students to use. This can include a

mini vacuum, handheld broom, dustpan, wipes, or disposable gloves.

But What If . . .

. . . I Do Not Have Enough Storage Space?
Many of us do not have the privilege of a storage closet, cabinets, shelves, or matching buckets. Our carpets might not match a single thing in the room, and desks may be a variety of heights. But let's make lemonade out of the lemons we've been given! I for one have a cabinet with only two out of four doors hinged properly, have desks of at least four different heights, and have never been blessed with a storage closet. I am forced to be creative. See if you can get high and wide shelving units from your district's warehouse. Use floating shelves, stackable buckets, large storage containers, and file cabinets that double as a magnetic surface for learning centers.

. . . I Don't Have a Budget for Bins and Buckets?
Organizing with sturdy buckets, baskets, and bins can be extremely expensive. Try shopping at the dollar store, asking local grocery stores for extra crates, or creating buckets out of cardboard boxes. Cut off the flaps, cover with construction paper or wrapping paper, and smack a label on it! Ask parents to donate buckets and containers they no longer need or save boxes that hold copy paper, containers, tissue boxes, and other recyclable products.

. . . I Feel Overwhelmed and Don't Know Where to Start?
Ask yourself one question: "What is *one* thing that my students need to help them be efficient in the classroom?" In my classroom right now, the biggest need is keeping track of pencils. Pencils in first grade are like socks in the dryer. Hundreds disappear into a black hole, never to be seen again. An organizational tactic would be to find a location for student pencils to be stored. I like to use duct tape and a quarter of a jumbo straw to tape a "parking spot" down on each child's desk, and voila! Pencil parking.

Real-World Connection

As an adult, how do you feel after cleaning and organizing your personal space or completing routines such as washing dishes, going grocery shopping, making your bed, or vacuuming? Although personally, I prefer to not do said routines, in the end they typically bring a sense of satisfaction.

Learning organizational skills and practicing routines can influence how we treat and respect our space at home, work, on transportation, and at public establishments. It can influence how we plan events, trips, and manage our finances. Simple strategies and systems can be learned from an early age and become a mindless routine for kids. We can set our kids up for success and give them ideas for systems such as alphabetizing, sorting, and color-coding, which can work in all areas of their lives!

Dear Families

Organization is *just* as important at home. Think about the time spent getting ready for school, picking out an outfit, cleaning up toys, and the donation pile that continuously grows.

There are many child-friendly, accessible ways to implement organizational systems at home:

- ♦ Create a basket of supplies to help complete chores or household tasks. Add in non-toxic, child-friendly items that can be used to assist with cleaning. Give your child small tasks such as making the bed, wiping the countertops, or using a mini vacuum to clean up crumbs after snack time.
- ♦ Hang a sticker chart incentivizing homework completion, getting positive reports from the teacher, helping a parent, listening the first time asked, or going above and beyond with chores. Set a goal with each incentive so your child knows exactly what they are working toward (see *I is for Incentives* chapter for more).

- Label all buckets with text and a visual as your child learns to read and navigate their environment
- Specify which shelves/areas are for toys, art supplies, books, and technology. Ensure that the items you want your child to use are accessible to them.
- Talk about boundaries with your child, clearly sharing which space is theirs and which space is yours

O is for Organization Wish List

- Classroom dividers/partitions
- Clear, stackable storage bins with lids
- Colored painter's tape
- Dry erase incentive charts
- Floating bookshelves
- Jumbo straws and colored duct tape for pencil parking
- Large storage bins with lids
- Plastic stacking desk drawers (three-drawer storage)
- Student-friendly cleaning supplies: non-toxic wipes, brooms and dustpans, a handheld vacuum, disposable gloves, hand sanitizer, or a duster
- Three-ring binders

Extra! Extra! Read All About It

A Little Spot of Organization (Inspire to Create a Better You!)
Written & illustrated by Diane Alber

Kiki & Jax: The Life-Changing Magic of Friendship
Written by Marie Kondo & Salina Yoon; Illustrated by Salina Yoon

Llama Llama Mess Mess Mess
Written by Anna Dewdney; Illustrated by Reed Duncan

Organized Ninja: A Children's Book About Organization and Overcoming Messy Habits
Written & illustrated by Mary Nhin

The Pout-Pout Fish Cleans Up the Ocean *(A Pout-Pout Fish Adventure, 4)*
Written by Deborah Diesen; Illustrated by Dan Hanna

A B C D E F G H I J K L M N **O** P Q R S T U V W X Y Z

is for **Organization** because . . .

The way *we* and our *students* set up and take care of our space matters

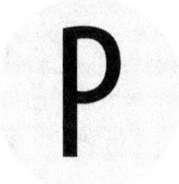

P is for Partnerships

[PARTNERSHIP]: 1) The state of being a partner; 2) The persons joined together in a partnership (Merriam-webster.com, 2025)

Similar to . . . participation, connection, link, alliance, bond, collaboration, cooperation, or togetherness (Word-Hippo, 2025)

I can <u>build strong partnerships with staff, students, families, and the surrounding community</u> so my *students* can . . .

- Build long-lasting friendships and relationships
- Feel loved, safe, and supported in the classroom
- Observe positive interactions between adults
- Practice social and emotional skills
- Understand the benefits of teamwork and community

"Why be a star when you can make a constellation?"
—Mariam Kaba (Kaba, 2021)

Working in a school setting is a unique experience. Every day, we are face-to-face with people who are *not us*. Whether it be staff members, students, or their families, we are constantly meeting and forming relationships with people from various perspectives, personalities, cultures, races, and life experiences.

What makes the school setting unique is that the people we meet *change* every single year. After working hard to establish loving and trusting partnerships, we are forced to start over from the beginning. With a new year comes a new class of students, families, staff members, volunteers, and school partnerships.

Building substantial partnerships with our students is at the center of everything we do as teachers. Studies show that when students feel their teacher is engaged, supportive, and cares about them, they are more motivated to come to school and be involved in the classroom (Klem and Connell, 2004).

FIGURE P.1: Our chapter P *why*

Successful teaching isn't a solo act or one-person show. It can't be done on an island. To reach our fullest potential, we need community and partnerships that help us and our kids to feel loved, connected, and supported. Not only does building partnerships make our lives and jobs easier, but it also helps us grow and learn as teachers and human beings. In this chapter, we will explore the importance of connecting through **The Five Hearts of Partnerships**: The student–teacher, teacher–teacher, family–teacher, student–student, and community–school partnerships.

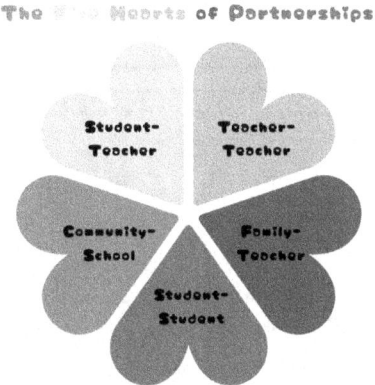

FIGURE P.2 The Five Hearts of Partnerships

Student–Teacher Partnerships

Student–teacher partnerships are the connections built with students both inside and outside of the classroom. Building a strong student–teacher partnership helps students feel important, loved, and safe. It allows them to feel like an integral part of the classroom—someone who holds *value*.

From day one of school, our goal is to get to know each student: their interests, strengths, favorites, and what makes them tick—so we can pour into them. During the first week, I like to send home a "Getting to Know You" survey for families to fill out. I want to know from the get-go what motivates each student, how they show love, what movies they enjoy, and what their favorite hobby is. When completed, this survey lives in their data folder so I can reference it throughout the year (see *G is for Goals & Growth* chapter for more information on data folders).

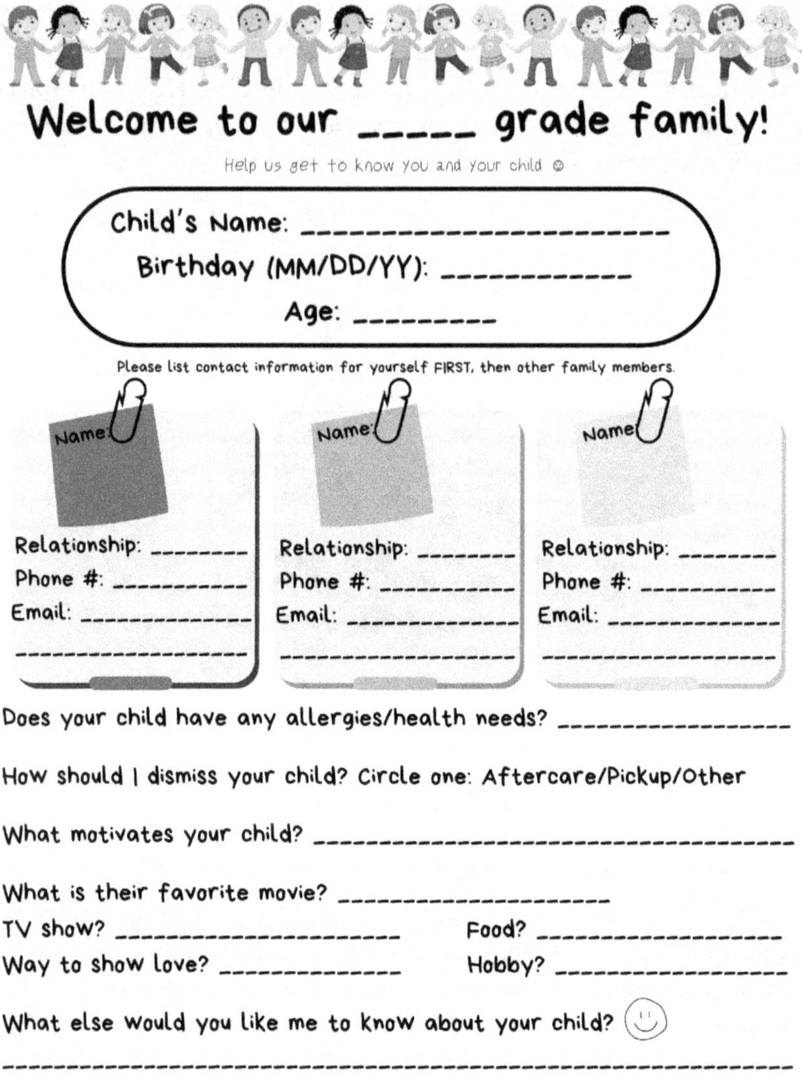

Welcome to our _____ grade family!

Help us get to know you and your child ☺

Child's Name: _____
Birthday (MM/DD/YY): _____
Age: _____

Please list contact information for yourself FIRST, then other family members.

Name: _____ Name: _____ Name: _____

Relationship: _____   Relationship: _____   Relationship: _____
Phone #: _____   Phone #: _____   Phone #: _____
Email: _____   Email: _____   Email: _____
_____   _____   _____

Does your child have any allergies/health needs? _____

How should I dismiss your child? Circle one: Aftercare/Pickup/Other

What motivates your child? _____

What is their favorite movie? _____
TV show? _____   Food? _____
Way to show love? _____   Hobby? _____

What else would you like me to know about your child? ☺
_____

FIGURE P.3 Example of a "Getting to Know You" survey

Simultaneously, while collecting this information, begin forming connections with each child. Here are ways to jump-start your connections with students:

- Actively listen when they talk about how they are feeling
- Ask about their family and "best friends" (these can change daily)

- Attend extracurricular events such as football games or recitals
- Celebrate big events such as family birthdays or moving to a new home
- Check in with students each morning
- Collaborate with them one-on-one when needed
- Compliment them for who they are, beyond outer adornments
- Contact families when a child is absent to remind them that they are missed
- Craft vision boards of hopes and dreams, and anchor them in the classroom
- Create unique handshakes to greet students
- Host a lunch bunch: Eat lunch with a small group of students
- Interact with students during lunch and recess duty
- Make a list of *why* you value each student and anchor it in the classroom
- Read books with characters that share students' names
- Read with them during Books and Blankets (see *B is for Books and Blankets* chapter for more)
- Share your life with them: pictures of your family, pets, trips, hobbies, interests, or bring in meaningful artifacts for them to see and touch
- Stock up on classroom materials that align with their interests. For example: superhero stickers or football-shaped erasers
- Tell students "We missed you!" and "It wasn't the same without you!" when they return to school after absences
- Use incentives that align with student interests (see *I is for Incentives* chapter for more)
- Use their name in word problems during math instruction

Teacher–Teacher Partnerships

Teacher–teacher partnerships are the connections built with other adults in the school building, such as teachers, student teachers, administrators, janitors, front office staff, school support staff, school counselors, and instructional aids. Investing in these relationships is key to establishing a community within the school walls. It provides support, trusted individuals to talk to, and a sense of belonging to the place where you spend seven-plus hours every day. Take the time to invest in those you work with by trying some of the following ideas (PSA: This is not me telling you to date your co-workers):

- Be a listening ear when a co-worker needs to vent
- Collaborate on special events or projects
- Form a tight-knit bond with your grade-level team
- Hand out homemade treats or cards around special holidays or breaks
- Keep track of life event dates and follow up after. For example: anniversaries, birthdays, weddings, due dates, or celebratory trips
- Make a class card for special occasions, such as birthdays, marriages, new babies, or running a marathon
- Mentor a new teacher*
- Offer teachers a quick water/bathroom break when walking by their classroom (Some of us just need a minute!)
- Pair with a **buddy classroom**—partner with another class (see student–student section for more details)
- Share resources. For example: "I have a great book on *xyz*. I'll bring it down so you can take a look!"
- Shout out teammates during staff meetings, on the morning announcements, or on online platforms such as Microsoft Teams
- Simply smile and say, "good morning!" (You wouldn't believe how many people *don't* do this!)
- Split grade-level planning responsibilities amongst teammates. For example: Team up to create newsletters or plan events
- Vertically plan: Meet, plan, and check in with teachers of other grade levels
- Write handwritten notes or thank-you cards

Mentor teachers can be a blessing to new teachers. My first year teaching at a public charter school, I was paired with a brilliant mentor teacher who taught me everything I needed to know. She taught me how to manage behavior, demand respect, and even how to dress appropriately (I'll admit being a Florida girl experiencing her first winter in Washington, DC, required far too many conversations). She showed support, listened when I cried, gave me tough love when I needed it, shared her knowledge and resources, and continued to partner with me years down the road. My relationship with my mentor teacher was irreplaceable. She taught me how to be the teacher I am today. Are there opportunities for mentor teaching at your school? What would it look like to pilot similar partnerships?

Establishing strong teacher–teacher partnerships creates the safe space to grow as an educator and opens doors to observe, learn, discuss, and process the many responsibilities (or hats) we wear. It pours into us as *humans*, who need connection just as much as our kiddos do.

Family–Teacher Partnerships

Family–teacher partnerships are the connections built between the teacher and parents, stepparents, grandparents, foster parents, extended family, guardians, or caregivers. Partnering with families shows how much you care for the child as well as the people who mean so much to them. Here are ways to continue building family–teacher partnerships:

- Ask what strategies are working well at home
- Be open and honest
- Book home visits if it is within your school policy
- Connect families with resources. For example: grief and trauma resources, outside tutoring, summer camps, and special education resources
- During arrival and dismissal, ask families how *they* are or how *their* day was

- Follow up when you say you will and send resources home when promised
- Keep families informed about all school and classroom events
- Meet or connect with families before the school year begins to let them know you are looking forward to partnering with them
- Organize the names and contact information for all families by saving them in a phonebook, phone, or tracker
- Reach out when a child is sick or has an exciting event like a recital or big game
- Send positive notes, texts, pictures, or emails. Try to make positive phone calls at least two times per month. A little goes a long way!
- Use your calendar to write down family events such as birthdays, trips, and weddings. Then *follow up* to ask how it went!

Student–Student Partnerships

Student–student partnerships are the opportunities built between peers inside and outside of the classroom. As adults, we can teach how to navigate relationships by giving examples of words to use when expressing feelings, setting boundaries, showing empathy, and helping others.

How we establish our culture within the classroom radiates outside of our four walls. When our kids honor, respect, and care for each other, it translates throughout the building. Encourage a strong classroom culture through some of these one-liners . . .

- *We are a family and a team*: The classroom has a bond like no other. We might not always like each other, but we can still respect each other.
- *We help each other, not hurt each other*: I like to ask my students, "Was that helpful or hurtful?" and discuss why.

- *We guide instead of give*: I think partner work is incredibly important when developing student–student relationships, but it is important to model how to help a friend with their work. Show students how to *guide* toward an answer, as opposed to *giving* it away.
- *How can I help?* Show students how to come from a place of kindness and offer help to others.

You can also try encouraging student–student partnerships by making time for . . .

- Buddy classrooms*
- Group work, projects, or challenges
- **Lunch bunches**
- Small-group teams: I like to have my daily small groups *name their team* and decorate their supply drawer to encourage working together from the very beginning
- Talk time: Moments for students to share their opinion with a partner

Buddy classrooms are when two classrooms—one younger and one older—form an ongoing classroom-to-classroom relationship. Students can meet to share and present projects, read together, or celebrate special events. When pairing with a buddy classroom, students can connect with others they wouldn't typically see or talk to and establish a big brother/big sister relationship—someone who can watch out for them around the school and have their back.

Buddy classrooms have worked best for me when they meet once a week on the same day and time (For example: every Friday at 2 pm). This builds consistency as well as excitement. Students start to look forward to the next meeting as relationships grow. Try partnering with a buddy classroom for . . .

- Art projects
- Culminating unit projects
- Dance parties

FIGURE P.4 Fifth and first grade buddy classes get to know each other through a *"Find Someone Who activity"*

- Fundraising or community service projects
- Holiday celebrations
- Making gifts for students to give their families
- Movie and popcorn days
- Publishing parties after writing books
- Reading buddies
- Relay races or field games
- School performances
- Science experiments
- Writing letters

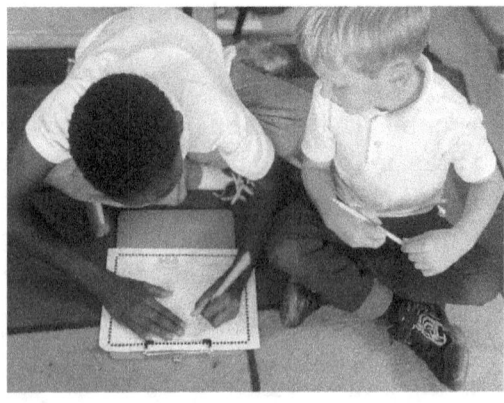

FIGURE P.5 Fifth and first grade buddies write letters for soldiers for Veterans Day

Community–School Partnerships

Community–school partnerships are the connections built with outside organizations and volunteers—anyone outside the school who wants to walk alongside you on a similar mission. Look into partnerships your school/district has already established or contact local organizations to see if they would like to form a partnership. You can also connect with . . .

- Companies that offer reading incentives, such as Pizza Hut's BOOK IT! program
- Extended family members and friends who want to volunteer
- Local bookstores, libraries, sports teams, restaurants, churches, or other religious establishments that are looking to donate their time and resources
- Local festivals and events
- Military bases
- Neighborhood businesses willing to donate items to the classroom or open their doors for a walking field trip
- Non-profit organizations that provide books and resources for schools, such as First Book or Dolly Parton's Imagination Library
- Non-profit organizations that focus on gardening, cooking, or nutrition education, such as FRESHFARM FoodPrints
- Police or fire stations
- Volunteers who want to visit the classroom as a mystery reader and surprise students with a read-aloud

Where to Start

1. Pick one way to continue building strong student–teacher partnerships. For example: Can you greet students every morning with a unique handshake or host a lunch bunch?
2. Connect with each family in your classroom, get to know them, and ask how you can support them at home

3. Find a buddy classroom and agree on a recurring day/time to meet

But What If . . .

. . . A Staff Member, Teacher, or Parent Has Overstepped the Boundary in a Partnership?
It's okay to respectfully protect your peace and set boundaries. That's what we are teaching our students! Clearly state what you need from them, provide a next step/solution, and ask administration for support if needed.

. . . My School Has Regulations, and I Am Unable to Bring in Volunteers/Local Organizations?
Connect with speakers, picture book authors and illustrators, and mystery readers through Zoom meetings or take virtual field trips.

. . . My Co-worker/Teammate Prefers to Work Solo?
All we can do is try! If someone has set a boundary and prefers to work alone, see if another adult is willing to partner with you.

Real-World Connection

Partnerships, relationships, and connections are how we navigate life as adults. Relationships with our coworkers, friends, significant others, children, animals, neighbors, and bosses are where we find comfort, joy, safety, and a shoulder to lean on. This is where we learn to communicate, love others, show kindness, and empathize. As human beings, we yearn for connection.

Our students learn these skills firsthand from us and their family. When they see us open up to others, befriend other teachers, talk to students in other classes, and connect with their parents, they can see the importance of connection. But to build these skills in our kids, we first must look at ourselves.

Dear Families

You are the first relationship your child has. They look to you to learn how to connect and form new friendships in their youngest years. Encourage your child to try new things with new people. Teach them how to ask kids to play with them on the playground, plan games and activities, speak up for themselves, set boundaries, and express their emotions using their words rather than hands.

Schedule playdates, register for team sports or extracurricular activities, and talk to their teacher about specific social-emotional skills you can work on at home. Show your child what healthy partnerships and friendships look like in your life and explain *why* they are that way.

P is for Partnerships Wish List

- Classroom materials and incentives that align with student interests (For example: superhero stickers or football-shaped erasers)
- Thank-you cards or blank cards

Extra! Extra! Read All About It

A Teacher Like You
Written by Frank Murphy & Barbara Dan; Illustrated by Kayla Harren

Hey Wall: A Story of Art and Community
Written by Susan Verde; Illustrated by John Parra

The Circles All Around Us
Written by Brad Montague; Illustrated by Brad Montague & Kristi Montague

We Are Together
Written & illustrated by Britta Teckentrup

We'll Make Things Better Together
Written by Ben Gundersheimer (Mister G); Illustrated by Dow Phumiruk

A B C D E F G H I J K L M N O **P** Q R S T U V W X Y Z

is for **Partnerships** because . . .

The way *we* and our *students* interact with each other m a t t e r s

Qu

Qu like in Conse/qu/ences

> [CONSEQUENCE]: 1) A conclusion derived through logic; 2) Something produced by a cause or following from a set of conditions (Merriam-webster.com, 2025)
> **Similar to** . . . result, outcome, conclusion, by-product, effect, or repercussion (WordHippo, 2025)

I can <u>use natural and logical consequences in the classroom</u> so my *students* can . . .

- Distinguish between helpful and unhelpful choices
- Practice responsibility and self-regulation
- Relate actions to consequences
- See firsthand that their actions have power
- Understand cause and effect

"Life might take you down different roads.
But each of you gets to decide which one to take."
—Gayle Foreman (Foreman, 2009)

The word **consequence** causes quite the debate these days. Some people believe children should sit in a time-out and think about what happened or that children should never hear the word *no*. But when you take the adult out of the equation, what happens in the real world when a less-than-desirable decision is made? With every choice we make, a natural or logical effect follows.

FIGURE QU.1 Our chapter Qu *why*

Early in my teaching career, I learned that punishments and consequences are two *completely* different things. *Punishments* are a form of payback for an act considered wrong by someone else. They remove the child's right to decide and are typically given out of fear or anger. *Consequences* are outcomes that result from our choices. They help us learn a lesson and grow from our experience (Pincus, 2021).

Our classroom culture can truly thrive when we use consequences as a learning opportunity to cultivate responsibility, ownership, independence, and empathy—characteristics that help our students grow. But here's the secret to the sauce: This only happens when a genuine connection or partnership is built with the child (Bailey, 2018). Students need to know you—not just as their teacher, but as someone they have shared experiences, conversations, and meaningful moments with. When students feel seen, heard, and understood, that's when the magic happens. Let's keep this key ingredient in mind: *connection*.

In this chapter, we will discuss three types of consequences and their unique time, place, and purpose: **natural**, **logical**, and **problem-solving** consequences. Although these terms are widely known in the world of education, my favorite advice and research stems from Dr. Becky A. Bailey's book, *Conscious Discipline*.

Natural Consequences

Natural consequences happen *naturally*, without the involvement of an adult (Bailey, 2018). For example: When you drink piping hot tea, it burns your tongue. Natural consequences are never a setup for a child or used to put a child in harm's way. They create a space for awareness and reflection over an experience.

When a child experiences a natural consequence, it's important to respond with empathy and narrate what happened (Bailey, 2018). For example: "You were spinning when walking in line and bumped your head on the wall. That seemed painful! Ow!"

It's also important to respond without bringing guilt or shame to the child. Rather than saying, "I told you that would happen" or "That's what happens when you don't listen," try saying "Next time, remember to _____, so you can _____."

Logical Consequences

Logical consequences are *pre-determined* by an adult and directly related to the action done (Bailey, 2018). For example: If you make a mess, you will need to clean up.

Logical consequences give kids an experience resulting from *their choice*. They connect the dots between *what was done* and *what happened because of their action*. These consequences are intended to help kids reflect on their choices, behaviors, and what can be done differently next time. But what makes logical consequences unique is that they are directly tied to an action. They must make sense! For example: If you use too much glue after learning that we use "just a dot," you will lose the privilege of using it for the rest of the activity.

When practicing the *art* of giving logical consequences in the classroom, I like to stick to **The Five Logical Consequence Commandments**.

FIGURE QU.2 The Five Logical Consequence Commandments

1. *Thou shall make it make sense*: When deciding on a logical consequence, remind yourself to *make it make sense!* For example: "If you don't pick up your toys, you will lose recess" would not connect to the action of leaving toys out. But "If you don't pick up your toys, I will have to keep them behind my desk for the rest of the morning" connects to the choice. The consequence chosen needs to relate to the action and serve a learning purpose.

2. *Thou shall not engage in a back-and-forth*: Refrain from a back-and-forth power struggle between you and the child. State what is happening, what will happen next, and *why*, while standing firm that the logical consequence will not change. For example: "I still see toys on the floor. Now, I must hold the toys behind my desk *because* someone could step on them and get hurt."
3. *Thou shall communicate clearly*: A logical consequence ends with an *action* or *loss of a privilege* for a short and clear period of time. The amount of time must make sense for the child to connect their action to the consequence. Continuing our toy example: "I will keep the toys with me for the rest of the morning. After recess, I would like you to try again and show me you can clean them up."
4. *Thou shall only make promises you intend to keep*: If you say it, follow through and *do it*. The students in your room should believe that their teacher is true to their word. They should be able to trust the words you say. Be careful what you promise, especially if it works against you. For example: "If you can't finish this assignment, you'll have to stay after school" puts you in a position to follow through with something you probably *don't* want to do—stay after hours!
5. *Thou shall stay calm—despite reactions*: When giving a logical consequence, ensure it is done respectfully and in a calm, yet firm tone. How the child chooses to react is their choice and can be learned from so that the outcome next time is different (see *D is for De-escalation* chapter for more).

Problem-Solving Consequences

Problem-solving consequences are *created* during a *group brainstorming time* for issues that repeatedly happen and involve a majority of the class. They motivate and invite our students to be a part of the solution and work together as a team to solve a problem (Bailey, 2018).

When meeting with the class or group, express the problem and impact. For example: "A lot of friends are feeling sad after recess because of teasing. Recess should be a safe place where we take care of each other and have *fun*. What do *you* think we should do to solve this problem?" Collect student solutions on the board or on an **anchor chart**—a handwritten chart that captures information. As a group, decide on solutions as well as a *logical consequence* for if it happens again.

In my classroom, we had an event I like to call "The Case of the Missing Fidgets." A few Pop It fidget toys disappeared from a literacy center, so students thought we should deep clean the classroom to look for them, ask the aftercare teachers if they had seen them, and send a message to parents in case they accidentally came home in a backpack. Our agreed problem-solving consequence became: *next time a fidget goes missing from a center, Ms. Meyers will put them in her teacher drawer* until we find it or it is replaced.

After creating solutions together, post the list of ideas for students to reference and discuss progress during future group meetings.

Where to Start

1. Reflect on your responses to behavior. Would they fall under a *punishment* or a *consequence*?
2. Problem-solve with students and ask for their opinions. What logical consequences make sense to them? Collect answers and anchor them in the classroom.
3. Brainstorm a list of logical consequences for recurring actions you see in your classroom. For example: *If you . . .* misplace your pencil three times, *then, logically you will . . .*use a crayon for the day instead.

But What If . . .

. . . A Student Refuses to Do Something They Are Told to Do?
This is a terrific opportunity to use logical consequences. Try saying, "You are showing me that you need more practice" or "Do

you need me to show you how one more time?" When the child is ready to follow expectations, keep your consequence the same and pick up where you left off.

. . . A Student Responds Saying, "I Don't Care"?
Tell them that you are hearing them say they don't care—*and the consequences still stand*. Ask them if they need something from you before you enforce the logical consequence. Do they need a minute to themselves? A hug? A drink of water? Give them that minute, but do not let it distract you from what you said will happen.

. . . The Child Responds With Defiance or a Tantrum?
Try to lead the child through *The Flow of De-escalation* (see *D is for De-escalation* chapter for more) but do not allow the consequence to change because of their reaction. Keep toward the goal! When the child is calm, re-visit the initial choice and logical consequence given, checking for student understanding.

Real-World Connection

In the real world, there are real consequences. When we run a red light, we get a ticket—not a time-out in a corner. When we take something, we don't have to miss play time—we have to find a way to return it or work to replace it.

Our most memorable lessons are learned through logical or natural consequences that directly relate to the thing we did. For example: We learn to wear a helmet after falling off a bike without one or we learn to create a budget after getting into credit card debt. Our kids deserve the same opportunities to learn from their mistakes and make sense of them. That's how, like us, our kids will learn that their actions have *power* in this world. Every decision comes with an outcome, whether positive or negative.

Dear Families

Using natural, logical, and problem-solving consequences is just as important at home. Your child will experience natural consequences for their actions every day. You can help them learn and reflect by talking to them about the *how* and *why* of their action and consequence.

Reflect on some behaviors that consistently happen at home and jot down some logical consequences that make sense and relate to the action you are seeing. For example, mirroring our classroom scenario: After playing with blocks, they need to be cleaned up and on their assigned shelf. If you continue seeing the toys not cleaned up, the blocks will need to be stored away for the weekend and returned on Monday to try again.

Create an "If _____, then _____" chart that both you and your child can reference. Hang it on the fridge for a gentle reminder. For example: If homework is not complete, then the television remote will not be available to use.

Qu like in Conse/qu/ences Wish List

- Flip chart markers
- Sticky easel paper for anchor chart

Extra! Extra! Read All About It

A Bad Case of Stripes
Written & illustrated by David Shannon

If You Give a Mouse a Cookie
Written by Laura Numeroff; Illustrated by Felicia Bond

No, David!
Written & illustrated by David Shannon

The Busy Beaver
Written & illustrated by Nicholas Oldland

What If Everybody Did That?
Written by Ellen Javernick; Illustrated by Colleen Madden

A B C D E F G H I J K L M N O P **Qu** R S T U V W X Y Z

is for **Conse/qu/ences** because . . .

The way *we* and our *students* reflect and learn from our choices matters

R

R is for Representation

> **[REPRESENTATION] (In Education):** 1) A school culture that is free from bias and limitation—benefiting all students (Newleaders.org, 2024)
>
> **Similar to** . . . picture, embodiment, exemplification, resemblance, personification, portrayal, or perspective (WordHippo, 2025)
>
> **For this chapter, it is important to also look at antonyms of the word representation:** dissimilarity, discord, inequality, misconception, concealment, camouflage, misrepresentation, or masking (WordHippo, 2025)

I can <u>create a safe space where every student feels represented</u> so my *students* can . . .

- Build inclusivity and challenge stereotypes
- Celebrate diversity
- Connect with characters in books that look or think like them
- Feel a sense of belonging
- See themselves reflected in their space

"Be somebody who makes everybody feel like a somebody."
—Kid President (Novak, 2013)

In a single school year, a child spends over one thousand hours in their classroom (Ed100.org, 2023). That's one thousand hours of feeling safe or unsafe. Loved or unloved. Encouraged or discouraged. Welcome or unwelcome. One hour can change a child. So, imagine what over *one thousand* can do!

The classroom can make or break how children feel about school and how they view themselves. It's important that our students feel respected, represented, and reflected in the space they spend so much of their time.

FIGURE R.1 Our chapter R *why*

How would you feel if you walked into your home and saw *no* recollection of you living there? No pictures of you, items you remember, or reflections of your hobbies and interests. These things might sound small, but they provide the feeling of *belonging* and *importance*.

My first year of teaching, I spent every penny I had to make my space color-coordinated, and of course, *cute*. I hung up posters of my alma mater (GO NOLES!), framed pictures of my family, and filled the walls with pre-made anchor charts. But when my kids entered the classroom, the only person it truly represented—was *me*.

I quickly noticed that my students thought of the classroom as *my* space, when I wanted them to feel like it was *ours*. I wanted them to take ownership of the space and share it with me.

In this chapter, we will brainstorm how to create a classroom that reflects our students. A space where they feel loved, accepted, seen, safe, secure, and most importantly—*represented*. A place where students can dream, make mistakes, take risks, and discover who they are. A space that celebrates and appreciates diversity.

Why Is Representation so Important?

Bishop (1990) describes children's literature using an analogy of mirrors, windows, and sliding glass doors. He sees some children's books as *mirrors* that reflect a child's world back to them, some as *windows* that look into other's experiences, and some as *sliding glass doors* that allow readers to step into a character's life and experience.

School is not a place where kids need to conform, feel insignificant, or less-than. School should be a safe place where kids get to grow in their character, learn about who they are, and feel special. We, as adults, have the power to create an environment that builds students up and expands their way of thinking about the world using a variety of books, resources, materials, anchor charts, and tools to represent every child in our classroom.

Representing Every Child

Think about your classroom space. Do you view it as *your* classroom, *your* rules, because *you* say so? Or, as *our* classroom, *our* rules, because *we* say so, *together*? Building a representative space is key to creating a culture where students see themselves reflected, miss being in the environment, and see their classroom as a place they are excited to come back to. Ask yourself, *is every child reflected here in this space*? Here are a variety of questions to think about when committing to representing all students in your classroom:

- *Are diverse characters represented in books?* In an article in *Literacy Today* on building inclusive classroom libraries, Havran writes: "Our goal as teachers and advocates should be to make our classroom libraries as diverse as the students within them and the world in which they live." Ensure that your selection of books includes a wide range of people from around the world and includes neurodiverse characters. Even if your students primarily come from a similar background, it's important to have diverse books that reflect the world and allow them to step outside of what they know.
- *Are there a variety of cultures and traditions represented in your classroom?* If your school allows it, recognize and learn about important cultures, traditions, holidays, and celebrations from around the world
- *Are words around the room written in student handwriting?* Ask for student volunteers to write labels for buckets, the word wall, and anchor charts
- *Are families reflected in the classroom?* Keep a photo album in the Zen Den (see *Z is for Zen Den* chapter for more) where students can add a picture of their family and look at it when they are feeling sad
- Ask students, "Where do you see yourself reflected in our classroom or library?" Use their response to find and fill picture book gaps
- *Do books have a range of authors and illustrators with personal or cultural experiences relevant to the story?* When reading the author or illustrator's biography, notice the personal connections that will bring heart and experience to the story

- *Do students have access to each other's work?* After students publish books for Writer's Workshop, can other students read them? Create a bucket with student-made stories.
- *Do students have a space and items to call theirs?* If not, give them a space with their name on it. Give them materials to be responsible for such as pencil boxes, pencils, notebooks, or crayons.
- *How are books sorted in my classroom?* If books are sorted by generic genres, how can you make the categories even more specific? For example: If a library bucket is labeled as *Life Lessons*, could books be categorized into *Celebrating Differences, Accepting Others,* or *Showing Kindness* instead?
- *How are books stored in my classroom library, and are they accessible to my kids?* Ensure that students can easily access, browse, read, and re-read books available to them (Henderson, 2020)
- *How do the identities of characters in these books align with my students' identities?* Do the characters in your classroom library represent a wide range of genders, races, incomes, families, abilities, and neurodiverse conditions? (Henderson, 2020)
- *If you have students that speak different languages, are there ways to incorporate their language into the classroom?* Try adding words from other languages into the morning message and find picture books that represent their language and culture
- *Is their name and picture visible around the room?* Allow them to write their name on desk tags, cubby spaces, anchor charts, goal charts, line spots, and pick-me sticks
- *Is their hard work displayed?* Post superstar work, projects, and art on the walls to show how proud you are of their effort. Hang goal charts and progress toward their goals to remind them what they are working toward
- *Is time allotted for students to share with their peers?* Create time for students to share about themselves, their families, cultures, traditions, and items that are important to them. Try incorporating a *share time* that allows questions

and conversation rather than *show and tell* into your morning meeting

New Year, New You

Keep in mind that every year, we get new students with new stories and new personalities. No two groups are the same. Every year, start fresh and allow students to make the classroom their own. Here are ideas to kick off the new school year:

- Ask for student support when designing and organizing spaces. I like to set up the room in a basic layout at the beginning of the year and let kids vote on where things should go. For example: *Would you rather have desks in table teams or rows*, or *should we keep computers together or spread them out so you can concentrate?* Similar to the Reggio Emilia and Montessori philosophies, try creating an environment that is personally reflective of the children, parents, and teachers by starting with an empty classroom or blank canvas and allowing students to transform it into their own space (Exchange Press, 2024).
- Create vision boards or "All About Me" boards during the first week of school. Set them up like a museum display so kids can learn about each other
- Give away last year's anchor charts to past students and start anew, allowing students to help write and re-make the charts as they learn
- Let students decorate and design their small-group journal or homework folder during the first week of school
- Make *word bank boards* as a class: Take a side-profile picture of each child and print it out in black and white. Give them magazines and a powerful bank of words to represent how they want to feel in the classroom Then, laminate each one and hang it up to display.

FIGURE R.2 Example of a word bank board

- Once you meet your new students and learn more about them, find picture books that reflect and represent them. Move chosen books to the forefront of your bookshelves
- Take pictures of each child. Hang them around the room and use to label spaces

Where to Start

1. Start fresh: Take off any name tags, labels, or anchor charts written primarily by you. Try asking students, *what do you feel our classroom still needs?*
2. Go through your classroom library and ensure there is a balanced selection of picture books with ample representation of your students. Re-label, re-group, and re-organize so that books are accessible to students. Families: grab the last three picture books you have read with

your child or your child's favorite titles. What trends do you notice?
3. Take pictures of each child in the classroom and print out a few copies. Use for cubby tags, anchor charts, bulletin boards, and homework folders

But What If . . .

. . . My District Has Regulations on Picture Books, and Many Are Banned?
Review your district's policy and stance on books used in the classroom and their criteria for banning books. Build a case for specific books, authors, and topics that benefit students and present the information to your school board. Attend board meetings, connect with school officials, and use your platform to advocate against book bans of books that you believe belong in the classroom. Reach out to organizations like the American Library Association (ALA) or the National Council of Teachers of English (NCTE).

. . . A Parent Is Upset About Another Child's Identity, Culture, or Religion Being Read About or Spoken About in Class?
Listen and try to hear their point of view. Ask them what *specific* part of the book is of issue. Explain *why* diverse books and representation are so important in the classroom, allowing children to see a wide view of the world, while developing empathy and understanding of others around them. Explain *how* you personally select the books in the classroom or the school/district's procedure and stance on culturally responsive teaching, diversity, and inclusion.

. . . My Funding for Books Is Limited and My Library Doesn't Feel Representative of My Students?
Partner with non-profit organizations such as First Book or We Need Diverse Books. Connect with your school librarian about your book requests. Apply for a local library card educator account if available and check out a large amount of books that

you swap in and out. Create an Amazon wish list of picture books you would like and send it to families, organizations, or social media accounts that promote teacher wish lists and sponsor classrooms. Stop at a Little Free Library in your neighborhood to see the current selection of donated books.

Real-World Connection

People in our world still fight to be seen, represented, and treated as equal. They feel disparity in places where they should be treated with respect—like walking down the street, eating at a restaurant, visiting the doctor, or interacting with neighbors. As adults, we have the power to make school and home a place where our children can breathe easy and know they are safe, seen, and loved. Representation is key as our kids move into adulthood as respectful individuals that know how to listen and learn from others. The classroom is just a starting point.

Dear Families

Creating a space where your child feels seen and represented is just as important at home. Representation can be difficult in tight spaces, such as when siblings share a room, in temporary housing locations, or when experiencing homelessness. If space isn't available to hang pictures or decorate to reflect personalities, try designating an object that can move from place-to-place with your child that helps them feel seen and loved. If a child shares a bed, can they have a blanket, pillow, or stuffed animal that they can call their own?

Even though *sharing is caring*, write or print your child's name on items that are owned. If possible, hang their artwork up on the fridge or wall. Frame it or use a digital frame.

Create a space—whether a room, corner, chair, or basket—and allow them to use this space when needed. Find picture books that have main characters that look like your child or speak on cultures, religious holidays, and traditions that your family or friends celebrate.

R is for Representation Wish List

- ♦ Book bins
- ♦ Diverse picture books
- ♦ Photo album or digital picture frame

Extra! Extra! Read All About It

A Space for Me
Written & illustrated by Cathryn Falwell

Freddy the Not-Teddy
Written by Kristen Schroeder; Illustrated by Hilary Jean

My Very Own Space
Written by Pippa Goodhart; Illustrated by Rebecca Crane

The Day You Begin
Written by Jacqueline Woodson; Illustrated by Rafael López

Where Are You From?
Written by Yamile Saied Méndez; Illustrated by Jaime Kim

A B C D E F G H I J K L M N O P Q **R** S T U V W X Y Z
is for **Representation** because . . .
The way *we* and our *students* see and respect one another
matters

S is for Self-Talk

> **[SELF-TALK]**: 1) An inner voice/monologue; 2) Talk or thoughts directed at oneself (Merriam-webster.com, 2025)
>
> **Similar to** . . . personal empowerment, self-guided improvement, self-support, betterment, transformation, evolving, or breakthrough (WordHippo, 2025)

I can <u>model and encourage positive self-talk</u> so my *students* can . . .

- ♦ Develop intrinsic motivation and emotional regulation
- ♦ Encourage themselves to persevere
- ♦ Practice positive self-talk
- ♦ Speak kindly to themselves using affirmations
- ♦ Transform their inner monologue

In summary of Author A. A. Milne's words from *Winnie-the-Pooh*:

> *"You are braver than you believe, stronger than you seem, and smarter than you think."*

When you look in the mirror, what do you see? How would you describe yourself? Would your words leave you feeling empowered or deflated? When we talk kindly to ourselves, we move in the direction of our words. If we think we can do it, then we are far more likely to do it. If we love and build ourselves up, then it will radiate when we go out into the world. This is especially important for our kids as they grow up and discover who they are and who they want to be. The way we speak to ourselves and the words we use matter.

FIGURE S.1 Our chapter S *why*

What would it be like to be a fly on the wall in your classroom? What would you hear as students work independently on difficult tasks? Words that tear down or words that build up? Would you see kids slamming down their pencil in frustration or kids pausing, reflecting, saying they can do it, and persevering with grit?

During the pandemic, when virtual learning was in full force, I asked my students to write a three-sentence speech to themselves using encouraging words, the way we would want someone to speak to us. We talked about phrases to use such as *you can do it* and created a word bank for other possibilities. Then, students were asked to stand in front of a mirror and record a video speaking to and celebrating themselves.

I teared up watching video after video. The words that my six- and seven-year-old learners were speaking were powerful. Life-altering. One of my students spoke triumphantly, "You are SOOOO beautiful. Look at you! Your hair is beautiful, and your brain is beautiful!"

FIGURE S.2 A first-grade student filming a video affirmation

Our inner voice and monologue are similar to a friend in the passenger seat helping us navigate and arrive safely at our destination. But if that passenger is more hurtful than helpful, it can steer us in the wrong direction entirely.

If we give our kids examples of words they can use when making friends, resolving conflict, and advocating for their needs, why wouldn't we also give them words they can use to speak kindly to themselves? In this chapter, we will take a deep dive into **The I Ams**: a collection of "I am" phrases that students can use to speak kindly to themselves.

The I Ams:

I am adventurous: I take risks and try new things
I am ambitious: I want to work hard and make things happen
I am artistic: I use my imagination to make things beautiful and meaningful

I am awesome: I am impressive and inspiring
I am bold: I take risks and speak up when I need to
I am brave: I persevere when things feel hard or scary
I am caring: I show kindness and think about others' feelings
I am clever: I think of quick solutions to solve problems
I am compassionate: I show concern for others when they are feeling sad or sick
I am confident: I believe in myself
I am considerate: I think about others and how my actions affect them
I am creative: I use my imagination to create and explore
I am curious: I want to learn more
I am dependable: I mean what I say, and I say what I'll do
I am determined: I follow through and finish tasks to completion
I am eloquent: I speak and write with clarity and power
I am empathetic: I try to understand what someone is going through even if it didn't happen to me
I am encouraging: I support others and help them feel stronger
I am enough: I know my worth, and I am confident in everything I am
I am enthusiastic: I show excitement and interest about things I do and see
I am expressive: I show how I feel through my words, body, and facial expressions
I am flexible: I can go with the flow and be open to changes
I am friendly: I treat others with kindness
I am forgiving: I move forward and try to let go of frustration when my feelings are hurt
I am funny: I like to be silly and laugh
I am generous: I give without needing someone to give something back to me
I am genuine: I am me—I say what I think and act how I feel
I am giving: I give to others without expecting something in return
I am hard-working: I try and try and don't give up
I am helpful: I do things for others to help make their life better or easier

I am honest: I tell the truth even when it's hard
I am imaginative: I explore, create, and think of new ideas
I am important: I matter to others and am needed
I am inclusive: I include and welcome others when playing and learning
I am intelligent: I know a lot about a lot
I am inventive: I find new ways to solve problems
I am kind: I talk to others with respect and do nice things for others
I am a leader: I motivate and inspire others
I am loved: There are people who love and care about me
I am loving: I help others feel loved and safe
I am loyal: I keep my promises and stand up for my friends
I am missed: When I am not at school, my teacher and class wish I were there
I am motivated: I am excited to work toward something
I am optimistic: I am hopeful and can look for the bright side
I am organized: I keep track of my belongings and know where they are
I am patient: I try my best to stay calm when I have to wait
I am persistent: I refuse to give up
I am polite: I listen, share, and say "please" and "thank you" to others
I am powerful: I have the power to change and do
I am respectful: I show people I care by the way I treat them
I am responsible: I can do things independently and be trusted to make the right choices
I am safe: I am with someone I trust who will do their best to protect me
I am sincere: I am truthful, honest, and mean what I say
I am strong: I power through hard things and show courage and bravery
I am supportive: I help, encourage, and celebrate others
I am talented: I have the ability and power to learn and practice new talents and skills
I am thoughtful: I think about others and what they need
I am trustworthy: I can be responsible with my choices

I am understanding: I listen to others and acknowledge how they feel
I am unique: There is no one else like me

When to Use the *I Ams*

All day, our brains brew as we process words and actions. Think through ways you might process information (Ewu.edu, 2023). Do you typically . . .

- Aim for perfection?
- Believe something will happen before it does?
- Compare yourself to others?
- Discredit compliments given to you?
- Exaggerate a problem?
- Generalize how the world might see you? ("Everyone thinks I am _____.")
- Let your emotions navigate what happens next?
- Mind-read by assuming something without proof?
- Think cut and dried or black and white? ("If it's not *x* then it has to be *y*.")
- Use the words *should have*, *must have*, or *ought to have*?

These moments are opportunities to use the *I Ams*. Once you identify how you process your own thoughts or how a specific student tends to respond to frustration or disappointment, you can begin teaching how to catch negative thoughts and flip them into *I am* statements.

How to Teach the *I Ams*

Begin by modeling how to catch a negative thought like a baseball in a mitt—the moment it comes. For example:

> "UGH! I ripped my paper! I can't do *anything right*!
>
> WAIT!

> *This* is the moment I can catch and change how I talk to myself. Let me try again.
>
> I ripped my paper, but *I am creative*. I can find a way to tape it back together."

To *hook* your learners, make a **T-chart**—a two-column table that organizes information—of unkind words we say or think to ourselves starting with the word "I." Then, ask students what a cheerleader would say if they were standing right next to them and cheering for them. Frame it using the sentence starter, "But what if I can?"

For example: If a student thinks "I can't read," what would a cheerleader say instead that is encouraging? Have students practice *flipping the thought* from negative statements to positive "I am" statements using "But what if . . ." to connect the thoughts. "I can't read" could become *"But what if I can read? I am smart!"*

To *teach* The *I Ams*, list them on an anchor chart. Talk about the meaning of each statement and have them repeat the words with expression and excitement. Discuss how these words reflect our hearts, minds, and who we are. It's not about what we wear or look like. Talk about when and how to use the statements. For example: "Try pointing to your brain or looking in a mirror to say these words and eventually you will think them in your brain!"

To *model* the *I Ams*, pick a scenario to act out. Start with the negative thought and model how you flip the script to a positive *I am* statement. For example: Model breaking a pencil by accident, ripping your paper, struggling to sound out a word in a sentence, or missing a basket when playing basketball.

To *reinforce*, create an anchor chart with a picture of a road that splits into two paths. Label one road "I'm not" and the other "I am." Add words along both roads and show how a driver can decide which street to turn down. We always have a choice!

FIGURE S.3 The self-talk split with dividing roads

How to Practice the *I Ams*

Once students learn how to catch a negative thought and flip it into an *I Am* statement, provide opportunities for practice and continue to reinforce using the following ideas:

- Designate a "talk it out" spot with a stuffed animal, plant, or poster of someone that students can talk to and will listen to them (Leonard, 2024)
- Hang index cards on a string with a negative thought on one side and a positive thought on the other. Then, physically flip the cards like an open/closed sign on a storefront when practicing how to flip the script
- Measure the size of the problem: Attach meaning through a number scale, color scale, or by sizes of animals to measure how big the thought is. For example: "Is this an ant-sized problem or an elephant-sized problem?" (Leonard, 2024)
- Motto of the month: Pick one *I am* statement per month to practice both at school and home. Add it to your classroom newsletter, post it in the room, read it daily for morning meeting, and praise students who use it throughout the day.

- Keep two puppets available for students to practice *talking it out* to change a negative thought into a positive thought
- Read affirmational picture books that use *I am* statements, including the titles listed at the end of this chapter
- Talk to students about the feeling of rejection or disappointment. Ask them what they can do if they feel they aren't good enough. What *actions* can be taken when self-confidence feels low? Make a list!
- Use a plastic name badge holder with a lanyard for each *I am* statement. Allow students to pick the one they need at that moment and put it around their neck for extra encouragement
- Velcro the *I Ams* around a handheld mirror so students can read the words while looking at their reflection

FIGURE S.4 First-grade student smiling at her reflection in the *I Am* mirror

Where to Start

1. Make a list of the *I Ams* you want to use in your classroom. Start with five to ten that you think are the most important for your current class
2. Hook, teach, model, and reinforce how to use the *I Ams*

3. Create a space with tools to help students practice speaking kindly to themselves

But What If . . .

. . . A Student Is Non-verbal?
Self-talk is intended to be non-verbal and spoken internally. Post visuals of the *I Ams* and words that match with a special pointer. Use the necklaces recommended above so students can wear the statements. Use voice recording buttons that speak the affirmations aloud so students can hear them.

. . . A Student Refuses to Flip Their Negative Statement?
Tell them you are here to help and can see what they might not about themselves. Speak affirmational phrases to them like "I believe you are _____" or "We believe you are _____."

. . . A Student Tries to Sabotage Another Child's I Am Statement?
Self-sabotage can give us insight into a child's comfort level when receiving praise. Is there another way to make this child feel loved? Maybe they've normalized negative statements, and positive statements make them uncomfortable. Maybe they tend to think negatively rather than positively or struggle with depression. Observe if their reaction is directed toward one child, the class, or only themselves. Talk to them about ways we can receive praise, even if we disagree. Build a relationship with the child and connect with a school counselor or school psychologist for support and new ideas.

Real-World Connection

Many of us talk to ourselves in a negative light but would never tolerate our children or students doing the same. We pick apart our bodies, abilities, and decisions, but we tell our kids they are *perfect*. We and our children can benefit from positive self-talk that flips the script.

Think about what the world would be like if our next generation of kids weren't focused on social media and the validation it brings. Imagine if they could look at themselves in the mirror, love themselves without worrying about others, and speak words that build up instead of tear down. We have the power to provide the words and phrases to our kids that could potentially change the world, the way we interact with others, and the way we interact with ourselves.

FIGURE S.5 First-grade student writes an affirmational message for the surrounding community during a grade-level service project

Dear Families

As you know, kids are like sponges. They notice everything from the way we walk to the way we talk. Our youngest learners tend to mimic what we say and how we react. Think through these instances and your typical responses. What is your child seeing, hearing, or feeling? How do you typically react when *you* . . .

- Do something that feels difficult?
- Don't win or get first place?
- Forget something?
- Make a mistake?
- Take the wrong turn while driving?

Now, think about how you can *flip the script* out loud in front of your child, modeling how The *I Ams* can be used in real time. For example:

- If you make a mistake, say: "I made a mistake! Let me try again. *I am persistent.*"
- If you forget something, say: "Sometimes I forget things, but *I am responsible*, and will try to remember next time."
- If you take the wrong turn, say: "I missed my turn, and it may take longer this way, but *I am patient*, and *I am safe* when I drive."
- If you do something that feels difficult, say: "I can do this. *I am hard-working. I am determined* to finish this."
- If you don't win or get first place, say: "It's okay, I'll get it next time! *I am enough. I am talented.*"

S is for Self-Talk Wish List

- Affirmational picture books
- Chart paper
- Index cards and string
- Handheld or standing mirror
- Plastic name badge holders with lanyard necklaces
- "Talk it out" tools: stuffed animal, plant, or poster of someone for students to talk to
- Two puppets

Extra! Extra! Read All About It

I Am Enough
Written by Grace Byers; Illustrated by Keturah A. Bobo

Maybe You Might
Written by Imogen Foxell; Illustrated by Anna Cunha

The Koala Who Could
Written by Rachel Bright; Illustrated by Jim Field

The Power of Yeti
Written by Rebecca Van Slyke; Illustrated by G. Brian Karas

Who I Am: Words I Tell Myself *(I Am Books)*
Written by Susan Verde; Illustrated by Peter H. Reynolds

A B C D E F G H I J K L M N O P Q R **S** T U V W X Y Z

is for **Self-Talk** because . . .

The way *we* and our *students* speak to ourselves m a t t e r s

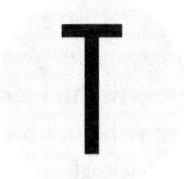

T is for Teachable Moments

> [TEACHABLE MOMENT]: A time that is favorable for teaching something, such as proper behavior (Merriam-webster.com, 2025)
>
> **Similar to** . . . a learning opportunity, teaching moment, learning experience, growing experience, or important life lesson (WordHippo, 2025)

I can <u>create time and space for teachable moments</u> so my students can . . .

- Build healthy curiosity about the world around them
- Deepen understanding of the here and now
- Feel comfortable asking questions
- Practice life and social skills with the guidance of a trusted adult
- Relate experiences to their learning

"Education is learning what you didn't even know you didn't know."
—Daniel J. Boorstin (Boorstin, 1970)

As teachers, we are responsible for the *whole child*. Our teaching goes far beyond mandated learning standards, district requirements, standardized tests, report card grades, scopes and sequences, and timelines. Our students look up to us for inspiration, praise, answers, and explanations of how the world works.

In this chapter, we will talk about **teachable moments**—the *little* moments that offer a *big* opportunity for learning. These moments don't need a PowerPoint, handout, or exit ticket. They are memorable, impactful explanations built on real-life, in-the-moment experiences. They are about what is happening in the here and now.

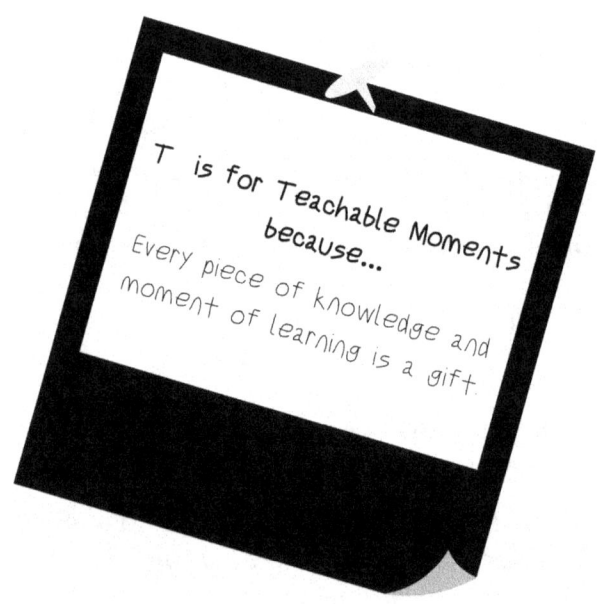

FIGURE T.1 Our chapter T *why*

Years ago, my kindergarteners received bagels and cream cheese for breakfast in the classroom. When we unzipped the breakfast bag, one student excitedly shouted, "YES! DONUTS!"

This was my golden opportunity to discuss the similarities and differences between bagels and donuts. My moment to press pause and teach, baby, teach!

"Donuts are delicious and look similar," I began. "*This* is a *bagel*. It has the same shape as a donut but tastes more like bread. It can be eaten with cream cheese, butter, jelly, or used to make sandwiches! Today you have cream cheese to dip your bagel in. You can break it in half to dunk it in cream cheese or eat it plain. Who wants to try first?"

As they took big bites of their bagels, chatter filled the room about who liked it the most and which they preferred: a bagel or a donut. Later, during our morning meeting time, we looked at pictures of bagels and donuts and compared how they are made, where you can buy them, and what people like to pair them with. This small moment could have been glossed over as we started our day, but instead, students learned to compare, contrast, make predictions, and share their opinions.

Teachable moments can be serious or silly. Some can have a momentary impact, while others have a lifelong impact. It's up to us if we want to catch them like a Frisbee and make something of them. Let's use this teachable moment about teachable moments as a teachable moment.

The Equation for a Teachable Moment

OPPORTUNITY + CONNECTION = TEACHABLE MOMENT

A teachable moment is a spontaneous time that brings forth learning and understanding. It is unique to the child and meets them where they are at that exact moment.

A teachable moment begins with an *opportunity* that comes from a child—whether an action, question, or statement. Maybe they saw something new and need help naming it, are curious and want to know more, or have an unanswered question about the world. These opportunities happen naturally, and without prompting, but with a classroom culture that cultivates curiosity, we can inspire students to have a mindset of wanting to learn more. Here are ways to create opportunities for teachable moments:

- ♦ Add sensory tables and exploration centers into your center/workstation rotation
- ♦ Ask students to respond during and after a lesson and open the floor for questions

- Create a "Curiosity Box" with sticky notes and pencils next to it. When students have a question, allow them to write it down and add it to the box.
- Create a space on chart paper where students can list what they want to know *more* about. Take moments to read and answer their questions
- Discuss current events happening in the world
- Do hands-on, STEAM-based projects that allow students to explore outside the curriculum, make mistakes, practice trial and error, and learn to fix problems using critical thinking skills
- Explain that there are *no silly questions*. Our brains are full of thoughts—big and small
- Have open conversations about cultures, traditions, people, and places around the world
- Read a variety of picture books that ignite thinking
- Reframe and reflect on moments of failure, frustration, and disappointment

Once you identify the *opportunity* for learning, it's time to make the *connection*—a guidance/direction toward new knowledge. The *connection* is guided by the teacher and allows for questions, connecting dots, relating to the real world, and naming how new information can help. Here are ways to help students connect the dots and make connections:

- Bring hands-on examples to touch, feel, and explore
- Connect learning with nature by taking students outside
- Look for information *together* when you don't have the answer
- Make a list with students to record information learned
- Open the floor so students can share their past experiences
- Role-play a scenario to promote understanding
- Show examples through art, videos, and photographs
- Take time to respond to student misconceptions and help them understand the information that replaces or adds to their prior knowledge

- Teach research skills using encyclopedias, dictionaries, books, newspapers, magazines, interviews, online search engines, or by asking an expert
- Tell a story about your own personal experience
- Use graphic organizers to collect and record new knowledge
- Watch a movie that links the teachable moment to real life

A few years ago, I went to France for a dear friend's wedding. But when I realized my students had never heard of the country, a light went off—my *opportunity* for a teachable moment!

Leading up to my departure, we used maps to plan my trip, researched facts about France, and made a list of activities I should do while visiting. This teachable moment built excitement and increased curiosity about France and other surrounding countries. But the learning didn't stop there!

When I returned from the trip, I devoted the entire morning to sharing about my adventures and answering lingering questions. I showed my favorite pictures and videos I took around the city and took students on a virtual field trip to the Eiffel Tower. We wrote about what it would be like to take a trip to France and three things we would like to see or taste. We read a nonfiction book about Paris landmarks, built our own towers with toothpicks and clay, and collected data on a tally graph about which classic French meal would be our first choice: Croque monsieur—similar to a grilled cheese sandwich, a savory crêpe, or Quiche Lorraine, made with ham and eggs.

Teachable moments like this come from opportunities and shine light on new understanding and relevant knowledge for our kids. But you have to create this time for kids to learn what the curriculum won't teach them—to allow for moments that speak to their needs, interests, questions, and concerns. We can make teachable moments intentional and meaningful if we just press *pause*.

Where to Start

1. Teach students that questions typically begin with the words *who, what, when, where, why, how, do,* or *can*. Practice framing questions versus making a statement.

2. Catch teachable moments throughout the day and continue to expand upon learning
3. Share your personal experiences with students and model how *you* enjoy finding opportunities to learn. Your enthusiasm will give *them* enthusiasm!

But What If . . .

. . . A Child Has a Question, But I Don't Have the Answer?
Be honest that you are not sure of the answer and would love to find it alongside them. Model how you will find the answer. Will you search for it online? Look inside a book? Ask another teacher? Ask an expert? Find the answer in real time with them or on your own, returning to share what you learned, and how you discovered the answer.

. . . My Schedule Doesn't Allow Time for Teachable Moments?
Teachable moments can be done *anytime*. Because they are moments, they do not need a scheduled time block. Take a moment during morning meeting, breakfast, lunch, or snack time, while transitioning to/from recess, closing circle, or dismissal time. Take a moment one-on-one with a child, in a small group, or with the whole group. The opportunities are endless—if you are open to finding them.

. . . My Students Are Uninterested in What I Am Teaching?
Teachable moments need a direct connection to student learning. The more interesting and relatable you make it, the better! Can you relate information learned to their life inside or outside of school? A sibling, parent, or pet? A television show or movie they love? Their neighborhood or community? When teaching through these moments, utilize what you know about their learning style to explore information. For example: If a child is a kinesthetic learner and learns best through hands-on exploration, bring in a model or sensory example to further explore.

Real-World Connection

As adults, we have the world at our fingertips. When we want to know something, we can type it into a browser, and *poof!* Ask virtual assistants, and *ta-da!* Immediate answers. But researching, discovering, critical thinking, and problem-solving are crucial skills that our kids need as they grow into adults.

Yes, our kiddos can easily find answers online or with artificial intelligence. But how else can we open them up to the world of discovering new things and searching for answers? We can teach how to search an encyclopedia, ask others for deeper explanations, think critically, solve problems, and find answers in books.

My challenge to you is, how can you create these moments of deeper knowledge and understanding as often as possible? How can you reveal the treasures of inquisitiveness and curiosity within your classroom?

Dear Families

A curiosity for learning stems from creating a non-judgmental, open space to ask questions and live a life of wonder.

Let that sink in. Curiosity and inquisitiveness are wonderful qualities to have and continually help a child's world and mind expand. Take the time to answer the little questions, as well as the big ones. Try to be as flexible as possible, even if that means re-routing and rearranging your plans for the day if there is something your child is interested in. Allow your child the space to try new things and decide what they like and don't like. Many of our ideas for creating opportunities and making connections can be done at home, but you also can have teachable moments at the park, in the car, or at the grocery store!

Before a child comes through the school doors, they have experienced thousands of teachable moments at home. How can you support and encourage their life of wonder?

T is for Teachable Moments Wish List

- Sensory table
- Sticky notes
- Student dictionaries
- Student encyclopedias

Extra! Extra! Read All About It

Ada Twist, Scientist
Written by Andrea Beaty; Illustrated by David Roberts

Just Because
Written by Mac Barnett; Illustrated by Isabelle Arsenault

The Curious Why
Written by Angela DiTerlizzi; Illustrated by Lorena Alvarez Gómez

The Girl with Big, Big Questions
Written by Britney Winn Lee; Illustrated by Jacob Souva

What If . . .
Written by Samantha Berger; Illustrated by Michael Curato

A B C D E F G H I J K L M N O P Q R S **T** U V W X Y Z

is for **Teachable Moments** because . . .

The way *we* and our *students* seek opportunities for learning matters

U is for Unfairness

> **[UNFAIR]**: 1) Marked by injustice, partiality, or deception; 2) Not equitable (Merriam-webster.com, 2025)
> **Similar to** . . . biased, inequitable, unequal, or preferential (WordHippo, 2025)

I can <u>teach the difference between unfairness and inequality</u> so my *students* can . . .

- Build resilience in the face of unfairness
- Develop compassion and empathy for others
- Learn to advocate for themselves and others
- Self-regulate when coping with disappointment
- Understand the difference between fair and equal, equality and equity

As John F. Kennedy once said:

"Life isn't fair. It never was and never will be."

When I was a child, the words "It's not fair!" would be followed by a *hmph* and a *humph*. Without missing a beat, my grandfather would reply with the ultimate eye-rolling phrase, "Life's not fair."

He was right. Life *isn't* fair, and plenty of people have experienced this firsthand in traumatic and life-altering ways. The world is full of terrible, horrible injustices, inequities, and disservices, with clear divisions between privilege and poverty. But when a child mutters the words "It's not fair," it can come from an innocent place. A place where a child simply wants to feel *heard*, *seen*, and *loved*.

Within the four walls of the classroom, in a safe environment with a loving adult, children can learn to distinguish the daily differences between *fair* versus *equal*, *equity* versus *equality*, and *fair* versus *unfair*.

FIGURE U.1 Our chapter U *why*

In this chapter, we will focus on the child-like feeling of *unfairness*. For example: getting called on last during carpet time, not getting picked for a classroom job, or not earning a sticker while another friend did. The baseline for this chapter is an environment where every child feels seen, heard, represented, and loved. It is a space where there are no prejudices or judgments attached and where kids can truly explore their emotions and feelings.

In Jean Piaget's study of The Developmental Theory, he labels a particularly important stage in child development called The Preoperational Stage. From ages two through seven, children struggle to see another person's point of view. Piaget called this **egocentrism** (Piaget, 1952).

A child experiencing egocentrism thinks it's *their way or the highway*. They believe everyone hears, feels, and operates the way they do. Not until age seven does the child begin to see other points of views. But teachers in preschool through first grade can anticipate this developmental change and lay the groundwork for students as they grow and learn about the world. Educators and families can teach learners how to cope with the feeling of disappointment, model how to celebrate others' wins, and show solid sportsmanship (Kurt, 2023). We must remind ourselves that although we cannot control the unfairness of the world, we *can* control how we respond and react to it (Holiday, 2014).

Our ultimate goal for this chapter is for our kiddos to understand the difference between two key terms: fairness and equality.

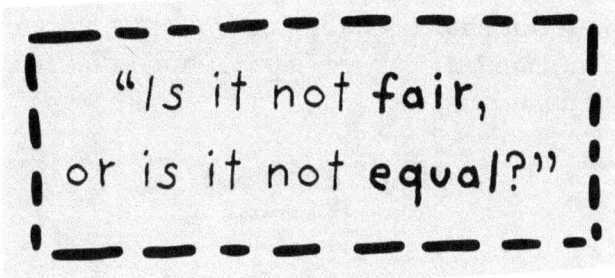

FIGURE U.2 Our reflecting question of fairness vs. equality

To teach this difference, we must, as adults, have an understanding between **equity** and **equality**. *Equity* means everyone should be able to *access* the resources and opportunities they need to have a chance to succeed, while *equality* means everyone should be given the chance to try (Marin Health and Human Services, 2021). For example: During a whole-group lesson on the carpet, *equity* means that a child needing glasses can sit closer to the board so they can see, while *equality* means every child deserves a spot on the carpet where the board is visible (National University, 2023). Once we understand the key difference between *equity* and *equality*, we can begin to teach about *fairness* vs *unfairness*.

The phrase "It's not fair" comes in many forms for our kids:

- When feeling left out of a team or group
- When someone earns a reward that they did not
- When someone else gets chosen first
- When someone else gets a thing or privilege they want
- When someone makes a decision for them

In these moments, you can see alarm bells sound. A child might react with tears or a tantrum, pouting or pleading, whining or *why*'ing, and cry out "IT'S NOT FAIR!"

A famous quote by Charles R. Swindoll comes to mind for me in these moments: "Life is 10% what happens to you and 90% how you react to it." This reactive moment is when we get to help our kids process their big feelings and remind them that *how we respond* to our feelings is of the utmost importance.

To guide our students through this process, we will utilize *The It's Not Fair 1–2–3s*: three steps to support the response to feelings of unfairness.

The *It's Not Fair* 1–2–3s
1. Express
2. Encourage
3. Elevate

1) **Express:** *Use words to explain how you feel*
   Finding the right words to describe how you feel is *hard*—even for adults. Encourage students to express how they feel by using words or choosing an emotion from a feelings chart. Pay close attention to what the child says and

needs. Are they expressing that they aren't understanding and need support? That they feel unloved or unsafe? Are they feeling triggered from something else entirely? Ask guided questions to find the hidden layer before responding and moving into the second stage. Our responses hold a lot of weight in navigating feelings of unfairness and disappointment (see *D is for De-escalation* chapter for more).

2) **Encourage**: *Listen and affirm*
Actively listen, acknowledge their feelings, and say, "It's okay to feel (emotion)." Use I am statements to ensure understanding. For example: I am hearing that it makes you sad when _____." Acknowledge when things aren't fair by validating their feelings. Then, thank them for sharing with you and make necessary changes if you have the power to.

3) **Elevate**: *Think about how you will react and respond*
Ask the child, "What can you do to *elevate* yourself?" "What can you do to show love to yourself?" or "What can you say to pick yourself back up?" Can they celebrate others? Show kindness? Choose a way to calm down before continuing? Give kids the words to say when things feel unfair, such as, "I'll get it next time," "Maybe next time," or "Just because I didn't . . . doesn't mean I couldn't have." When you hear them use these phrases, praise them for their kind, self-affirming words.

After going through these three steps with your students or child, try role-playing different scenarios. For example: If they want to be student leader of the week, but someone else is picked, or if the teacher calls on a friend to answer a question when they wanted a turn.

Where to Start

1. Continually practice expressing feelings and adding feeling words to your word wall or classroom anchor charts to develop emotional language.

2. Teach students how to affirm others using sentence stems and I am statements. Show them how to listen, even if they disagree.
3. Pick two or three sentences that students can repeat to "elevate" themselves and others after experiencing something that feels unfair. For example: "I'll get it next time." Anchor these sentences in the classroom so students can easily reference them.

But What If...

...I Witness Unfairness and Inequalities Toward a Child?
Talk to the child, listen to them, and affirm how they feel. Advocate for the child the best you can, speak up to administration, brainstorm how to support them, and use any privilege you have to make a change and help others.

...A Child Receives Accommodations for Their IEP and Others Claim, "It's Not Fair"?
Discuss the meaning of *equity* and how learning tools support friends so they can reach their goals. Ask questions and relate scenarios to the real world. For example: "Have you ever felt like you needed support to understand something?" "Tell me about a time when you needed something to help you reach a goal."

Real-World Connection

As teachers and parents who know what our complicated world entails, we can respond to our youngest learners by acknowledging, discussing, and supporting our children through their feelings. This begins with understanding the differences between equity and equality and where we see both in the world around us. Think about the causes that mean the most to you. What things feel unfair to you as an adult, and do children feel the weight of those same concerns?

Reflect on your reactions when something feels unfair. How do you react when someone gets the thing *you* want, is chosen for a job or project before you, earns a reward you believe to be more deserving of, or makes a decision that takes away your voice? Our kids are watching how we, as adults, respond and react to unfairness and follow suit.

Dear Families

You can model using the *It's Not Fair 1–2–3s* when you feel something is unjust or unfair. Think about how to narrate your thought process and reactions to express, encourage, affirm, and elevate yourself in a healthy way. The more your child sees you model this behavior in real time, the more likely they are to respond similarly.

Share how *you* cope with disappointment and what your child can do when *they* experience disappointment. Encourage them to support others when they win something and practice good sportsmanship through extracurricular activities and hobbies.

U is for Unfairness Wish List

- ◆ No items are needed for this chapter

Extra! Extra! Read All About It

Amazing Grace
Written by Mary Hoffman; Illustrated by Caroline Binch

Fair is Fair
Written by Sonny Varela; Illustrated by Peter Mahr

It's Not Fair!
Written by Amy Krouse Rosenthal; Illustrated by Tom Lichtenheld

No Fair!
Written & illustrated by Jacob Grant

The Little Red Hen
Written & illustrated by Paul Galdone

A B C D E F G H I J K L M N O P Q R S T **U** V W X Y Z

is for **Unfairness** because . . .

The way *we* and our *students* process, reflect, and react to unfairness m a t t e r s

V

V is for Virtual Learning

> **[VIRTUAL LEARNING ENVIRONMENT]**: A digital learning environment with virtual classrooms that allow students and teachers to communicate and collaborate. Virtual classrooms are highly customizable and accessible to users on a variety of devices such as smartphones, tablets, and laptops (Top Hat, 2019)
>
> **Similar to** . . . distance learning, adaptive learning, synchronous and asynchronous learning, e-learning, blended learning, remote learning, or digital learning (WordHippo, 2025)

I can <u>mirror my virtual classroom with my physical classroom</u> so my *students* can . . .

- Access their work and lessons using different modalities
- Be held to high expectations no matter the environment
- Develop skills and interests for future jobs with a virtual component
- Feel set up for success with their peers
- Practice productivity on a variety of platforms

*"Technology will not replace great teachers,
but technology in the hands of great teachers can be transformational."*
—George Couros, author of *The Innovator's Mindset*
(Couros, n.d.)

In March of 2020, life for both educators and families changed as we knew it. Our idea of teaching flipped on its head. A curtain pulled back, revealing a whole new world of classroom management, expectations, and teaching as a whole. Educators had to master new programs, translate lessons to virtual platforms or slides, find new ways to keep kids motivated, and teach new expectations for this classroom in the clouds.

In our **V is for Virtual Learning** chapter, we will dive into the tips and tricks, hows and whys, and ifs and buts of a virtual classroom setting, so that we as masterful teachers can continue sharpening our acquired technological skills.

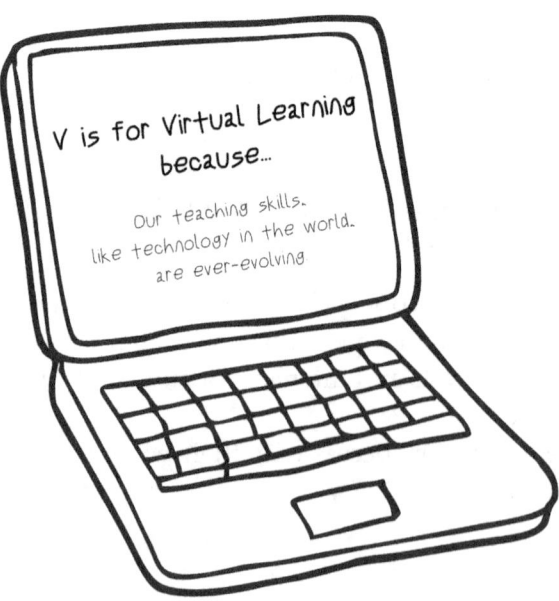

FIGURE V.1 Our chapter V *why*

I, for one, felt unprepared for the changes the pandemic brought to teaching. What I thought I knew about the classroom and successful teaching was questioned and forced to be re-imagined. Teachers had a front-row seat to students in their home setting and parents had a front-row seat to their child in the classroom setting.

The pandemic of 2020 brought a time of trial and tribulation, revealing even more inequities between families, students, and teachers. Not every child or teacher could access technology, internet, printers, school supplies, or a quiet environment. But as difficult as this time was, I like to remember it as a gift that also brought *insight*, *understanding*, and *empathy* for one another. As post-pandemic teachers, it's our job to ensure education is accessible and equitable for *any* and *every* child.

The most important piece to successful virtual learning is *mirroring* your physical and virtual classroom environments. Ask yourself the continual question, how can what I'm doing *right now* be modified and done virtually? For example: If you do calendar time every morning with your students, can you make a virtual calendar for your students to use? If you go on field trips throughout the school year, can you incorporate virtual field trips/experiences with your students? If you use classroom jobs, can you also give students responsibilities in the virtual environment?

Transitioning to virtual learning called for educators and families to be flexible, patient, and open-minded. We tried and failed (a lot), reshaped our thinking, and learned valuable lessons. Let's reflect on some *Virtual Lessons Learned* that can help merge our virtual and physical learning spaces in the current classroom and continue strengthening our post-pandemic teaching.

Virtual Lessons Learned

> Tips and tricks to help mirror the physical and virtual classroom setting:

Anticipate the little things: In the physical classroom, lots of little things can distract our lessons and learners. For example:

When the intercom calls a child down for early dismissal, the fire alarm goes off, a pencil breaks and needs sharpening, or a marker dries out. We also see little distractions happen in the virtual classroom. For example: When a website refuses to load, the sound can't connect to a video, a video call drops, or the camera doesn't work. Do your best to anticipate and prepare for these little moments by making a list of if/thens. For example: *If* the sound does not work for the digital story → *Then* I can pause the video on each page and read the story aloud myself.

Assign work using both paper and virtual platforms: When assigning work, use platforms with submission flexibility to balance assignments on paper versus assignments on a device. Use a digital platform like Seesaw that allows students to upload a photograph of their completed work if they prefer to do it on paper. Ask yourself, *Can I send a PDF or make the activity downloadable for families who would prefer to do it on paper? Can the assignment be completed on a blank piece of paper or simplified? Can the child send a picture of their work for credit?* This also works when students are absent for extended periods of time and need make-up work.

Balance the use of technology: In our technology-heavy era, a great deal of teachers and families want to be cognizant of screen time. Try going back and forth between **synchronous** and **asynchronous** learning—learning that happens at the same time versus learning that happens at different times. Teach, model, try together, and then give students ample time to complete work free from their device. If necessary, they can stay logged on, turn off their camera, or mute their microphone, with the understanding that the work will be completed.

Continue to use randomizers for equity purposes: If you use **equity sticks**—popsicle sticks that randomly select student names—in your physical classroom, try using online randomizers—name wheels, spinners, and shufflers—to choose music, activities, and more, in the virtual classroom.

Discuss expectations with families and caregivers: Connect with families and caregivers to discuss your expectations for virtual learning. For example: An adult is nearby; the child is in an independent space, if possible; the student should is sitting up at a table; background noise is kept to a minimum; and the camera is on.

Incentivize learning and increase motivation: No matter the environment, incentives motivate students to do their best, participate, and finish strong. When using digital incentives, feel free to get creative! Prepare a visual that reveals mystery incentives behind a curtain or trophies of incentives on a shelf. Award incentives such as taking a virtual roller-coaster ride, playing a virtual game, or picking the next brain break song.

FIGURE V.2 Virtual trophy incentives

Use www.classdojo.com to track positive behavior using a point system and award points when students are going above and beyond (see *I is for Incentives* chapter for more ideas).

Incorporate hands-on learning projects: Think about how students can further explore learning by doing a step-by-step project with everyday items. This not only encourages kinesthetic learning but also gives students creative time away from technology. During the pandemic, in science, my first graders learned about force and gravity. We studied the parts of a roller coaster and built our own coaster using toys, tools, and recyclable materials from around the house. These engineers drew blueprints, gathered materials, made models, assessed problems, made improvements, and culminated their project by filming a video presenting their coaster.

Integrate social-emotional learning, social skills, and play skills: Continue to teach, model, give sentence stems, and provide examples to students for making friends, taking turns, speaking up, and asking to play. Talk about what this looks like in both the physical and virtual space. For example: Muting your microphone until someone has finished talking, raising your hand and waiting for the teacher to call on you, or cheering for and encouraging classmates.

Offer support with computer literacy: Take time in the physical classroom to teach your students the basics to computer, tablet, and iPad use. Show them how to power devices on and off, toggle between applications, charge their device, log in and log out, open browsers, search for information, and type on the keyboard.

Practice and reflect on your own teaching: Just like our students, we are all learning and there is always room for growth. Practice your lessons before going "live," record yourself teaching, watch it back, and reflect on a few questions: *Do I need to tighten any transitions? What student behaviors did I overlook while teaching? Which students seemed distracted or confused with the content? What do my students need extra support with?*

V is for Virtual Learning ◆ 241

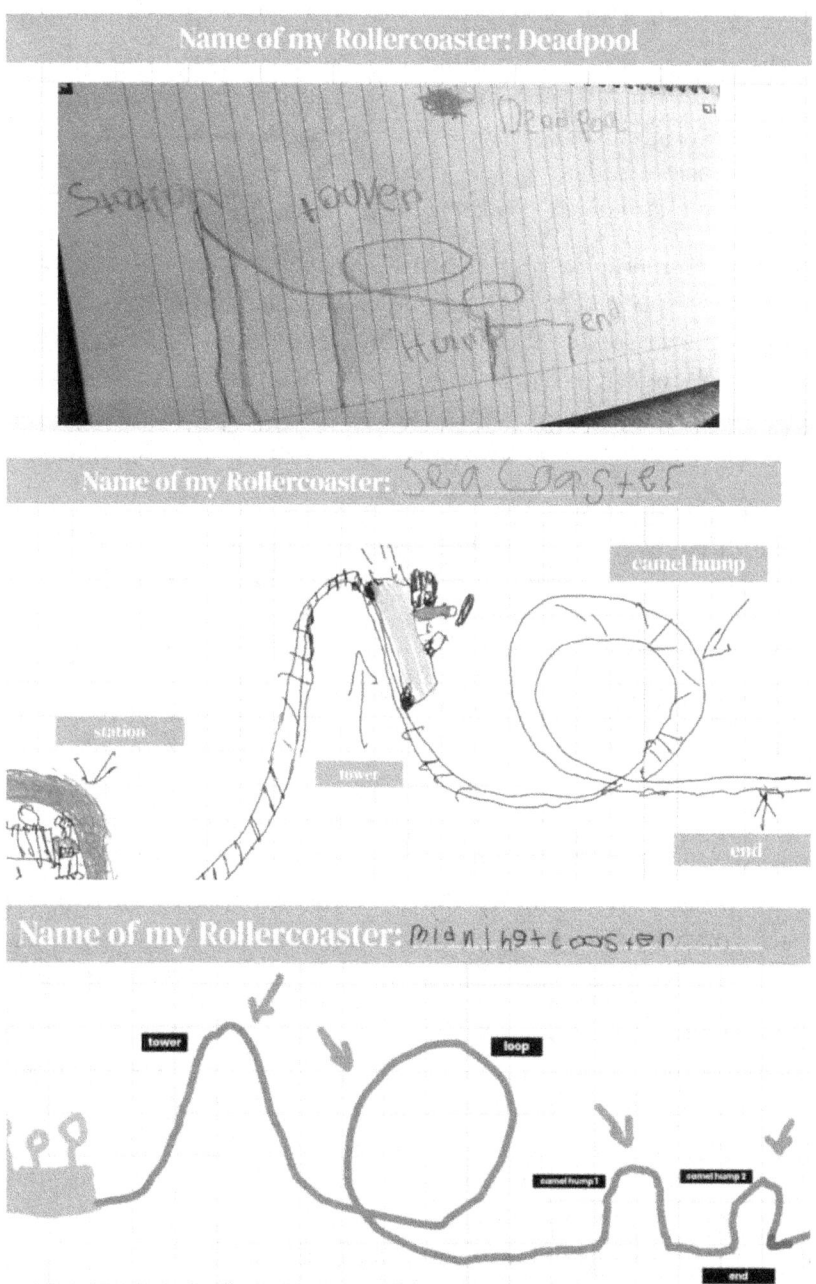

FIGURE V.3 Student roller-coaster blueprints

Provide movement and brain breaks: In my experience, students can only sit for a few minutes at a time without moving their body. Try incorporating movement every five to seven minutes by stretching, mirroring body movements, or taking brain breaks using Cosmic Kids Yoga on YouTube, Go Noodle videos, or the Kidz Bop channel on YouTube.

Record lessons for asynchronous learning opportunities: Record videos for specific skills that need extra practice, such as using a finger space (a space the size of your finger) between each word when writing or decoding a word sound by sound and blending it together. Send the video to families for additional, optional practice. If you feel comfortable, record your whole-group lesson for students who were absent or tardy to class.

Take advantage of training resources: If you are using a new program or platform, watch pre-recorded videos provided by the website or read the "Frequently Asked Questions" for instructions, tips, and tricks. Do a run-through of your lesson before using the program or platform before bringing it to your students to ensure it goes as smoothly as possible.

Track growth and monitor progress: Create virtual portfolios for each student by saving assessments and pictures of important work. Create a spreadsheet with your class roster. Track growth scores with aligned dates as students take their required performance assessments or take anecdotal notes as they work with you in small groups (see *G is for Goals* chapter for more).

Utilize virtual platforms for books and manipulatives: A myriad of manipulatives and books we know and love are available online through platforms such as Vooks, Epic, Storyline Online, MagicBlox, or through your local library on Sora or Overdrive. You can also substitute physical manipulatives with digital manipulatives such as virtual magnet letters, letter tiles, counting cubes, teddy bear counters, rulers, and dice.

Virtualize your whole-group lessons: Create slideshows to make your lessons as visually pleasing as possible. Add in picture and video examples, agendas, objectives, and links to all websites needed. Lesson slideshows can be used in the physical classroom as well to guide your whole-group lessons. Sign up for a Canva educator account to have access to a variety of premium images and graphics.

Where to Start

1. Make a list of your school-mandated, required platforms and platforms you would like to weave in. For example: In my district, I am required to use Microsoft Teams, iReady, and Canvas, but I additionally use Seesaw for posting work and Go Noodle for brain breaks.
2. Peruse all platforms you have decided to use, gain permissions if needed, and look through their available resources to get you started
3. Connect with each family and give a brief overview of your virtual expectations. Ask them to share *their* expectations as well. Take notes so you can remind learners what is expected of them both at home and at school.

But What If . . .

. . . I Want to Limit the Use of Technology?
Think through other learning modalities. For example: Can students listen to an audiobook while sitting in a cozy spot rather than watch a read-aloud on the screen? Can you play music while students work independently on a project? Can you shorten lessons to allow for more asynchronous learning time?

. . . Families Are Without Access to Technology, Paid Platforms, or the Internet?
Connect them with the school for support and resources. Are there extra devices that can be borrowed, connections that can be made with local internet companies, or funding that can be used to buy a paid program and create logins for students to use at home? There are free resources out there as well that do not require a paid membership (see *V is for Virtual Learning Platform* section for ideas).

. . . I Prefer Not to Incorporate Technology Into My Lessons?
The world is ever-changing and ever evolving. It is important that we prepare our students for the world both as we knew it *and* know it. Continue to teach in the way you do best, but think about where you can incorporate pockets of technology and digital modifications to set up your students for success in our modern, technological world. For example: After writing a narrative story, can students type it on the computer? Can they create a slideshow to pair with a book report? Can they record a video to explain how they solved a math problem?

Real-World Connection

Technology has taken over our youngest generation. What we knew and used ten years ago has transformed in drastic ways. Who knows where we will be in five, ten, or twenty years! As technology develops, let's prepare our students to be flexible and open to learning more. Literacy is all-encompassing and reaches far beyond reading and writing. Our students need to build skills for the future by learning how to type, program, code, and use a range of devices.

It's important that we learn from younger generations. Technology is intended to be user-friendly. The more you use it, the easier it becomes. Our students know a lot about a lot, and many are willing to explain steps. How can you learn from your students and develop your personal technology skills?

Dear Families

Balancing virtual learning is *especially* important if you homeschool your child or enroll them in online courses. Here are ways to set up your child for successful virtual learning at home:

- ◆ Allow your child, when able, to complete assignments on paper and give their eyes a break from the screen. Speak

with their teacher to see if assignments are available in PDF form or printable at home without asking that they create more work for themselves.
- Designate a quiet space for learning that is separate from a play or dinner space. If you have limited options, use a special carpet, mat, cushion, or chair to mark the space.
- Encourage problem-solving with technology instead of jumping to fix the problem for your child. Can your child brainstorm a solution on their own?
- Give incentives for your child to look forward to like wearing a crown at supper time, playing with their favorite toy after school, or playing outside for ten extra minutes
- Keep extra materials nearby like sharpened pencils, a backup glue stick, or scrap paper in case your child needs it mid-lesson
- Limit background noise to the best of your ability. This includes music, television, talking to other family members, or taking phone calls near the learning space.
- Practice typing and mouse-clicking skills at home
- Provide opportunities to practice social skills face-to-face. Encourage playtime with siblings, neighbors, and other friends.
- Set learning expectations for your child. Think of the three most important things they need, write them down, and practice the expectations with them. For example: how to listen to directions the first time, raise their hand, or sit safely at their learning space
- Show your child how to use their device independently and how to fix problems such as the camera or microphone not working

V is for Virtual Learning Platforms

Skip the wish list—let's get techy! In the spirit of all things virtual, here is a roundup of some of my favorite online platforms that enhance virtual learning and make teaching (and learning) a whole lot more *fun*!

- BookFlix by Scholastic
- BrainPOP and BrainPOP Jr.
- Canva (to create slideshows)
- Class Dojo (to track positive behavior points)
- Cosmic Kids Yoga
- Didax (virtual manipulatives)
- Down Dog Yoga app
- Epic!
- Flip Simu's Coin Flip Simulator
- Flipgrid
- Flippity.net
- GoNoodle
- Google Classroom
- Kahoot!
- Kodable Education
- MagicBlox
- Math Playground
- Mystery Science
- Nearpod
- Online-Stopwatch.com
- PebbleGo
- Prodigy Education
- RAZ Kids/Reading A-Z
- Room Recess (virtual manipulatives)
- Seesaw (to collect and assign work)
- Sora/Overdrive
- Storybird
- Storyline Online
- Teacherled.com (virtual manipulatives)
- TPT: Teachers Pay Teachers (for downloadable PDFs)
- Toy Theater (virtual manipulatives)
- Vooks
- Wheel of Names (name randomizer)
- YouTube

Extra! Extra! Read All About It

A Little Spot Learns Online: A Story About Virtual Classroom Expectations
Written & illustrated by Diane Alber

eNinja: A Children's Book About Virtual Learning Practices for Online Student Success
Written & illustrated by Mary Nhin

Once Upon a Time Online: Happily Ever After Is Only a Click Away!
Written by David Bedford; Illustrated by Rosie Reeve

The Fabulous Friend Machine
Written & illustrated by Nick Bland

Unplugged
Written & illustrated by Steve Antony

A B C D E F G H I J K L M N O P Q R S T U **V** W X Y Z

is for **Virtual Learning** because . . .

The way *we* and our *students* succeed through this technology-heavy era m a t t e r s

W is for Writing to

> [WRITING]: 1) The act or process of one who writes, 2) The act of forming visible letters or characters; 3) The act or practice of literary or musical composition; 4) A style or form of composition (Merriam-webster.com, 2025)
>
> **Similar to** . . . handwriting, printing, recording, composing, or creating (WordHippo, 2025)

I can <u>teach and model the multi-purposes of writing</u> so my *students* can . . .

- ♦ Communicate ideas through various writing styles
- ♦ Explore various writing opportunities
- ♦ Learn to express themselves and share their opinions
- ♦ Take action through writing
- ♦ Tell their own story and relate to others' experiences

"Create something that will make the world more awesome."
—Kid President (Kid President, 2013)

Every day, we *write*. We sign our names, type out emails and text messages, create captions on social media, jot down grocery lists, reflect in journals, write commitments on calendars, take notes in class, and the list goes on. Whether we handwrite, type, voice

DOI: 10.4324/9781003617204-24

record, or use dictation tools, formulating thoughts and transferring them to words is a skill that our students can practice in a multitude of ways.

With the development of artificial intelligence and other technologies, we inch closer to the danger of writing becoming a lost art. Our **W is for Writing to** chapter is a call-to-action for our young writers. But how do we get our kiddos to *want* to write beyond the daily necessities or current trends?

FIGURE W.1 Our chapter W *why*

As teachers, it can be hard to remember that writing exists outside our lessons on letter formation, shared writing, test preparation, and post-reading comprehension checks. These forms of writing are important, *absolutely*, but writing goes far beyond this. Writing is also a way to communicate, keep memories alive, track information, create, and dream.

My goal as a teacher *and* writer is to build a long-standing passion for writing that goes far beyond responding to questions on a standardized test. The idea is to create a balance of academic, creative, and thought-collective writing.

When I think of writing, I think of the *verb*. The *action* it takes. Writing makes things *happen*, and we can teach our kids that they can write to *do*. In this chapter, we will walk through a variety of action-based, verb-filled reasons to write, such as writing to advocate, ask for information, share information, teach, entertain, publish, communicate, organize data, respond, and process.

Writing to Advocate

We can write to advocate for our wants or needs, big or small. I once received a text from a parent on a Saturday night asking for another family's phone number. Her son wanted to have a *mega playdate* and used his dry-erase board to list his requests. He wrote down who he wanted to invite, as well as the food, music, and proposed day of the week for the event.

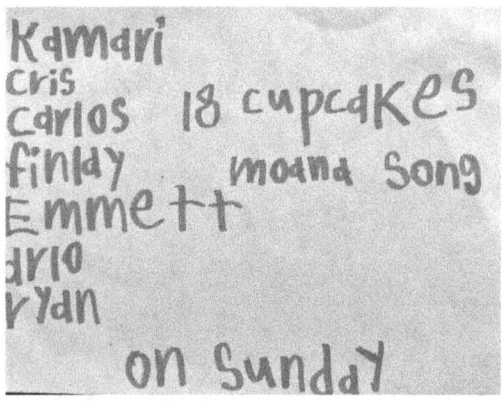

FIGURE W.2 Example of a student writing to his parents to advocate for a *mega playdate*

This child *advocated* for his desires through his writing. He presented his requests in an organized, detailed way and convinced his mother to make it happen for him. But this is only one example. Writing to *advocate* could also look like . . .

- ♦ Creating signage for protests and marches within the school building

- Opinion writing tasks: Having students journal about their opinions on different topics ranging from serious to silly. For example: Which dessert is better—cookies or cake?
- Writing letters requesting something students *want* or *need*: Creating a space in the classroom where kids can advocate for change by leaving you suggestion notes
- Writing petitions for change when students see a need
- Writing to process a big decision: When making changes in the classroom, consult your kiddos and ask for their opinion. Have them write to explain what they want and why. Share what details in their writing convinced you to make your final decision

Writing to Ask for Information

We can write to ask for information and learn more. If you have used K-W-L charts in the classroom that list what kids *know*, *want to know*, and what they have *learned*, you are likely already doing this! Before learning, in the "W" column, ask students to write what they *want to know* in question form. Then, when learning is complete, the teacher can ensure they have answered all ruminating questions.

During Hispanic Heritage Month, I connected with my brother living in Argentina and asked him to FaceTime with my first-grade students. With a GoPro and his scooter, he took us on a tour around the city streets, through a local park, and answered their questions. When the call was complete, the students were fired up to learn more.

After the call, each child wrote down lingering questions on a sticky note, and we sent them to my brother so he could answer them. Invested in the country of Argentina, they asked if we could "learn about it forever."

Writing to *ask for information* could also look like . . .

- Creating interview-style questions and hosting an interview
- Handwriting a letter to someone asking for information

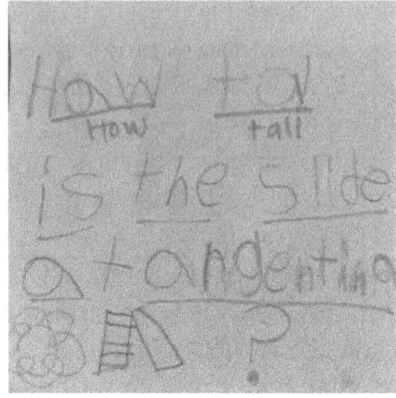

FIGURE W.3 Student question written on a sticky note about life in Argentina

- Inviting a special guest to the classroom and writing down questions beforehand
- Typing and sending a text or email with questions
- Writing down questions on sticky notes to give to someone

Writing to Share Information

We can write to share thoughts, events, and details. This can include writing reports, articles, invitations, or details of an event that happened.

Speaking of events that happened, let's talk about the tattle-tale epidemic continually taking place in the first-grade classroom (*especially* after recess). *He said, she said; they did, they didn't; I heard, she told me that . . .* it goes on and on.

Along with having students use their words (see C is for Conflict Resolution chapter for more), I ask them to write me a tattle note. **Tattle notes** are sticky notes that students use to jot down the gist of what happened. In a tattle note, one needs to list the perpetrator, the action, and what the writer *already did* to try and resolve the conflict.

When finished, the child sticks their note on my desk, and I call them up to talk through the details. This process proves they can write to communicate, update, and share information because *their words hold value*. Writing to *share information* could also look like . . .

- Adding back matter to student-made Writer's Workshop books
- Collecting information on a graphic organizer or note-taking sheet
- Informational writing units and tasks: Teaching others about a topic using facts and research
- Writing about the weekend, an upcoming event, or a vacation they recently took and sharing it with the class or teacher
- Writing a podcast episode on a specific topic
- Writing "Breaking News" as if they are a news anchor sharing current events

Writing to Teach

We can write to teach others how to do something. When we cook, we read steps. When we play a board game, we read directions. When we do a project, we follow a guide. Steps, directions, guides, manuals—these are all *written* by someone to help us learn how to do something. Writing to *teach* could also look like . . .

- Crafting a how-to PowerPoint or Canva presentation
- Creating a class game and writing down the step-by-step instructions
- Digging into how-to picture books and writing units
- Re-writing directions to a class activity after experiencing it
- Shared writing on something the entire class wants to learn (for example: tying shoes)
- Writing an advice column
- Writing a list of tips and tricks for an activity/craft
- Writing a recipe
- Writing to share an expertise/special skill

Writing to Entertain

We can write to provide entertainment. Comedy movies, television shows, scripts, commercials, and stand-up shows are all written words first. Give your kiddos opportunities to write new material or create a collection of entertaining writing. Writing to *entertain* could also look like writing a/an . . .

- Advertisement
- Commentary to a video or sports game
- Commercial/jingle
- Extension or alternate ending to a book
- Jokes/stand-up comedy sketch
- Plan to develop a video game
- Reader's Theater script
- Script to be an emcee for a school show or parent event
- Television, movie, musical, or play script

Writing to Publish

We can write to publish our work. When I was in first grade, my teacher had us publish books every time we completed the writing process. As an adult, I still have my pile of 12 laminated and spiral-bound books I published throughout my first-grade year.

Provide opportunities for your aspiring authors to publish their work. Take them through the writing process: planning, drafting, editing, revising, and publishing. Explain each step and its importance toward the end goal. Writing to *publish* could also look like . . .

- A daily Writer's Workshop block focused on the full writing process to publication
- Narrative writing units and tasks
- Submitting to kids' writing contests and magazines
- Writing for the school website or social media page

- Writing backstories of characters to deepen world-building
- Writing to perform at an open-mic event or poetry slam

Writing to Communicate

We can write to communicate with others through letters, emails, text messages, social media, or by using augmentative and alternative communication devices (AAC) to enhance communication and language for non-verbal learners.

Social media has become the main mode of communication for our youngest generation, but to write posts, emails, and hashtags, you first must know *how to write*! This includes how to spell, sound out words, formulate a sentence, use proper punctuation, and string sentences together that others will understand. Writing to *communicate* in the classroom could look like . . .

- Crafting emails and text messages
- Creating hashtags to describe the theme of a story and ensure comprehension
- Exploring hieroglyphics and other symbolic languages
- Typing emails to school administration to ask for something or say "Thank you"
- Typing letters to write a word or pressing visual cues on an AAC board to communicate
- Writing a newspaper column or magazine article
- Writing a social media post about a topic
- Writing comments in the back of a peers' published book, celebrating their hard work

Writing to Organize Data

We can write to organize our thoughts. Writing down our thoughts helps us keep track of information and reference it when we need it again. Writing to *organize data* in the classroom could look like . . .

♦ Creating a shopping list

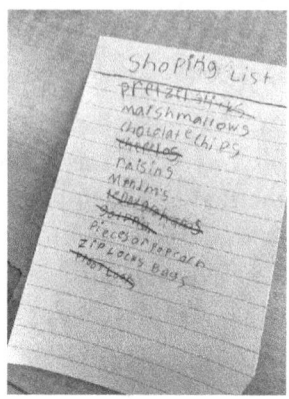

FIGURE W.4 Example of a student's handwritten shopping list

♦ Creating checklists or to-do lists
♦ Jotting down thoughts and notes
♦ Organizing a classroom calendar or individual student calendars and writing in important dates and reminders
♦ Planning a class celebration: To celebrate Lunar New Year in my classroom, we read corresponding picture books

FIGURE W.5 First graders plan for food and decorations needed for their Lunar New Year feast

about traditions, food, music, and decorations. Then, as a class, we made a list of all the items we would need if we were having our own feast and celebration. We collected donations, handmade decorations, planned outfits, and had our very own Lunar New Year feast—all stemming from learning to organize data and write down *thoughts*. When planning a class celebration, ask students to write down all food and decorations wanted/needed. Let them add visuals to the chart and then celebrate together as a class.

FIGURE W.6 Lunar New Year table based on written list

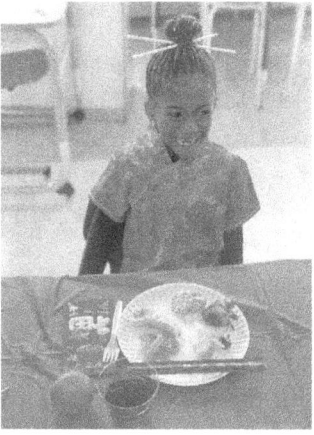

FIGURE W.7 First grader enjoying her Lunar New Year feast

- Teaching note-taking strategies
- Writing about how to solve a problem
- Writing in response to data seen in math problems

Writing to Respond

We can write to respond to text or videos. We already do this in our day-to-day teaching as we prepare for standardized tests, classroom assessments, and teach how to respond to reading. Writing to *respond* in the classroom might look like . . .

- Checking a classmate's work: Writing one thing they did well and one thing they could do next time
- Paragraph or essay writing
- Retelling or summarizing a story in one's own words
- Using details to describe learning or plot points
- Writing a review for a book, movie, or video shown in class
- Writing an introduction or conclusion to a text/book read
- Writing *before*, *during*, or *after* reading a text
- Writing to answer *who*, *what*, *when*, *where*, *why*, and *how* questions

Writing to Process

We can write to process our thoughts and keep our calm. When I put my innermost thoughts down on paper and brain dump, I feel a sense of relief because I got them out of my system. Explain to your students that releasing words into the world can make us feel lighter and calmer. Writing to *process* in the classroom could look like . . .

- Responding to a quote, verse, statistic, or meaningful word
- Using a reflection paper to process an event, feelings, and next steps
- Writing a journal or diary entry

- Writing music lyrics to express a feeling/emotion/experience or composing music for instruments to play
- Writing in the Zen Den space (see *Z is for Zen Den* chapter for more) to process a recent conflict or current emotion
- Writing a blog post for others to identify with
- Writing to vent thoughts/feelings: Remember—writing can be *personal*. We don't have to read everything we ask our kids to write. Give them space to write for *their eyes only*!

Writing is not one-size-fits-all. It's multi-faceted. So, whether our kids are writing by hand, in cursive, typing on a computer, or on a tablet/phone, the act of writing opens them up to a world of *verbs*. A world of writing that *does and* young writers that *do*.

Where to Start

1. Post all the actionable ways we can use "Writing *to* ____" on an anchor chart
2. Play with your daily schedule. Are there pockets of time that can be used for different purposes of writing? For example: journaling time in the morning, narrative writing time during Writer's Workshop, or reflection time after a read-aloud. Try adding a writing component to each part of the day.
3. Create a "Writing Corner" of special supplies. For example: scented pens/markers, feather pens, colored paper, sparkly pencils, clipboards, special stools, or materials like brown paper bags, Ziploc bags, and index cards to make homemade books

But What If...

. . . There Is No Writer's Workshop Block or Flexibility Within My Schedule?
Try to create pockets of writing time that allow you to meet all requirements. Incorporate writing into morning arrival or

breakfast time. Give each student a journal and allow them journaling/reflection time, use sticky notes to have students write questions, comments, and concerns, or send writing tasks in homework and incorporate them into projects. If time allows, host a writing/publishing club at school focused on creative writing and other styles.

. . . My Students Are Not Forming/Writing Complete Sentences Yet?
Empower our youngest learners to use what they know. Encourage and praise when they write a sound they hear, add the beginning sound, a string of letters, or put spaces between words. Ask them to read it to you and respond to what they are saying.

. . . My Students Need Physical Supports/Modifications to Assist Them?
Some students may need to trace letters, have the teacher dictate for them, or use dictation technology. Have supports available, such as voice-to-text dictation, tablets, computers, magnet letters, or alphabet sound and formation charts.

Real-World Connection

As adults, we navigate life and communicate with the world through writing. We keep relationships strong through snail mail, postcards, emails, text messages, social media messages, comments, and posts. We write letters to advocate for causes we care about, sign our names on checks and contracts, and journal our deepest thoughts, desires, and prayers. We write in some way, shape, or form countless times a day.

Think of all the jobs that require strong writing skills: a reporter, contractor, lobbyist, newspaper/magazine writer, editor, blogger, songwriter, screenwriter, lawyer, doctor, grant writer, columnist, assistant, professor/teacher, content marketer, the list goes on. Using writing as an action verb can open a world of opportunities for our kids.

Dear Families

Action-based writing can be done at home with your child. Think about their skills and interests. How can you add a level of writing to them? For example: If your child loves music and singing, encourage them to write lyrics in a notebook. If your child likes football, encourage them to write commentary for their favorite football interception video clip.

When offering opportunities to write, let the creativity flow! Try not to correct every little spelling or grammar error but instead compliment the writing goal. For example: If they wrote a shopping list, focus less on whether the words are spelled correctly and more on whether it is organized, orderly, and useful to collect items while shopping.

Last, celebrate your child's writing by displaying, publishing, taking pictures, and encouraging them to share it with others. If they want to keep it private, that's okay, too! Some writing is meant for the world, while some is meant for the writer alone.

W is for Writing to Wish List

- Augmentative and alternative communication devices (AAC) for non-verbal students if needed
- Chart paper
- Poster boards
- Sticky notes
- Several types of paper, templates, and writing tools for the writing corner. For example: gel pens, dual-tip markers, or blank comic book planning sheets

Extra! Extra! Read All About It

A Day with No Words
Written by Tiffany Hammond; Illustrated by Kate Cosgrove

Click, Click, Moo: Cows That Type
Written by Doreen Cronin; Illustrated by Betsy Lewin

Dear Dragon
Written by Josh Funk; Illustrated by Rodolfo Montalvo

I Wanna Iguana
Written by Karen Kaufman Orloff; Illustrated by David Catrow

More than Words: So Many Ways to Say What We Mean
Written & Illustrated by Roz MacLean

A B C D E F G H I J K L M N O P Q R S T U V **W** X Y Z

is for **Writing To** because . . .

The way *we* and our *students* use writing as an action verb matters

X like in E/x/pectations

[EXPECTATION]: 1) Basis for expecting; 2) Assurance; 3) The state of being expected (Merriam-webster.com, 2025)
Similar to . . . requirement, desire, wish, necessity, or readiness (WordHippo, 2025)

I can <u>set/teach clear expectations</u> so my *students* can . . .

- Feel safe, stable, and supported in their learning environment
- Go *beyond* what is expected of them
- Thrive academically and socially
- Understand the purpose and process of classroom routines
- Work together to take care of their shared space

"Nobody rises to low expectations."
—Calvin Lloyd (Lloyd, n.d.)

Some see expectations as restrictive, like a fence keeping them inside. But what if we thought of expectations as a safe, protected space to explore and create?

Clear expectations give guidelines and a direction to go in, while still giving freedom of how to get there. When expectations are easy to understand, taught, modeled, and practiced regularly, students are free to think about other things like *learning* and *discovering*.

FIGURE X.1 Our chapter X *why*

In the classroom, I like to think of **expectations** as the actions you want students to *do* and helpful words they can *say*. But before we *expect*, we need to clearly *teach*, *model*, and *practice* said expectations. In this chapter, we will imagine classroom expectations like the parts of a tree—with healthy roots, a trunk, branches, leaves, and fruit.

The roots of our tree are the *clear expectations* we set in the classroom, the trunk of the tree is the strong *support* that expectations create, the branches represent our kids aiming higher and freely growing, and the leaves and fruit are the *benefits* to our students' learning. But the key to our tree is that the leaves and fruit grow due to the *strength of the tree as a whole*.

FIGURE X.2 The Tree of Expectations

The Roots

To grow a strong tree, we need a foundation of strong roots. These roots are our *must-haves*. The *what* we want and the *why* behind it. What holds high value to you? What are the biggest needs right now for students? Your expectations should carry weight and meaning. We are going to call these **The Fundamental Five**: the most meaningful and important expectations that set the tone of your space and give roots to your tree.

When thinking through your **Fundamental Five** expectations, it's important to ask yourself, "What do I want to *see*, *hear*, and *feel* in my classroom space?" "What will I tolerate?" Because what you *allow* in the classroom is what you'll *receive*.

My **Fundamental Five** would begin like this: *I want to* . . .

1. *See* students working together to solve problems
2. *See* students finishing tasks to completion
3. *Hear* words being used to solve problems
4. *Hear* and *see* students affirming one another and themselves
5. *Feel* like my students take care of our shared space

What would *your* **Fundamental Five** look like? *I want to* . . .

1. _____
2. _____
3. _____
4. _____
5. _____

Now, look at each must-have and rephrase, ensuring it is . . .

- Achievable: Every child can do it
- Age-appropriate: Developmentally appropriate
- Clear: Every word counts
- Directional: Tells students *what to do* rather than what *not* to do
- Easy to remember: Uses rhyme, rhythm, or alliteration
- Personal: Uses "I . . ." or "We . . ."
- Logical: Makes sense
- Meaningful: Helps you and others as a whole
- Short: Can be said in *one* sentence

Here's how I would rephrase my Fundamental Five:

1. When we need somewhere to lean, we work hard with a team.
2. If we don't do it *now*, we're gonna do it *later*.
3. We use our words, not our hands.
4. We flip *I can't* to *I can* and flip *I'm not* to *I am*.
5. We play an important part and lend a helping hand.

How can *you* rephrase your **Fundamental Five** to give roots to your tree?

1. _____
2. _____
3. _____
4. _____
5. _____

The Trunk

Once our expectations take *root*, we can focus on growing a strong, supportive tree trunk. This is when we teach and model each expectation, provide examples, and role-play scenarios with students. The strength and structure of the tree depends on how you introduce each expectation and the time you take to teach it.

- After introducing each fundamental, ask students for their opinion: Give each child a small sticker and let them vote by putting it next to their favorite fundamental
- Ask students to explain the expectations in their own words: How would they teach their baby brother, sister, or cousin how to do it?
- Follow through: This is crucial to making expectations stick. If you say you are going to do something, do it. If you say you will *not* do something, stand strong. I like to tell my students, "I mean what I say, and I say what I'll do." Only make promises that you intend to keep.
- Give positive reinforcement when students are practicing the fundamentals: Narrate what you see that you like and be specific
- Read, teach, model, and role-play each expectation so that students can see what it looks like or hear how it sounds: Demonstrate with a range of examples and have students act out both the good and bad choices
- Take pictures of students meeting your expectations: Add pictures to anchor charts, morning messages, PowerPoint slides, or classroom newsletters
- Use sentence strip paper to write strong sentence starters that students can reference

The Branches

Once our tree trunk is strong and secure, kids can freely grow like branches, practicing what they've learned and finding ways to navigate various scenarios. Stemming from our Fundamental Five, we can begin to add smaller branches of additional expectations.

Think about the **parameters** of your classroom—where you want students to walk and go; the **daily schedule**—what you expect during certain blocks; and **attention-getters**—how you want to gain student attention in interesting ways.

Parameters

- Flexible seating: Are there areas of the room designated for flexible seating? What times of the day can students work there?
- Bathroom usage: How many students can leave the room at a time? Is there a hall pass to take? Can they leave without permission? How do they ask?
- Entering and exiting the classroom: Where do students stand to line up? What are the expectations before they enter or exit the space?
- Walking in the hallway: What should the line look like and sound like? I like to say, "When there's quiet, we walk; when there's talking, we stop."
- What areas are off limits? For example: behind the teacher's desk, the filing cabinet, or near electrical outlets
- Where should students stand? For example: on assigned number spot stickers or a line of painter's tape on the floor

Daily Schedule

- Closing up shop: What are the end-of-day cleanup expectations? What needs to be done before backpacks are put on? After cleaning the space, I like to ask my students, "How does it look?" so they can respond with, "So fresh and so clean!"

- Folders/Homework: Where do students put their folders and completed homework? Do they bring it every day or on one day of the week?
- Materials: Does every material have a home? How are students expected to clean up materials? What can they do to take care of classroom materials?
- Technology: What devices are available to students? Are they color-coordinated or labeled with names? How do they log on to platforms independently?
- Transitions: How do students know when to transition from point A to point B? Is there music, a rhyme, chant, or sound to listen for? Is a visual timer used? How much time do they have? What should the classroom sound like during this transition?

Attention-Getters

- Call and Response: What phrases elicit a group response? For example: When the teacher says, "Holy moly," students say, "Guacamole!"
- Focus: What should students be doing with their eyes/body when you are talking? I like to say, "Where am I?" while the students turn their body and eyes toward me and respond with, "There you are!"
- Giving directions: Will you talk over students or wait until you have their full attention? My students know that I will wait until *everyone* is ready. Why? Because I deserve respect. The same goes for students—I teach them to say, "I'll wait," when leading something or sharing during carpet time.
- Greetings: How do you want students to greet you at the door threshold? For example: with a handshake, hug, high-five, meow, or smile?
- Non-verbal signals: How should students get your attention during carpet time, independent work time, center time, or while walking in line? How can they quietly ask

to use the bathroom, get water, sharpen their pencil, or get a tissue?

Leaves and Fruit

Once our tree has roots, a strong trunk, and branches of a variety of expectations, over time—it will grow leaves and bear fruit. The leaves and fruit on our tree are the *benefits* we see after planting, teaching, and allowing students to practice meeting expectations.

You'll likely *see* less breakdowns/conflicts and notice students are willing to take risks and try new things. You'll likely *hear* respectful exchanges between peers or students reminding you of expectations, routines, and transitions. You'll likely *feel* consistency when you are both in and out of the classroom, as the students know what to do with or without you there. And you'll likely *do* more teaching—because there is a baseline understanding of how, when, and why we strive to meet expectations in the classroom.

Where to Start

1. Reflect on your personal values. Do your expectations reflect what you value, believe, or view as non-negotiables or must-haves?
2. Make your expectations *zing* by turning them into one-liners starting with "I" or "We." Write them on an anchor chart and hang it in the classroom.
3. Schedule time to teach, model, and practice each new expectation

But What If . . .

. . . A Student Refuses to Meet the Expectation?
Meet one-on-one with the child to explain why the specific expectation needs to be met. They may need a moment to de-escalate

first and *that's okay*! When meeting, discuss how the expectation can benefit them and their friends and how doing the opposite could affect them. Dig deeper to find out why they don't want to follow the expectation. If the student still challenges the expectation, this is the perfect opportunity to use logical consequences (see *Qu like in Conse/qu/ences* chapter.) Try saying, "You are showing me that you need more practice," "Do you need me to show you how one more time?" or "If you don't do it now, you'll still do it later."

. . . I Need to Change My Expectations Mid-year?
Your expectations should constantly change as your students grow. What a child needs in the beginning of the year will be different by the end. Expectations may become habits that no longer need daily practice—freeing up space for new ones. Don't be afraid to switch it up!

. . . A Student Joins My Class Late in the Year?
Create a one-pager for each expectation with simple directions, a photograph of a child modeling it, and ideas for how students can go above and beyond. When a new student joins your class, go through one to two expectations per day and teach them one-on-one. You can also choose a leader to be their *buddy* and model how to follow the fundamentals.

Real-World Connection

As adults, learning to abide by others' expectations and respect boundaries is part of our day-to-day life. By practicing how to meet expectations from a young age, students can build up and equip the next generation. We can teach and build skills such as listening, honoring words and time, not talking over others, following directions, and setting and respecting boundaries. I wish *all* adults would follow suit, don't you? As teachers, we have the time and space to teach our students about following and setting expectations—a skill they will need in the real-world, just like us.

Dear Families

Setting and modeling clear expectations is just as important at home. With clarity and reinforcement, your child will know and understand what is expected of them both inside and outside of your household.

What are your non-negotiables, beliefs, and values? How do you want your child to speak or act in different environments? How do you expect them to behave when you are not around? Think about your Fundamental Five expectations that you want to use at home, write them down, and stick them to the fridge or create a note in your phone.

Ask your child for their opinion. Can they help you set a household expectation for a chore, pet, or family member? And most importantly, when you see your child exceeding expectations, praise them, and tell them exactly what you are seeing.

X like in E/x/pectations Wish List

- Colored sentence strips
- Consecutive number stickers for number line spots
- Small stickers to vote on favorite expectation/fundamental
- Sticky easel pad paper/chart tablet paper
- Visual countdown timer/sand timer

Extra! Extra! Read All About It

Clark the Shark
Written by Bruce Hale; Illustrated by Guy Francis

Howard B. Wigglebottom Learns to Listen
Written by Howard Binkow; Illustrated by Susan F. Cornelison

How Do Dinosaurs Stay Safe?
Written by Jane Yolen; Illustrated by Mark Teague

The Book of Rules
Written by Brian Gehrlein; Illustrated by Tom Knight

We Don't Eat Our Classmates
Written & illustrated by Ryan T. Higgins

A B C D E F G H I J K L M N O P Q R S T U V W **X** Y Z

is for **E/x/pectations** because . . .

The way *we* and our *students* follow/set clear expectations and boundaries m a t t e r s

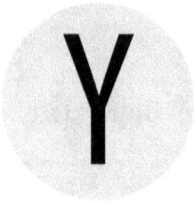

Y is for You

> [YOU]: This word speaks for itself. There's only *one* you!
>   **Similar to** . . . yourself, personally, or your own self (WordHippo, 2025)

I can <u>prioritize taking care of myself and setting boundaries</u> so my *students* can . . .

♦ Learn about setting and respecting boundaries
♦ Prioritize their own self-care
♦ Support their teacher's health and well-being
♦ Understand the importance of overall well-being
♦ Use their energy productively and creatively

"The greatest act of self-care is to believe that we are worthy of care."
    —Tara Westover, Author of *Educated* (Westover, n.d.)

After boarding our flight and buckling our seatbelts, we hear the same safety spiel before take-off: "Should an emergency occur, please put on your *own* oxygen mask first before helping those around you." This mindset especially rings true in teaching.

As teachers, we carry a ton of responsibility on our shoulders. Not only do we have to take care of ourselves, but we are responsible for each little life that walks into our classroom.

Then, add on our own family, friends, pets, and side-hustles. It's important that we *take care of ourselves* and fill up our own tanks before those around us.

FIGURE Y.1 Our chapter Y *why*

It sounds like the premise to a horror movie, but our kids are *always* watching us. They watch how we react, solve problems, interact with people around us, and respond to making mistakes. They notice how much we pay attention to them versus our technology. They sense when we are stressed, checked out, or sick. They can tell when we are excited—or feeling down.

Taking care of our own mental, physical, and emotional health makes us stronger teachers and sets the example that the way we treat and take care of ourselves *matters*. In our Y is for You chapter, we are going to think like mathematicians using **The Pieces of You Pie Chart**: A tool for achieving balance with one-third of our focus on work-life balance, one-third on health, and one-third on stress management—helping us build balanced lives as creative, authentic educators.

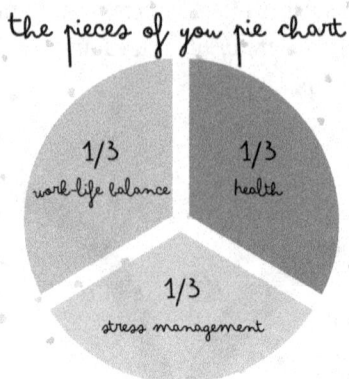

FIGURE Y.2 The Pieces of You Pie Chart

Work-Life Balance

It took me far too many years to realize it, but work and life don't have to blend together. My first five years in teaching, you'd catch me grading and writing lesson plans on the couch at home, cutting laminate during a rom-com movie, spending Sunday evening at Target shopping for weekly materials, and taking phone calls at all hours of the night. I was so exhausted by the time I finished preparing for school and completing tasks that I had *nothing* left. I was running on empty. One day, a trusted co-worker sat me down and whispered wise words: "If it doesn't get done tonight, everyone will live."

I decided it was time to make changes that helped me work smarter, not harder, and set some boundaries to bring balance back to my life. That's why *work-life balance* is the first third to our *Pieces of You Pie Chart*. Here are ideas to help you balance it all and reclaim your time:

- *Commit to a "work-late" or "work-early" day*: Gone are the days of me leaving Monday through Friday at 6 pm as the building is closing. Now, I routinely stay after-hours one day a week with a lengthy task list and knock it all out. I like to do this mid-week, on Wednesdays, as I find myself more tired on Thursdays and Fridays. On work-late days,

I make important after-hour parent phone calls, schedule meetings, prepare for school events, complete grading, and start thinking about next week's lesson plans.

- *Create a space you love that reflects you*: Do you enjoy being in your own classroom/space? Is your personality reflected there? Students may spend an average of six hours a day in their classroom, but you as the adult spend far more time there. If you're going to be working from your desk or small-group table and not your couch, make it a comfortable space that feels like home. I like to call this **The Sprinkles of You**. Sprinkle your personality around the room to ensure it is a place that provides respite, peace, belonging, and reflects *you* as well as your students. Choose your color scheme, put pictures up of the people/things you love, get matching office supplies, and add a decorative pillow to your chair to make it cozy. Make your space a place where you *enjoy* working.
- *Pick a 15- to-30-minute block of* "**Untouchable Time**": I need time to call mine during lunch, recess, or planning periods. Time to take a breath, walk, put my feet up, socialize with coworkers, or read a few pages of a book. The kids get brain breaks, why can't we? Carving out untouchable time helps me be the best teacher I can be for my students during the remainder of the day.
- *Set a hard stop time:* My motto is, *I can try again tomorrow*, or *it can be done tomorrow*. If a task is unfinished, I add it to my morning task list, "To-Do" bucket for daily tasks, or work-late/work-early day list before leaving school for the day.
- *Set certain days for certain tasks:* Write down your recurring tasks and weekly routines. Then, schedule them on a Monday through Friday calendar. This helps visualize your available gaps of time and brings routine to your week. Remember to recreate this every new school year, as each group's needs are different and duty schedules/school calendars can change. For example:
    - On Tuesdays, at 1 pm, I lead a grade-level meeting.
    - On Wednesdays, in the morning, I hang classwork.

- On Thursdays, during my planning, I make copies for the following week.
- On Fridays, at lunch, I insert grades into my gradebook.
♦ *The Friday close-out:* Before leaving on Friday, I write a new, fresh task list for the following week—making note of all the things that need to be done Monday morning and beyond. I also put materials needed in a "To-Do" bucket and leave it at school—checking out for the weekend. Bye-bye, Ms. Meyers—*Hello, Alicia!*

This is what works for *me*. But this chapter is all about YOU. What work-life boundaries resonate with you? What methods do *you* want to put in place?

Stress Management

Just because we leave the school building doesn't mean our school-brain turns off. It can be difficult to manage stress after-hours and not take it home with you. But when we are stressed, it's impossible for the people we love to get the best version of us. Those around us can sense, see, and feel our stress. I admittedly am terrible at this. I can go from zero to a meltdown in ten seconds flat if I don't catch myself and put strategies in place to de-stress.

In the same way we teach our students to use de-escalation strategies (see *D is for De-escalation* chapter for more), we as adults need a collection of strategies that help us lower our stress levels and de-compress. My personal favorites are . . .

- Calling/FaceTiming a friend or family member
- Cuddling with a pet
- Decluttering a space
- Doing a creative activity such as coloring or crafting
- Drinking cold water
- Eating/cooking a healthy meal
- Exercising/moving my body

- Getting a massage
- Going on a walk/getting fresh air
- Journaling
- Listening to music
- Listening to a podcast
- Meditating/practicing breathing exercises
- Reading/listening to an audiobook
- Squeezing a stress ball/playing with a fidget toy
- Taking a hot bath
- Taking a nap
- Watching a movie/television show

Pick your favorite strategies that work for *you*. Then, identify a few that can benefit your students, such as breathing exercises or squeezing a stress ball. Think about how you can model these strategies for your students. For example: When I feel frustrated, I say to the kids, "Ms. Meyers is feeling overwhelmed. She needs a minute to relax and (action)." They love it, copy it, and even follow up by asking, "Do you feel better now, Ms. Meyers?" or "Do you need a hug?"

Health

Y'all, this is by far my weakest category. I refuse to act like I have mastered health myself. But, over the years, I have thought through how my health affects my students' views of their own health. I encourage us as educators to reflect on a few questions:

- *Do we have someone to talk to?* Do we have a friend, family member, coworker, counselor, or therapist who we can talk to about what's going on in our lives?
- *How do we process feelings and emotions?* Can we identify what we are feeling and use strategies to de-escalate the way we ask our students to? Or do we let our frustration bubble and explode or passively accept behaviors?
- *How do we take care of ourselves physically?* Do we tell our students to stand up, move around, take a walk, run, and

play at recess—all the while sitting down in our cozy teacher chair?
- *What foods/drinks do we consume in front of our kids?* Do we tell them not to eat junk food and then eat it ourselves? When we eat something we deem as "unhealthy," do we comment on it or talk about how we will gain weight?
- *What happens when we are sick?* Do we allow ourselves to rest? Change routines if we don't feel well? Take a day off? It's important that we take care of ourselves when our body is asking us to and allow our students to as well.

Let's ensure as educators that we are putting on our own oxygen mask first and balancing our **Pieces of You** by focusing on our *work-life balance, stress management,* and mental, physical, and emotional *health*. It will only make us stronger, more impactful teachers for our students. Self-care isn't selfish—it's necessary.

Where to Start

1. Pick a space in the classroom that belongs to *you* and add *The Sprinkles of You* to it. Decorate your desk according to your personality, add pictures of friends, family, or favorite memories, and display knick-knacks that pay tribute to your hobbies and interests.
2. Schedule your *untouchable time*, daily hard-stop time, routine tasks, and work-late or work-early days
3. Think through de-escalation strategies that you can use in front of your students

But What If . . .

. . . It's My First Year of Teaching?
Borrow ideas from other teachers or social media teaching accounts, ask for advice from expert teachers, request a veteran

teacher to be your first-year mentor, and save everything you do in an organized fashion, so you don't have to reinvent the wheel the following year. Put in place as many boundaries as possible to create a work-life balance, take care of yourself, and respect your time. The first year of teaching is tough but makes you stronger!

. . . Leading a Before or After-School Activity Is Required for Me?
At one of my previous schools, volunteering for an *unpaid* after-school club used to be required in order to get a highly effective score for our end-of-year evaluation. In instances like that, my advice would be to spend time in pre-existing clubs that align with your passions or start a club yourself. For example: I volunteered for years as the music director for our annual spring musical because I love to sing. I also love to read books, so I started a club called Books and Blankets (see *B is for Books and Blankets* chapter for more), where older and younger students were paired together to read with blankets and snacks after school.

. . . I Lose My Cool in Front of the Kids?
You are human! Sit down with them, discuss what happened, apologize sincerely, and tell them what you will try to do better next time. Model how you would want them to handle the situation. *This in no way insinuates the permission of any form of abuse or inappropriate teacher-student behaviors.*

Real-World Connection

As adults, it's important that we know who we are, what we value, and what our boundaries are. As one of their safe adults, kids closely observe us and watch how we operate and move throughout the day. I consider it a *huge win* when my students recognize they need a mental break, ask to lay their head down, visit the Zen Den (see *Z is for Zen Den* chapter for more), or re-prioritize tasks. This prepares them for the world outside of school walls.

Dear Families

Taking care of yourself so you can be an example for your child is of the utmost importance. They view you as their hero and look up to you! How you take care of yourself, process emotions, deal with challenges, speak, and talk about others is taken in by them. Take time for rest and relaxation, eat foods that fuel your body, talk kindly about others in front of your child, and model how you work through conflict. Talk to your child about the importance of setting clear boundaries and choosing what feels right for them. Ask them how *they* feel, what *they* want, and what *they* need during difficult moments, after you, yourself, have reflected on the same questions.

Before texting or messaging your child's teacher, ask yourself if the timing feels appropriate or if the need is urgent. After school hours or on a weekend, send an email that your child's teacher can answer on Monday.

Y is for You Wish List

- Bucket for to-do, work-late, or work-early tasks
- Fidget toys/stress balls
- Mindfulness coloring book for kids
- To-do list notepad

Extra! Extra! Read All About It

Breathe Like a Bear: 30 Mindful Moments for Kids to Feel Calm and Focused Anytime, Anywhere
Written by Kira Willey; Illustrated by Anni Betts

Good Enough to Eat: A Kid's Guide to Food and Nutrition
Written & Illustrated by Lizzy Rockwell

Holdin Pott
Written by Chandra Ghosh Ippen; Illustrated by Erich Peter Ippen Jr.

The Law of Birthdays: A Story About Choice
Written by Brenna Jeanneret; Illustrated by Marina Kondrakhina

When a Donut Goes to Therapy
Written by Erin Winters; Illustrated by Kaitin Bucher

A B C D E F G H I J K L M N O P Q R S T U V W X **Y** Z

is for **You** because . . .

The way *we* and our *students* take care of ourselves m a t t e r s

Z

Z is for Zen Den

> **[ZEN]**: A state of calm attentiveness in which one's actions are guided by intuition rather than by conscious effort (Merriam-webster.com, 2025)
>
> **Similar to** . . . comfort, comfortable, ease, or well-being (WordHippo, 2025)

I can <u>create a calm, relaxing, Zen-like environment</u> so my *students* can . . .

- Find refuge when feeling overwhelmed
- Focus on mindfulness
- Have a safe space to go when needed
- Practice self-regulation skills
- Relax and recalibrate their emotions

"You can't stop the waves, but you can learn how to surf."
—Jon Kabat-Zinn (Kabat-Zinn, 1994)

Early childhood and elementary classrooms are full of creativity, constant chatter, and collaboration. But to balance that comes the need for quiet, calm, and relaxing moments.

As an extrovert, I am social and extra-talkative. I work well in busy and bustling environments like coffee shops and bookstores. But even *I* need peace and quiet. We all do! The space we use to recalibrate, self-regulate, and self-soothe is important. It is where we give our body, mind, and heart the permission to think differently, release stress, identify emotions, and let it all out. In the classroom environment, I like to call this space the **Zen Den**.

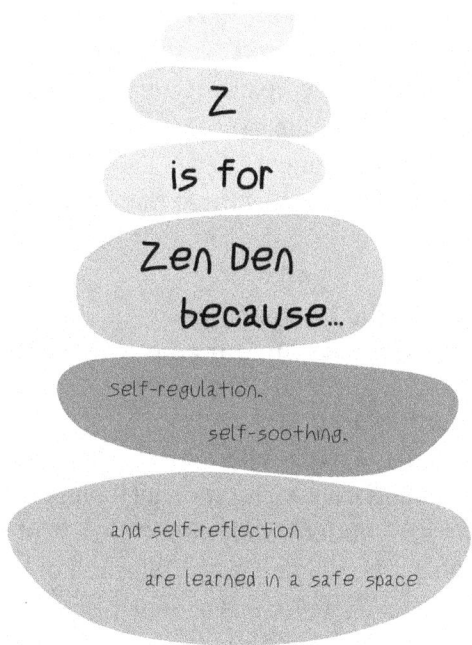

FIGURE Z.1 Our chapter Z *why*

Overstimulation and high stress levels are real. Personally, my level of stress and sensory stimulation can make or break my entire day if I don't take the time to wind down and process how I feel. Having a space to do this is important for all students, especially our neurodiverse students, many of whom are sensitive to light, sound, color, and the weight of an emotion.

As a child, living with Tourette syndrome, I didn't always *know* I felt overstimulated, but my body would tell me through tics. I would have to walk away to a quiet space where I could *let them out*. This helped me develop into the teacher I am today, understanding the importance of a quiet, private, safe, and comfortable space to let out your emotions.

You may already have a space like this in your classroom or home termed the calm-down corner, calm-down cave, calming corner, cool-down space, cool-down corner, cozy corner, Zen zone, or hygge space. We are not reinventing the wheel but walking through ideas to *modernize* this space.

The Zen Den we discuss in this chapter is inspired by mindfulness techniques and tailored to the needs of our youngest learners. Whether at a table, inside a pop-up tent, or on a mobile rolling utility cart, our goal is to create a quiet space for students to relax, recalibrate, and reflect.

Our classroom Zen Den has three main goals:

1) To *relax* the mind and body
2) To *recalibrate* the brain and body
3) To *reflect* and *respond* to our emotions and environment

1. **Relaxing the mind and body:**
   The Zen Den is a space where students can take deep breaths, stop their mind from racing, and let their body begin to relax. But to do this, students may need a variety of tools and strategies to help them. Here are a collection of tools that can be added to your Zen Den space to help students relax:
   - Expandable breathing ball: Expands and contracts when inhaling and exhaling

FIGURE Z.2 First-grade student breathing with an expandable breathing ball

- Fidget tools: Pop-Its, stress balls, sensory brushes, or even small, smooth stones that students can rub between their fingers
- Night-light projector: Use one with interchangeable films of calming scenes
- Quiet headphones: Use noise-cancelling headphones to block out noise
- Sand timer: Use a sand timer for students to track time
- Sensory bottles: Purchase liquid motion bubblers or make your own by filling bottles with food coloring, clear glue, baby oil, soap, glitter, or beads. Have students take **belly breaths** as the liquid drifts in the bottle.
- Sound machine: Use a small, rechargeable sound machine that plays white noise or nature sounds (Bonus points if it has a headphone jack!)
- Student offices: If your Zen Den is at a table or desk, let students decorate a file folder that can stand up and provide privacy when needed
- Touch lamp: Use a rechargeable lamp with a range of color options. Teach that each color symbolizes a different mood or feeling and let the students change colors to express how they feel
- Visuals: Print out pictures and steps for deep breathing techniques
- Weighted blanket: Use an easily washable weighted blanket to help support the release of stress and anxiety
- Yoga materials: Keep a yoga mat and resource of child-friendly yoga poses that students can do to stretch their body

2. **Recalibrating the brain and body**
   The Zen Den environment allows for recalibration of the brain and body—time to *build back up*. Here are ideas to create this atmosphere:
   - Basic building blocks: Provide blocks that students can stack in a tower. I like to add two colors of Unifix Cubes in case they want to make a pattern

- Calming lights: String lights, fairy lights, or lamps with a soft, white light
- Clear guidelines: Visual expectations regarding how to use the Zen Den
- Family photo album: Ask students to bring in one picture of their family and add it to a photo album that can be flipped through while recalibrating
- Flexible seating: Floor cushions, plush chairs, or beanbag chairs
- Furniture arrangement: Turn shelving furniture to create a cove or small space (Ensure that you can easily see inside!)
- Mobile rolling utility cart: If your classroom lacks space for a permanent Zen Den, fill a mobile rolling utility cart with all items and tools needed. Allow students to roll the cart to an empty or quiet space when needed.
- Pillows: Use decorative pillows to make the space comfortable and inviting. Choose calming colors and ensure that the pillowcase can be removed and washed.

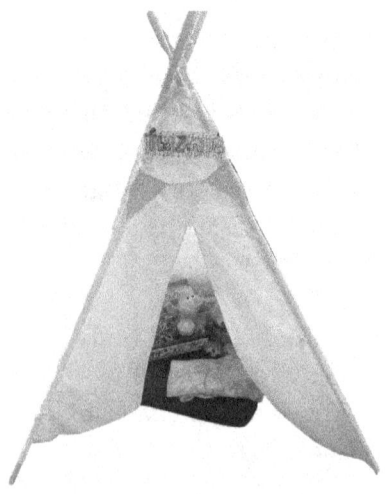

FIGURE Z.3 Decorative image of a Zen Den tent

- Plants: Add a live plant and pair it with a picture book like *Grow Happy*, written by Jon Lasser PhD and Sage Foster-Lasser, Illustrated by Christopher Lyles
- Plush blanket: Use a soft-textured, plush blanket that is washable
- Pop-up tent: Use a pop-up tent for extra privacy
- Soothing colors: Paint the wall, use peel-and-stick wallpaper, or hang a cool-colored bed sheet to create an inviting space. Use a color psychology chart to choose a color that reflects the goal of your space

3. **Reflecting and responding to our emotions and environment:**
   A Zen Den is a place where students can *reflect* and *respond* to their external environment—what they see, hear, and touch, as well as their internal environment—what they feel inside. Here are tools to support the act of reflecting and responding:
   - Affirmational/*I am* statements: Laminate a ring of affirmational statements for students to speak and declare (see *S is for Self-Talk* chapter for more)
   - Calming technique visuals: Whether on a chart or in a flipbook, provide visual examples of calming techniques and self-soothing strategies students can use
   - Coloring pages: Print social-emotional and affirmational-themed coloring pages or use an affirmational coloring book
   - Feeling visuals: Post visuals of feelings and feeling words that students can identify with
   - Handheld mirror: Use so students can see their reflection/facial expression or to read *I am* statements (see *S is for Self-Talk* chapter for more)
   - Picture books: Consistently switch out a small collection of picture books about mindfulness, self-regulation, and processing difficult emotions
   - Writing materials: Provide a notebook and pen, paper and pencil, or whiteboard and dry erase marker for

students to journal with—reflecting on what happened and how they feel

Where to Start

1. Designate a comfortable, private space for your Zen Den
2. Write and post your clear guidelines and expectations for the space
3. Design, decorate, and stock your Zen Den full of tools and materials

But What If . . .

. . . Students Visit the Zen Den to Play and Avoid Work Time?
Like all expectations, how and when to use the Zen Den must be taught, modeled, and practiced. When teaching about the space, show how to ask to visit it, set a timer, use one tool at a time, clean up, and re-join the class when finished. Teach phrases like, "Zen Den tools are used to help me feel calm." Talk about the difference between play toys and Zen Den tools. Ask students what questions they have about the space. If a child is playing, ask them how the items they are using can be used as a *tool* instead of a *toy*.

. . . My Students Do Not Identify When This Space Would Be Helpful to Them?
Guide them toward the space or ask if visiting it would feel helpful. Accompany the child and side-by-side coach them until they feel confident enough to go alone. Encourage them to express how they feel using feeling words or by pointing to a visual representation. For example: "I am feeling overwhelmed. Can I please go to the Zen Den?"

. . . I Do Not Have the Space to Set Up a Zen Den?
Use a bucket or rolling utility cart filled with tools that can move to any available space. Depending on the time of day, the available

space might change. Clearly tell and show students where they can take the bucket or cart. For example: On a three-tiered cart, the first shelf could have fidgets, sensory brushes, and stuffed animals, the second shelf coloring materials and journals, and the bottom shelf a collection of picture books.

Real-World Connection

Just like us, kids need downtime, too. Child or adult, introvert or extrovert, we all thrive from rest and relaxation. As a neurodiverse teacher, this is particularly important for me. Overstimulation can trigger a lot in my body and influence the rest of my day, health, sleep, and the attitude I show up with. For some students, this may be the only environment they can experience downtime in because they may come from a household with little to no privacy.

The pandemic changed our world, bringing a significant increase in the use of technology and social media. Life around us can be overstimulating and stress-inducing, and many of us are learning to self-regulate in our adult lives. Teaching mindfulness techniques helps our children develop into empathetic adults who go forth and teach healthy regulation skills to others in this modern world.

Dear Families

As the adult who your child loves and looks up to, it is important to model how *you* relax, recalibrate, and reflect throughout the day. Verbalize what you are doing and why. Show them *your* Zen space. Talk to your child about how *you* take a quiet minute, disconnect, and take deep breaths to feel calmer.

A Zen Den can be set up in the corner of your child's bedroom, under a table or desk, in a pop-up tent, or in another space in the home. Give your child free rein to design and decorate their new space. Make it a place that feels special to them and, when they choose to be in that space, let them have that moment independently. When they leave the space, talk to them about what they are reflecting on and feeling. Ask them what strategies they used to help them feel better.

Z is for Zen Den Wish List

- Building blocks
- Calming lights: string lights, fairy lights, or a lamp with a soft, white lightbulb
- Decorative or plush pillows
- Expandable breathing ball
- Fidget tools: Pop-Its, stress balls, sensory brushes, or small, smooth stones
- File folders
- Floor cushions, plush chairs, or beanbag chairs
- *Grow Happy* by Jon Lasser PhD and Sage Foster-Lasser, Illustrated by Christopher Lyles
- Handheld mirror
- Liquid motion bubblers
- Live plant
- Mobile rolling utility cart
- Night-light projector
- Noise-cancelling headphones
- Peel-and-stick wallpaper, paint, or a cool-colored bed sheet to hang on the wall
- Photo album
- Plush blanket
- Pop-up tent
- Sand timer
- Social-emotional/affirmational coloring books or coloring pages
- Sound machine
- Weighted blanket
- Writing materials
- Yoga mat and resource with kid-friendly yoga poses

Extra! Extra! Read All About It

Alphabreaths: The ABCs of Mindful Breathing
Written by Christopher Willard PsyD & Daniel Rechtschaffen MA; Illustrated by Holly Clifton-Brown

I Am Peace: A Book of Mindfulness
Written by Susan Verde; Illustrated by Peter Reynolds

Meditation Station
Written by Susan B. Katz; Illustrated by Anait Semirdzhyan

The Spaces in Between
Written by Jaspreet Kaur; Illustrated by Manjit Thapp

Quiet
Written & Illustrated by Tomie dePaola

A B C D E F G H I J K L M N O P Q R S T U V W X Y **Z**

is for **Zen Den** because . . .

The way *we* and our *students* learn to process and self-soothe matters

Conclusion

Now we know our ABCs! We have pulled out and put away 26 buckets on a shelf of A-to-Z systems, methods, and ideas to practice both in the classroom and at home. We have tried each one on for size, added our flair, and continued to be the exceptional educators, parents, guardians, counselors, coaches, writers, partners, and role models we are. But most importantly, we have focused on what truly *m a t t e r s* from A to Z:

Connecting to creativity through **Arts Integration**
Experiencing the joy of reading during **Books and Blankets**
Working through healthy steps of **Conflict Resolution**
Responding and resolving how we feel through **De-escalation**
Enjoying learning through **Engagement** tricks
Starting with momentum in the first week of school using **First Week Fundamentals**
Setting, working toward, and celebrating actionable **Goals and Growth**
Expressing ourselves through creativity and creation as we explore **Hobbies**
Motivating using meaningful **Incentives**
Practicing responsibility and accountability through classroom **Jobs**
Interpreting, challenging, and reflecting upon stories using **Kid-tiques**

Feeling confident in showing what we know during **Learning Checks**
Prioritizing and completing tasks on weekly **Menus**
Celebrating the uniqueness of **Neurodiversity**
Setting up and taking care of our space by using **Organization** tactics
Finding **Partnerships** that help us interact with each other and work together
Reflecting and learning from our choices using **Conse/qu/ences**
Ensuring the **Representation** of each child is seen and felt within the classroom
Speaking positively to ourselves using affirmational **Self-Talk**
Taking advantage of **Teachable Moments**
Processing, reflecting, and controlling our reactions to **Unfairness**
Continually learning in this digital age of **Virtual Learning**
Writing to encourage action
Setting clear **E/x/pectations** and boundaries
The importance of taking care of **You**
And processing feelings and self-soothing in a safe space like a **Zen Den**

We have followed *The Recipe for Resolution* to resolve conflict, filled our *Bag of Engagement Tricks*, and created our *Inventory of Incentives*. We have rolled out classroom jobs for every student, created menus for work time, and started monthly learning checks to break up our goals and encourage growth. We have ensured that our classroom celebrates and represents every unique child that walks through our door. We have taken the time to focus on ourselves before we put on our many hats. But above all, we have created a *community* of A-to-Z educators committed to working on their craft and families committed to learning more.

Just like you, I am constantly growing, trying new things, failing, and trying again. We are on this journey *together*, and I am rooting for you always.

In the words of T.S. Eliot in *Little Gidding*:

What we call the beginning is often the end. And to make an end is to make a beginning. The end is where we start from.
(Columbia.edu, 2025)

Although our alphabet is complete at 26 letters, our job as teachers is never over.

This is only the beginning.

A-to-Z Glossary

Anchor chart: A handwritten chart that visually captures information, giving students a go-to, accessible reference as they learn and practice new concepts.
Artistic avenues: The endless ways to infuse and integrate art into the classroom through theatre, music, dance, communication art, and visual art.
Asynchronous learning: Learning that happens away from the teacher at a preferred pace and time.
Attention-getters: A shortcut that grabs student attention whether through chants, call-and-response, songs, clapping patterns, sounds, mirrored body movements, or telling jokes.
Belly breaths: A simple trick to help students breathe from their diaphragm by placing two hands on their belly and focusing on its rise and fall while inhaling and exhaling.
Books and Blankets: A cozy, quiet reading time when students can read *what* they want, *where* they want, and *how* they want—without feeling the pressures of performance or perfection.
Brain breaks: A little learning break that relaxes the brain and provides movement opportunities for the body, such as singing, dancing, stretching, exercising, breathing, or taking a mindful moment.
Buddy classroom: A continual partnership between two classrooms of students: one older and one younger.
Conflict resolution: A gentle method of finding a peaceful solution to conflict, by listening, using words, taking turns, apologizing, asking for clarity, and ensuring resolution at the end.
Consequence: The unlikely result of a choice or circumstance.
Decluttering State of the Union: A spree of organization that consists of throwing away out-of-date papers, refurbishing or donating furniture, donating items that are no longer needed, and adding new systems that *just make sense!*

De-escalation: The process of calming down, unpacking big feelings, finding the root, and shrinking the situation.

Differentiation: Varying the modalities and methods of a child's learning to meet specific needs.

Engagement: The excitement and sense of joy in a space during learning time that piques interest and boosts motivation.

Equality: The understanding that all students should be given the same *opportunity to try*.

Equity: The understanding that all students should be able to *access* the resources and opportunities they need to have a chance to succeed—and *may need supports* to get there.

Equity sticks: Popsicle sticks with student names that can be pulled at random, to avoid favoritism or unintentionally calling on the same students.

Expectations: What you want to happen—what students can *do* and helpful words they can *say*.

Flexible seating: A range of seating options for students to take their pick of, giving them the freedom to move and engage in learning in a way that works for them.

Fun Friday: An end-of-the-week culminating incentive to engage in hobbies, interests, and social time with peers.

Hobby drawers: A collection of hands-on materials and picture books to explore and sharpen hobbies and interests.

Incentive: A perk presented *before* a behavior that motivates and encourages one to succeed.

Inventory of Incentives: A plethora of incentives that keep energy high and excitement alive.

Kid-tiques: An imaginative, artistic process consisting of six literary techniques that allow kids to visualize, internalize, and comprehend a story from all angles.

Learning checks: Monthly one-on-one check-ins that gather data and track progress toward the mastering of building block skills.

Logical consequence: A consequence that connects the dots between *what was done* and *what happened because of an action*.

Loving debrief: A one-on-one conversation between a child and adult held *after* the de-escalation process, focused on resolution and reflection.

Lunch bunches: Lunch with a small group of students to practice and apply social-emotional or behavioral skills.

Menus: A visual board of tasks presenting all student work/expectations for the week.

Modifications: Changes made to work, expectations, or teaching to better support learning.

Natural consequence: A consequence that happens *naturally*, without an adult involved.

Neurodiversity: The celebration of uniquely beautiful brains, skills, and abilities.

Non-verbal signals: Signals using the body that share thoughts, express emotions, and explain thinking without sound.

Parameters of the classroom: The boundaries to your space—where you want students to *go*, areas you want them to have *access* to, and the expectations you have for the classroom.

Problem-solving consequence: A consequence *created* during a group brainstorming time for issues that repeatedly happen and involve most of the class or group.

Reading behaviors: Practices toward reading: —how to hold a book, treat it with respect, distinguish between letters and words, turn pages one at a time, and read with a partner.

Reading perseverance: The act of reading and re-reading *strong*, refusing to give up.

Reading stamina: The act of reading *longer* and ignoring distractions.

Sensory stim toys: Toys and tools designed to activate one or more senses, support the release of energy, and heighten focus.

Student-friendly supplies: Supplies that can be safely managed, accessed, taken care of, and put away by children.

Supports: *Strategies* and *resources* that benefit the child and level the playing field for learning.

Synchronous learning: Learning that happens in real-time with the teacher.

Tattle notes: Sticky notes used for students to jot down the gist of what happened in a conflict. Includes the perpetrator, action, and what the writer *already did* to try and resolve the conflict.

T-chart: A table with two columns, making the shape of the letter t, used to organize information.

Teachable moments: The spontaneous *little* moments of the here-and-now that offer a *big* opportunity for learning.

The Five Hearts of Partnerships: Student–teacher, teacher–teacher, family–teacher, student–student, and community–school connections that work together inside and outside of school toward a similar goal.

The Flow of De-escalation: A sequence of steps that help calm the body, process emotions, and resolve a feeling within yourself.

The Fundamental Five: Five core expectations that hold high value to you. The must-haves and must-sees of your classroom environment.

The I Ams: A collection of "I am" phrases that students can use to speak kindly to themselves and flip thinking from negative to positive.

The Logical Consequence Commandments: Five *thou's* that advise the art of giving logical consequences in the classroom.

The Pieces of You Pie Chart: A representation of balance, where one-third of our focus is on work-life balance, one-third is on health, and one-third is on stress management, —helping us build well-rounded lives as creative, authentic educators.

The Recipe for Resolution: A four-step process to handling conflict in a healthy way, by using words to bring resolution, rather than escalation.

The Self-Talk Split: A crossroad with two paths: the road that states "I'm not" or the road that declares "I am."

The Sprinkles of You: The sprinkles of your personality around the classroom to ensure it is a place providing peace, respite, and a space that reflects who you are.

The Tree of Expectations: The roots, trunk, branches, leaves, and fruit of a tree that thrive only through strong and clear expectations.

Untouchable Time: A block of time during the school day to call *yours*.

Zen Den: A space for students to recalibrate, de-escalate, self-regulate, and self-soothe.

Q, R, S, T ... he End

Bibliography

Allington, R.L. (2013). 'What really matters when working with struggling readers', *The Reading Teacher*, 66(7), pp. 520–530.

Anderson, W. (dir.). (2009). *Fantastic Mr. Fox* (film). 20th Century Fox.

Andrews, E. (n.d.). *The More Difficult the Journey, the Sweeter the Reward*. [online] Available at: https://www.facebook.com [Accessed 11 Feb. 2025].

Armstrong, T. (2012). 'First, discover their strengths', *Educational Leadership*, 70(2), pp. 10–16. Available at: https://research.ebsco.com/linkprocessor/plink?id=82528ded-5020-3ff7-acc8-8ae78f81e642 [Accessed 30 Nov. 2024].

Bailey, B. (2015). *Conscious Discipline: Building Resilient Classrooms*. 2nd ed. Orlando, FL: Loving Guidance, Inc.

Bailey, B. (2018). *The Three Types of Consequences and How to Give Them*. Conscious Discipline. [online] Available at: https://consciousdiscipline.com/three-types-of-consequences/?utm_source=chatgpt.com [Accessed 22 Feb. 2025].

Beverlycleary.com. (2024). *Dear Day*. [online] Available at: https://www.beverlycleary.com/dear-day [Accessed 3 Dec. 2024].

Bishop, R.S. (1990). 'Mirrors, windows, and sliding glass doors', *Perspectives: Choosing and Using Books for the Classroom*, 6(3), pp. ix–xi.

Boorstin, D.J. (1970). 'A case of hypochondria', *Newsweek*, 6 July. [online] Available at: https://www.azquotes.com/quote/32145 [Accessed 23 Feb. 2025].

Bradbury, R. (2008). 'A conversation with Ray Bradbury', *Exchange Programs*, 12 March. [online] Available at: https://exchanges.state.gov/us/spotlight/conversation-ray-bradbury/transcript [Accessed 10 Feb. 2025].

Brand, M. (2007). *School Backs Peppermint for Student Alertness*. NPR. [online] Available at: https://www.npr.org/2007/03/21/9040969/school-backs-peppermint-for-student-alertness [Accessed 21 Feb. 2025].

Brightwheel. (2023). 'Loose parts play in preschool: A guide for educators and parents', *Mybrightwheel.com*. https://doi.org/1091391761/module_87098811510_Related_Posts.

Byrd, F. (2010). *Detecting Learning Disabilities*. WebMD. [online] Available at: https://www.webmd.com/children/detecting-learning-disabilities [Accessed 30 Nov. 2024].

Cambridge Dictionary. (2025). *Organization*. @CambridgeWords. [online] Available at: https://dictionary.cambridge.org/us/dictionary/english/organization [Accessed 2 Jan. 2025].

Cancer.gov. (2022). *Neurodiversity*. [online] Available at: https://dceg.cancer.gov/about/diversity-inclusion/inclusivity-minute/2022/neurodiversity [Accessed 30 Nov. 2024].

CDC. (2024). *Down Syndrome*. Birth Defects [online]. Available at: https://www.cdc.gov/birth-defects/about/down-syndrome.html [Accessed 30 Nov. 2024].

Clark, C. and Rumbold, K. (2006). *Reading for Pleasure: A Research Overview*. National Literacy Trust. [online] Available at: https://files.eric.ed.gov/fulltext/ED496343.pdf.

Cleveland Clinic. (2017). *Williams Syndrome, Williams Beuren Syndrome: Causes, Symptoms & Treatment*. [online] Available at: https://my.clevelandclinic.org/health/diseases/15174-williams-syndrome [Accessed 30 Nov. 2024].

Columbia.edu. (2025). *T. S. Eliot's 'Little Gidding'*. [online] Available at: https://www.columbia.edu/itc/history/winter/w3206/edit/tseliotlittlegidding.html [Accessed 21 Jan. 2025].

Confucius. (n.d.). *It Does Not Matter How Slowly You Go as Long as You Do Not Stop* (quote). [online] Available at: https://www.brainyquote.com/quotes/confucius_140908 [Accessed 6 Feb. 2025].

Corker, M. and French, S. (1999). *Disability Discourse*. Buckingham; Philadelphia, PA: Open University Press.

Couros, G. (n.d.). *Technology Will Not Replace Great Teachers, but Technology in the Hands of Great Teachers Can Be Transformational*. [online] Available at: https://www.georgecouros.ca [Accessed 19 Feb. 2025].

Crum, T. (1995). *The Magic of Conflict: Turning a Life of Work and Stress into One of Personal and Professional Growth*. New York: Penguin Group.

Disney. (1964). *A Spoonful of Sugar* (song). Performed by Julie Andrews. In *Mary Poppins* (film). Walt Disney Productions. [online] Available at: https://www.disney.com [Accessed 24 Feb. 2025].

Drjean.org. (2025). *June 2004 — Cheer Cards 1 to 3*. [online] Available at: https://www.drjean.org/html/monthly_act/act_2004/06_june/06_2004a.html [Accessed 6 Feb. 2025].

Ed100.org. (2023). *4.3 School Hours: Is There Enough Time to Learn?* ED100. [online] Available at: https://ed100.org/lessons/school-hours#:~:text=Most%20American%20children%20spend%20about,about%201%2C000%20hours%20in%20class [Accessed 7 Jan. 2025].

Epictetus. (n.d.). *It's Not What Happens to You, but How You React to It That Matters*. [online] Available at: https://www.brainyquote.com/quotes/epictetus_121101 [Accessed 20 Feb. 2025].

Ewu.edu. (2023). *Self-Talk—CALE Learning Enhancement*. [online] Available at: https://inside.ewu.edu/calelearning/psychological-skills/self-talk/ [Accessed 8 Jan. 2025].

Exceptional Individuals. (2023). *Neurodivergent & Neurodiversity: Meanings & Examples*. [online] Available at: https://exceptionalindividuals.com/neurodiversity/ [Accessed 30 Nov. 2024].

Exceptional Individuals. (2024). *OCD & Other Neurodivergent Disorders*. Exceptional Individuals. [online] Available at: https://exceptionalindividuals.com/neurodiversity/other-neurodivergence/ [Accessed 30 Nov. 2024].

Exchange Press. (2024). *Creating a Flexible Learning Environment: The Reggio Emilia Approach* (pdf). [online] Available at: https://hub.exchangepress.com/wp-content/uploads/2024/11/5020570.pdf [Accessed 20 Feb. 2025].

familydoctor.org editorial staff and Cook, S. (2024). *Sensory Processing Disorder (SPD)*. [online]. Available at: https://familydoctor.org/condition/sensory-processing-disorder-spd/#:~:text=Sensory%20processing%20disorder%20(SPD)%20is,that%20other%20people%20are%20not [Accessed 30 Nov. 2024].

Flanders, J. (2020). *A Place for Everything: The Curious History of Alphabetical Order*. Basic Books.

Foreman, G. (2009). *If I Stay*. New York: Dutton Books.

Franklin, B. (n.d.). *For Every Minute Spent in Organizing, an Hour Is Earned*. [online] Available at: https://thepeakperformancecenter.com/development-series/skill-builder/personal-effectiveness/time-management/managing-your-day/ [Accessed 19 Feb. 2025].

Hauser, A. (1951). *The Sociology of Art*. London: Routledge & Kegan Paul.

Havran, M. (2023). 'Centering neurodiversity: Building inclusive classroom libraries reflective of the world around us', *Literacy Today (2411–7862)*, 41(2), pp. 60–61. [online] Available at: https://research.ebsco.com/linkprocessor/plink?id=609211f8-6060-32de-ad1b-9658a6a0659f [Accessed 7 Jan. 2025].

Henderson, J.W. *et al.* (2020). 'Take a close look: Inventorying your classroom library for diverse books', *Reading Teacher*, 73(6), pp. 747–755. https://doi.org/10.1002/trtr.1886.

Holiday, R. (2014). *The Obstacle Is the Way: The Timeless Art of Turning Trials into Triumph*. Portfolio.

Kaba, M. (2021). *We Do This 'Til We Free Us: Abolitionist Organizing and Transforming Justice*. Haymarket Books.

Kabat-Zinn, J. (1994). *Wherever You Go, There You Are: Mindfulness Meditation in Everyday Life*. Hyperion.

Kagan, S. (2009). *Cooperative Learning*. Kagan Publishing.

Kennedy, J.F. (n.d.). *Life Isn't Fair: It Never Was and Never Will Be*. [online] Available at: https://www.jfklibrary.org [Accessed 21 Feb. 2025].

Khaliq, R. (2023). *MEDvidi Mental Health Telemedicine Provider*. MEDvidi. [online] Available at: https://medvidi.com/blog/types-of-neurodiversity [Accessed 30 Nov. 2024].

Kid President. (2013). *Create Something That Will Make the World More Awesome*. [online] Available at: https://www.youtube.com/watch?v=RwlhUcSGqgs [Accessed 14 Feb. 2025].

Klem, A.M. and Connell, J.P. (2004). 'Relationships matter: Linking teacher support to student engagement and achievement', *Journal of School Health*, 74, 262–273. https://doi.org/10.1111/j.1746-1561.2004.tb08283.x.

Kohl, M.F. (1998). *Children's Art: An Introduction to the Visual Arts*. 2nd ed. Wadsworth Publishing.

Kurt, D.S. (2023). *Piaget's Preoperational Stage of Cognitive Development — Education Library*. Education Library. [online] Available at: https://educationlibrary.org/piagets-preoperational-stage-of-cognitive-development/ [Accessed 23 Feb. 2025].

Lemov, D. (2010). *Teach Like a Champion: 49 Techniques That Put Students on the Path to College*. Jossey-Bass.

Leonard, D. (2024). *19 Ways to Help Elementary Students Self-Regulate*. Edutopia. [online] Available at: https://www.edutopia.org/article/elementary-student-strategies-for-self-regulation [Accessed 8 Jan. 2025].

Lloyd, C. (n.d.). *Nobody Rises to Low Expectations*.

Luccock, H.E. (n.d.). *No One Can Whistle a Symphony: It Takes an Orchestra to Play It* (quoted in various sources).

Manetta, N. (n.d.). *Those Who Do Not Think Outside the Box Are Easily Contained* (quote).

Marin Health and Human Services. (2021). *Equity vs. Equality: What's the Difference?* p. 1. [online] Available at: https://www.marinhhs.org/sites/default/files/boards/general/equality_v._equity_04_05_2021.pdf.

Martin, G.R.R. (2011). *A Dance with Dragons*. New York: Bantam Books.

Merriam-Webster. (2025). *Merriam-Webster's Online Dictionary*. [online] Available at: https://www.merriam-webster.com [Accessed 24 Feb. 2025].

Meyers, A. (2024). *Teaching Young Students About Classroom Expectations in the First Week*. Edutopia. [online] Available at: https://www.edutopia.org/article/catchphrases-that-teach-clear-expectations [Accessed 27 Jan. 2025].

Milne, A.A. (1926). *Winnie-the-Pooh*. London: Methuen & Co.

Misstechqueen. (2023). *Coding in the Elementary Classroom Made Easy — Miss Tech Queen*. Miss Tech Queen [online]. Available at: https://misstechqueen.com/2023/09/14/coding-in-the-elementary-classroom/ [Accessed 25 Feb. 2025].

Montessori, M. (1949). *The Absorbent Mind*. 1st ed. New York: Holt, Rinehart and Winston.

National Council of Teachers of English. (2021). *Independent Reading*. [online] Available at: https://ncte.org/statement/independent-reading/ [Accessed 3 Dec. 2024].

National University. (2023). *Equity in Education: Understanding Equity in the Classroom*. National University. [online] Available at: https://www.nu.edu/blog/equity-in-education/ [Accessed 23 Feb. 2025].

Newleaders.org. (2024). *Innovative Ways to Create a Positive School (and District) Culture*. [online] Available at: https://www.newleaders.org/blog/innovative-ways-to-create-a-positive-school-and-district-culture [Accessed 7 Jan. 2025].

Nicholson, S. (1971). 'How not to cheat children: The theory of loose parts', *Architectural Review*, 150(896), pp. 64–65.

NIDCD. (2023). *Developmental Language Disorder*. [online] Available at: https://www.nidcd.nih.gov/health/developmental-language-disorder#:~:text=Developmental%20language%20disorder%20(DLD)%20is,%2C%20understanding%2C%20and%20using%20language [Accessed 30 Nov. 2024].

Novak, R. (2013). *A Pep Talk from Kid President to You* (video). [online] Available at: https://www.youtube.com/watch?v=l-gQLqv9f4o [Accessed 20 Feb. 2025].

PBIS Rewards. (2023). *The Ultimate List of PBIS Incentives*. [online] Available at: https://www.pbisrewards.com/pbis-incentives/ [Accessed 12 Feb. 2025].

Piaget, J. (1952). *The Origins of Intelligence in Children*. International Universities Press.

Pincus, D. (2021). *Punishments vs. Consequences Which Are You Using?* Empowering Parents. [online] Available at: https://www.empoweringparents.com/article/punishments-vs-consequences-which-are-you-using/ [Accessed 25 Feb. 2025].

Plato. (2000). *The Republic*. Translated by B. Jowett, 1892. Dover Publications.

Rapposelli, M. (2021). *The Impact of Standardized Testing on the Mental Health of Students*. [online] Available at: https://spark.bethel.edu/cgi/viewcontent.cgi?article=1753&context=etd [Accessed 20 Feb. 2025].

Riley, S. (2024). *What Is Arts Integration?* The Institute for Arts Integration and STEAM. [online] Available at: https://artsintegration.com/what-is-arts-integration-in-schools/ [Accessed 30 Jan. 2025].

Roosevelt, T. (n.d.). *Believe You Can and You're Halfway There*. Theodore Roosevelt Center. [online] Available at: https://www.theodorerooseveltcenter.org/Learn-About-TR/TR-Quotes?page=16 [Accessed 24 Feb. 2025].

Singer, J. (2016). *Neurodiversity: The Birth of an Idea*. Lexington, KY: Amazon.

Svinicki, M. (2010). *Fostering a Mastery Goal Orientation in the Classroom*. [online] Available at: https://www.bu.edu/ssw/files/2010/10/Fostering-a-Mastery-Goal.pdf.

Swindoll, C.R. (n.d.). *Life Is 10% What Happens to You and 90% How You React to It*. [online] Available at: https://www.brainyquote.com/quotes/charles_r_swindoll_388332 [Accessed 23 Feb. 2025].

Tadesse, A. (2023). *What Are the Performing Arts? The Different Types of Arts*. ATX Fine Arts. [online] Available at: https://www.atxfinearts.com/blogs/news/performing-arts [Accessed 30 Jan. 2025].

Thesaurus.com. (2023). *The World's Favorite Online Thesaurus!* Thesaurus.com. [online] Available at: https://www.thesaurus.com/browse/quiet-time [Accessed 3 Dec. 2024].

Top Hat. (2019). *Virtual Classroom Definition and Meaning*. Top Hat. [online] Available at: https://tophat.com/glossary/v/virtual-classroom/ [Accessed 21 Jan. 2025].

Westover, T. (n.d.). *The Greatest Act of Self-Care Is to Believe That We Are Worthy of Care*. [online] Available at: https://mendingtimemama.com/be-your-best-self-quotes/ [Accessed 15 Feb. 2025].

What Are Learning Supports? (n.d.). [online] Available at: https://smhp.psych.ucla.edu/pdfdocs/whatlearnsupports.pdf.

WordHippo. (2025). *Synonyms and Antonyms*. [online] Available at: https://www.wordhippo.com [Accessed 24 Feb. 2025].

For Product Safety Concerns and Information please contact our EU representative GPSR@taylorandfrancis.com
Taylor & Francis Verlag GmbH, Kaufingerstraße 24, 80331 München, Germany